WRITING ON THE SOIL

AFRICAN PERSPECTIVES
Kelly Askew, Laura Fair, and Pamila Gupta
Series Editors

Writing on the Soil: Land and Landscape in Literature
from Eastern and Southern Africa
Ng'ang'a Wahu-Mūchiri

Lagos Never Spoils: Nollywood and Nigerian City Life
Connor Ryan

Continuous Pasts: Frictions of Memory in Postcolonial Africa
Sakiru Adebayo

Power / Knowledge / Land: Contested Ontologies of Land
and Its Governance in Africa
Laura A. German

In Search of Tunga: Prosperity, Almighty God,
and Lives in Motion in a Malian Provincial Town
André Chappatte

The Infrastructures of Security:
Technologies of Risk Management in Johannesburg
Martin J. Murray

There Used to Be Order:
Life on the Copperbelt after the Privatisation of the
Zambia Consolidated Copper Mines
Patience Mususa

Animated by Uncertainty: Rugby and the
Performance of History in South Africa
Joshua D. Rubin

African Performance Arts and Political Acts
Naomi André, Yolanda Covington-Ward, and Jendele Hungbo, Editors

A complete list of titles in the series can be found at www.press.umich.edu

Writing on the Soil

Land and Landscape in Literature from Eastern and Southern Africa

Ng'ang'a Wahu-Mũchiri

University of Michigan Press
Ann Arbor

Copyright © 2023 by Ng'ang'a Wahu-Mũchiri

For questions or permissions, please contact um.press.perms@umich.edu

Published in the United States of America by the
University of Michigan Press
Printed and bound by CPI Group (UK) Ltd, Croydon, CR0 4YY

First published May 2023

A CIP catalog record for this book is available from the British Library.

Library of Congress Cataloging-in-Publication data has been applied for.

ISBN 978-0-472-07620-8 (hardcover : alk. paper)
ISBN 978-0-472-05620-0 (paper : alk. paper)
ISBN 978-0-472-2214-1 (e-book)

Library of Congress Control Number: 2023931730

CONTENTS

Digital materials related to this title can be found on the Fulcrum platform via the following citable URL: https://doi.org/10.3998/mpub.12211422

ACKNOWLEDGMENTS

Thayũ na ngatho çia mwanya harĩ mũthoomi wa ibuku rĩrĩ.

Nitatoaje shukrani kwa wahisani wote walioniwezesha kukikamilisha kitabu hiki?

The ideas in this book lived many past lives, and with each rebirth my indebtedness grows. This book was once a senior English honor's thesis: shepherded by the indomitable Bryan Washington and Ian Smith. There have been many reincarnations since. Brenna Munro, Tim Watson, Subha Xavier, Evan Mwangi, and Pat Saunders midwifed the PhD dissertation version. To my graduate writing colleagues, especially the ever-supportive Josie Urbistondo, and the University of Miami Graduate School writing workshops: muchas gracias.

I also thank the following: Moses Sarara and Ruo Kimani Ruo, for an all-rounded introduction to the reading of Kiswahili literature. Myra Mutsune for turning ecology into narrative. The magnanimous Munungi Musee, for sharing your love of language, and for all the intellectual explorations since. The Bauers, for much-needed summer retreats, full of dominoes and laughter.

Gracious archival support by the Kenya National Archives, the University of Dar es Salaam Library, and the Africa/Middle East reading room at the Library of Congress. These research trips were generously financed by a Center for the Humanities Dissertation Fellowship at the University of Miami, and the University of Nebraska-Lincoln College of Arts and Sciences. To the numerous interlocutors of this work at conferences, my heartfelt gratitude for sharing so keenly. Ellen Bauerle, and your entire team at the University of Michigan Press: you have been such affable hosts. The care and attention you brought to this manuscript leaves me in awe. And to the reviewers who saw the potential: this monograph, and its author, owe you more than can ever be repaid.

The thread running through this work is my family's sense of place. I have no words for their constant, never-ending encouragement. Gĩçũhiro. Gĩkambura. Juja. Ngong'. Wangige. Kimana. Nkama. Chieko. Mayfield. I carry stories from those who have preceded us, and I feel their presence beside me. Mom, Dad, and the twins: home is that much sweeter for your affection and your companionship. And to Warũirũ—all my love; steadfastly beside me, here's to all we've dreamed of.

Introduction

Land and Landscape in Eastern and Southern African Literatures

> Our landscape is its own monument: its meaning can only be traced on the underside. It is all history.
>
> —Edouard Glissant, *Caribbean Discourse: Selected Essays*

IDENTITIES: A PLACE-BASED BIOGRAPHY OF MY KIN

The web of place-based identities that my family ascribed to was immensely fascinating to me as a child. Ethnically we were Gĩkũyũ, tracing long-lost roots to the rich lands around Mount Kenya, the Aberdare Ranges, and the ridges of Kiambu district. Congruously, other ethnicities in the Kenyan nation-state had their equivalent ancestral homes: the Dholuo-speaking regions around Nam Lolwe (Lake Victoria); the Abaluyha in spaces around Kakamega and Vihiga; the Maa communities in grazing pastures of the Rift Valley; and so on. Closer examination of this biography, however, complicated the simplistic collapsing of locale with identity. My father's people, though Gĩkũyũ, had also intermarried with the Ndorobo community—autochthons of Mount Kenya whose residence predated the Bantu migrations of the last two millennia. More recently, Mariibe, my great-great grandfather, and his son Karũgũ had moved their livestock from Gachie to Waithaka. After working for the Danish and English writer Karen Blixen, they subsequently resettled in Gĩkambura in the 1930s. Both my grandfather and my father tie their sense of belonging to Gĩkambura, the place they spent their childhood. But it was never clear to me how they arrived at that cutoff point; why not incorporate their sense of self to the entire migratory journey undertaken by Mariibe and Karũgũ?

My mother's relatives have a similarly picaresque history. Wahu, my great-grandmother, and after whom my mother is named, grew up in Rirūta, went to school a few miles away in Thogoto, and worked at the Scottish Church Missionary hospital. One of many children sired by Paramount Chief Kīnyanjui wa Gathirimū, her and her husband intermittently lived in colonial Nairobi, before eventually retiring in Gīkambura. Their first daughter, my maternal grandmother Maragret Wanjirū, went to school in Manguo, perhaps five years before Kenyan scholar and writer Ngũgĩ wa Thiong'o would study at the same institution. Eventually, Wanjirū would work in Nairobi—at the King George Hospital and the Transport and Allied Workers Union—before retiring first to Gīkambura, and eventually to Juja, the savanna lands northeast of Nairobi. My own upbringing began in Gīkambura, as my parents set up house close to their extended families, before moving to Ngong. Ngong, our new home, lies at the border of hereditary Maasai and Gīkũyũ lands. The region has continuously encouraged mixed farmers and pastoralists to settle as neighbors, to intermarry, and to trade. What these recollections demonstrate is that the "western concept of tribalism, which is usually taken to refer to closed populations reproducing fixed cultural characteristics, is not applicable" to familial histories (Thompson 2000, 25). In present-day South Africa, for example, there are living histories of aboriginal communities incorporated into herding or farming clans, or both, (15), while pastoralists often banded together with mixed farmers (29). Across all the spaces with which my family has associated itself, from the Ndorobo lands of Mount Kenya to the colonial capital in Nairobi, from the farmlands in Riruta and Thogoto, to the grasslands in Juja, there has emerged a rich network of memory, history, and identity. This is layered atop global geopolitical processes that not only brought the advent of British imperialism but also witnessed the rise of an independent Kenya.

Simultaneously, each of these locales—Gachie, Waithaka, Gīkambura, Rirūta, Thogoto, Nairobi, Manguo, Juja, and Ngong—maps out the complexity of tracing singular ethnic identities across several generations. Amid global politics, regional cross-cultural exchanges, and local migration, there exist key parallels between my ancestors' reaction and those exhibited by other ethnic communities not just in the Eastern African region but across the continent. These acts included resistance, collaboration, acquiring formal education, experimenting with the monetary economy, converting to Christianity, intermarriage, and much else besides. How did these four generations of Kenyans and proto-Kenyans signify their topographical surroundings?

The Gĩkũyũ language offers a lexicographic variety in describing lands and landscapes. The verdant valleys of Gachie and Waithaka were referred to as *ituamba* (*gĩtuamba*, singular). Upon their arrival in Rirũta and Thogoto, my extended kin were met by *mĩtitũ* (*mũtitũ*, singular). Mũtitũ is dense bush forest, spaces that had never been cleared for settlement or large-scale farming. The contemporary meaning of mũtitũ includes man-made forests. Beyond Gĩkambura were the lush pastures of *rũrie*: a flat plateau often composed of black cotton soil and so likely to flood. Advantageously, however, the grass in this terrain is favored by livestock and there were always plenty of watering holes. Rũrie is different from *werũ* in places like Juja. Werũ (singular and plural) is much closer to savannah. Werũ has low altitude, higher average temperatures, and is not favorable to indigenous Gĩkũyũ mixed crop agricultures. The Gĩkũyũ phrase "*kĩndũ gĩthaka*" describes a beautiful item. This applies to any material object. Gĩthaka, the modifier for beautiful, or appealing, comes after the noun. On its own, however, the word *gĩthaka* has an entirely different meaning. Gĩthaka is used interchangeably with *mũgũnda* (farm). Gĩthaka slightly differs from mũgũnda in that the latter has been cleared and put to agricultural use, while the former may still be uncultivated and populated by bushes and trees. Yet one can still speak of having bought gĩthaka, land. Gĩthaka (singular), *ithaka* (plural). *Waithaka*, where great-great grandfather Mariibe pastured his livestock, means one-who-owns/possesses/utilizes-many-lands. The Gĩkũyũ phrase *mũtumia wa ithaka* translates to "a woman with access to many lands."

Aside from this Gĩkũyũ vocabulary, my grandparents' generation also had increased access to a Kiswahili ontology. Originally an Indian Ocean trade language, Kiswahili made deep inroads into the Eastern African hinterland.[1] This resulted from Arab ivory and enslaving expeditions, European exploratory, missionary, and commercial voyages, as well as during indigenous markets for food, livestock, iron tools, and decorative beads. Kiswahili offered landscape representation of *milima* (mountain ranges), *mabonde* (valleys), *nyika* (arid and semiarid plains), *jangwa* (desert), and *chemi chemi* (water springs/swamps). There are distinctions between *kichaka, shamba, msitu,* and *mbuga* (bush, garden/farm, forest, and reservation, respectively). Each term denotes competing views of land use and attendant assumptions about the aesthetics, utility, and value of *ardhi* (land). Gĩkũyũ and Kiswahili are not unique in their representation of land and landscape. The Kikamba language demonstrates a similar capacity. In "Breathing Life into Dead Theories about Property Rights in Rural Africa," Celestine Nyamu-Musembi distinguishes at least five Kamba terms for depicting land and landscape: *weu, kisesi, kithaka, muunda,* and *ng'undu*. Weu is analogous to the Gĩkũyũ werũ; since both Kikamba and Gĩkũyũ are Bantu languages, they share many cognate words. Kisesi, though used for grazing, like weu, is unique in that a family, or groups of families, may reserve it for their own use. Kitheka, like the Gĩkũyũ gĩthaka, is used for harvesting timber, firewood, or honey (Nyamu-Musembi 2008, 25). Muunda and ng'undu are lands put to the same kind of use as mugunda; ng'undu differs in having been cultivated by the same family for a significant amount of time (25). What kisesi and ng'undu demonstrate is that land is not land is not land. Translating words like kisesi and ng'undu into English loses the nuance of corporate family ownership, an attribute strategically cultivated over time—often across several generations.

LAND AND LANDSCAPE IN AFRICAN LETTERS

Gĩkũyũ, Kiswahili, and Kikamba renderings of land and landscape influence Eastern African writing in English. Ngũgĩ wa Thiong'o, for instance, writes in Gĩkũyũ, Kiswahili, and English. Yvonne Owuor (2014) has incorporated Turkana land aesthetics into her novel *Dust*. Okot p'Bitek's lyrical poetry in *Song of Lawino* (1966) borrowed heavily from the Acholi language and the community's interaction with its ecological surroundings. Finally, the nineteenth-century Kiswahili artist Mwana Kupona binti Msham relied upon her Bantu and Arab heritage in composing "Poem to Her Daughter." Allegorical references to land in Eastern Africa are evident across various forms of language: literary, conversational, folklore, and so forth. The biography above demonstrates the extent to which land, migration, and perceptions of landscape color the fabric of African lived experiences. Movement and relocation feature in communal lore. Individuals express a range of emotions—from angst to jubilation and everything in between—as they recount their own peculiar peregrinations. Consequently, it is no surprise that communal knowledge— proverbs, riddles, poems, and songs—chronicles a similarly diverse scope of affect. What is of particular interest here is the literary depiction, allegorical or otherwise, of regional ecosystems.

Numerous African writers deploy the attributes of geography to illustrate kinship, friendship, or animosity among characters.[2] *The River Between* (1965) by Ngũgĩ wa Thiong'o relies on the confrontational positioning of two Gĩkũyũ ridges to demonstrate the social upheaval wreaked upon colonial Kenya by Pax Britannica. Chinua Achebe's *Anthills of the Savanna* (1987) and Yvonne Vera's *The Stone Virgins* (2002) both examine the postcolonial dystopia— elaborating particularly on the predatory manifestation of African politics from the 1960s to the 1990s. There is correlation between Achebe's solitary termite structure—standing tall in the grassland—and the indifference of rocks and boulders in Vera's title to the praxis of one-party totalitarianism in the regimes of Nigeria's Sani Abacha, Zaire's Mobutu Sese Seko, Kenya's Daniel Arap Moi, and Egypt's Hosni Mubarak. On the other hand, Margaret Ogola's *The River and the Source* (1994) engages the fluidity of water bodies to depict movement and dynamism across three fictional generations of Kenyan women. H. R. Ole Kulet's *Blossoms of the Savannah* (2008) invokes a fictional River Nasila to portray the pollution of Maa cultures, especially zeroing in on sexual violence against girls. Ngũgĩ, Achebe, Vera, Ogola, and Ole Kulet make use of topographical characteristics in their depictions of communal relationships. Additionally, there exist many points of connection between depictions of landscape and resistance against oppressive elites, including writers who allegorize weather patterns as political movements. For instance, Charles Mungoshi's *Coming of the Dry Season* (1972) and *Waiting for the Rain* (1975) articulate the Zimbabwean Chimurenga—war for independence—in the language of cyclical seasons. Predictably, twentieth-century European colonialism is akin to drought, which will end when the rains come—in the form of black self-rule. In poetry, *Mother Tongues* invokes "waves," "stones," "water," a "panther," a "banana tree," and a "cactus" (Jaji 2020, 15). Tsitsi Ella Jaji's poem "Daughtering" blends natural imagery to Zimbabwean metaphors of speech, language, and motherhood.[3] We can similarly map out the influence of South Africa's ecology on *Izibongo* (oral vernacular) poetry. Izibongo as a literary genre is "layered with names of ancestors, animals, and plants and rich with idiom and allusion. As such, it is intimately enmeshed with the Eastern Cape landscape and the lives and afterlives of the people and creatures who dwell there" (McGiffin 2019, xiv).

Finally, there are writers who invoke African self-rule and decolonization by attempting to literally name, or speak, the postindependence state into being through the metaphor of landscape. Jomo Kenyatta's *Facing Mount Kenya* (1938), Alan Paton's *Cry, the Beloved Country* (1948), and J. M. Coetzee and A. P. Brink's *A Land Apart* (1992) are exemplary of literary narratives deployed for political liberation. Each of these texts conjures a postcolonial nation that—at time of publication—was yet to be realized. While Kenyatta and Paton explicitly name Kenya and country, respectively, in their work, Grace Ogot's *The Promised Land* (1966) and Marjorie Macgoye's *A Farm Called Kishinev* (2005) rely on the terms "land" and "farm." Ogot and Macgoye foreground an imaginative reading of Kenyan landscapes in a literary activism that challenges British imperialism. Land performs metaphorical labor in twentieth and twenty-first-century African literature. The relevance that location has to family identities is hidden in plain sight; for example, in the short biography offered in this introduction. Elsewhere, Carola Lentz complicates our perception of mobility and autochthony when land and territory are used to underline ethnic nationalism. *Land, Mobility, and Belonging in West Africa* notes that "first-comer claims are inherently contradictory because they combine notions of mobility (having come 'first' implies having immigrated from somewhere) with the apparently natural legitimacy of being autochthonous (having been there before the arrival of others)" (Lentz 2013, 19). Hence, "Gods of Fiction" critiques the "language of dysfunction" that stunted parts of African literature as mere reaction to calamities (Edoro 2018, 4). Africanist scholars have variously attempted to comprehend connections between land, literature, and identity. This task is incomplete.

Unlike Enlightenment philosophies, which separated humans from their immediate ecologies, African ecocriticism explores the deep connections between communities and the ecosystem. Although the Enlightenment movement sought to decenter religious dogma, it paradoxically pedestaled white, male, aristocratic, heterosexual, and Christian ways of knowing. Ontologies unmatched to this approach have been suppressed, violently and systemically. The literature I discuss in this book explicitly seeks to reverse the culture/nature binary. Instead, these texts present a wide spectrum of human, animal, and plant life that often interacts with the mystical. "The Moral Status of Nature: An African Understanding" argues that "within the African ontological hierarchy, nonhuman animals and plants are vital forces by virtue of possession of life" (Chemhuru 2019, 65). Munamato Chemhuru contends for an appreciation of nonhuman agency—as encapsulated in the word "forces." What this suggests is that any definition of an African environmental ethics must be grounded in reverence for nature and recognition of its "moral status" (69). African ecocriticism, writ large, declares a dynamism in the ecosystem that a capitalist instrumentalization of the environment has always preferred to ignore.

WHY LAND? WHAT IS LANDSCAPE?

In the constellation of rites that a Kenyan child undergoes, owning a home is cardinal. The predetermined course progresses thus: birth; first day of school; completing the Kenya Certificate of Primary Education; puberty; going to high school and sitting for one's Kenya Certificate of Secondary Education; and completing a bachelor's degree. Marrying heterosexually and buying land—exercises that maintain middle class respectability—immediately follow several years of employment. Moving into a new home is often celebrated with a communal housewarming party.[4] Aside from reinforcing facets of an individual's identity, land also plays a key role in constructing the civic self. Historically, land anchored waves of political liberation in the first half of the twentieth century. Ethnicity as a marker of identity was increasingly challenged during this time, just as Kenyan citizenry gained ascendancy. Following Stuart Hall (1996), it is worth thinking of identity as "never complete [and] always in process" (110). Land and landscape served as cornerstones for a subjectivity that was incessantly mobile, migratory, transethnic, and transnational.[5] The regional movements undertaken by my extended families exemplify this fluidity; their spatial displacements catalyzed shifts in identity, and vice versa.[6] Amina Mama's (1995) work on subjectivity is instructive. Mama foregrounds the extent to which "multiplicity rather than duality" reigns in the Global South (6).[7] *Beyond the Masks* further argues that most postcolonial citizens embody

> not one but several contexts simultaneously . . . This is a world in which no context is as fixed or as static as is assumed by the Manichean and dualistic colonial frameworks that counterpoise west and non-west. Instead, cultural and social conditions are undergoing constant change and exchange. (13)

It is worth reaffirming the central role that land played in the politics and theatrics of African anticolonial resistance. Amilcar Cabral—a radical poet, agronomist, and revolutionary pan-Africanist from present-day Guinea-Bissau—underlined the importance that land held to independence movements across the African continent. "National Culture and Liberation" agitated for "complete liberation of the productive forces," with land and black labor as especially key in the struggle for cultural, economic, and social autonomy (Cabral 1994, 62). James Graham's *Land and Nationalism in Fic-*

tions from Southern Africa (2009) asserts that "land means much more, but also, in very important ways, often much *less* than the ideas of space, nation or property" (2, emphasis in original). This is imperative because land came to be a catch-all phrase upon which varied constituents projected (competing) ideals and desires. An African's ability to use land for subsistence and for a sense of belonging was, and still is, essential.

Graham's distinction between land and landscape as two "products of material historical and geographical processes . . . subject to potentially radical revisioning in the imaginable worlds of literary texts" (2009, 2) is crucial to the theoretical interventions that I undertake in this book. Furthermore, as earlier demonstrated in the biography at the beginning of this introduction, place "mediates the social and symbolic relationships among transnational experiences, spaces, identities and forms of power" (8). At this juncture in my introduction, it is imperative that I outline my use of the terms "place," "landscape," and "space." Place is multidimensional; it has geographic, environmental, genealogic, and phenomenological components (DeLoughrey and Handley 2011, 4). My family's biography at the onset of this introduction displayed knotted connections between place, identity, and community-building. Evidently, place is a complex ideational phenomenon that incorporates sensual input over and above the physical. I am particularly interested in what *The Empire Writes Back: Theory and Practice in Post-Colonial Literatures* portrays as the fissure "between the experience of place and the language available to describe it" (Ashcroft, Griffith, and Tiffins 1989, 9). How Eastern and Southern African authors attempt to bridge that experiential-linguistic divide has profound implications for how they illustrate lands, landscapes, and other topographical features. A common denominator across Anglophone postcolonial writing is "place, displacement, and a pervasive concern with the myths of identity and authenticity" (9). Land and landscape occupy a key role in the texts encountered. I define landscape as "predicated upon a particular philosophic tradition in which the objective world is separated from the viewing subject" (Ashcroft, Griffith, and Tiffins 2006, 345). What emerges from this is an understanding of place as a "complex interaction of language, history and environment" (345). Space, on the other hand, is an actionable entity; it is a dynamic component that shifts constantly. This amorphous characteristic is in fact shared between space and territory. The latter is premised upon "claims to land" (Gertel, Rottenberg, and Calkins 2014, 9). Achille Mbembe's "Provisional Notes on the Postcolony" (1992) notes that the *commandement* not only shares living spaces with its subjects but also devises "ways of getting into its subjects' most intimate spaces" (4, 19). There exists but a paper-thin barrier between elites and the masses. This porous frontier makes for great anxiety on both sides: grassroots efforts to prevent further insidious infiltration by the state, and top-down heavy-handedness to impede democratic and socialist reforms.

True decolonization demanded the dismantling of colonial modes of cultural/economic production. Card-carrying Marxist anticolonial platforms, such as Amilcar Cabral's, hyperfocus on issues of political economy. There are very good reasons for this. There was synergy between imperial cultural output and colonial economic productivity. As *Marxism, Modernity, and Postcolonial Studies* argues, cultural critiques of the quotidian cannot be divorced from interrogations of economic production (Bartolovich 2002, 6). This was a grievous charge laid against postcolonial studies. "What Postcolonial Theory Doesn't Say" points out "insufficient attention to the fact that colonialism is part and parcel of a larger, enfolding historical dynamic, which is that of capitalism in its global trajectory" (Lazarus 2011, 7).[8] Neil Lazarus notes that European imperialism foregrounded exchange-based productivity, monetizing labor, and fetishizing private property (11).[9] Robert Marzec's *An Ecologic and Postcolonial Study of Literature: From Daniel Defoe to Salman Rushdie* (2007) exposes the connection "between the enclosing of the land of the colonizer and the cultivation of the land in the colonized. This relation between enclosing and cultivation is an essential component of imperial expansion—of a widespread imperial culturalization" (11). Frantz Fanon's political apriorism in African decolonization was territorial sovereignty. Hence, "for a colonized people the most essential value, because the most concrete, is first and foremost the land: the land which will bring them bread and, above all, dignity" (Fanon 1963, 44). Fanon performs an ideational legerdemain whereby nutritional sustenance and civic autonomy are, although conceptually dissimilar, simultaneously engendered by one's geographical environment. To paraphrase James Graham, land means *so much more* than crop production and animal husbandry.[10] Aside from the material reality of land as a physical attribute, landscape's metaphysical significance is disproportionately large. Edward Said's *Culture and Imperialism* (1993) proposes that "land is recoverable at first only through the imagination" (77). Said highlights political agitation and civic empowerment as key prerequisites to the regime change and constitutional reform that heralded independence from colonial masters. Colonialism, like war, is real estate business. Pan-Africanism connects decolonial agendas to environmentalism. The *Routledge*

Handbook of Pan-Africanism frames Pan-Africanism as "simultaneously an idea *and* a movement, a kind of intellectualism *and* activism, a theory *and* a praxis . . . [that] exists wherever African people live, love, and fight for liberation, whether on the African continent or throughout the African diaspora" (Rabaka 2020, 5; emphasis in original). Rabaka's focus on liberation aligns with ongoing concerns that Africa's ecology is increasingly deployed toward goals that local communities have neither shaped nor prioritized.

ECOFEMINISM IN LITERATURES OF THE AFRICAN CONTINENT

In three separate property transactions that I have witnessed, I noticed that older men referred to the desired piece of land as *msichana*, the Kiswahili word meaning girl or young woman. All three negotiations occurred in Oloitokitok, a rural area bordering Tanzania. Historically, Oloitokitok was settled by Maa-speaking communities who used the rich grazing lands for pasture. There is deep local knowledge of migration by Chagga and Maasai ethnicities in present-day Tanzania, as well as by Kenya's Gĩkũyũ and Kamba communities, into Oloitokitok. Residents often trace the most recent wave of migration to the mid-Sixties, when individual Gĩkũyũ families bought farmland while escaping population pressure in the Central Province. Baba Njeri, to whom I was introduced through my mother, walks with me to Baba Lekina's house. Baba Njeri introduces me to his neighbor; he then declares "huyu kijana ameona msichana wako, na ako na haja." Baba Njeri is my spokesperson; he expresses my desire: I've seen a msichana in Baba Lekina's household and would like to negotiate for her. We then proceed into a back and forth on how much the half acre of land that Baba Lekina is selling will cost. This was in 2017. It was the second time that I was buying land in Oloitokitok, and just like the previous negotiations in 2016, land was invoked in the language of marriage. During my first experience, my interlocutor had urged the seller to deal fairly with me since—once the land deal went through—we'd become in-laws. The exchange of cash for land was interpreted using the registers that are common during bride price negotiations. Three years later David, a close friend, visits our new home in Oloitokitok. He's smitten by the views of Mt. Kilimanjaro. He asks my Dad to introduce him to anyone offering property for sale. In the subsequent conversation with Mr. James, my Dad narrates that the seller has a msichana in whom David is interested.

Allegorical references to land in Eastern Africa are varied across various forms of language: literary, conversational, folklore, and so on. These moments provide an examination of how communities discuss land. One way to explain references to land as msichana in the incidents related above is through the eyes of British imperialism. There already exists an established field of criticism that explores European colonial rhetoric and its positioning of African lands. For instance, it was common for male explorers to feminize the African continent into whose deserts, jungles, forests, and savannahs they deeply *penetrated*.[11] *Postcolonial Ecocriticism: Literature, Animals, Environment* argues that the aftermath of colonial experiences has not only been displaced and impoverished ecosystems but also the production of cutthroat, zero-sum views about natural resources, especially land (Huggan and Tiffin 2010, 136–37). Across varied colonial settings "female bodies [came to] symbolize the conquered land" (Loomba 2015, 154). Given the sociocultural history of patriarchy, however, there exists a long tradition of "women's material and intellectual exclusion" from the land: property rights, agricultural labor, domestic roles, and biased citizenship (Graham 2009, 110). Women's ubiquitous presence as *metaphors* in conversations about land disguises their pervasive absence as *stakeholders* in land ownership.[12] Africanist ecofeminism challenges colonial conflation of the African female body with African landscapes.

European settlers had prejudiced convictions about the insufficient husbandry skills of the peoples whose land they alienated. Colonial prejudice was premised upon the emasculation of African men. White males could, supposedly, copulate better with Africa—the land and the women—than black males. In Robert Ruark's oeuvre, for example, David Maughan-Brown (1985, 116) identifies "the myth of Gĩkũyũ agricultural incompetence [as opposed to] white farming expertise." Across white colonial fiction by Isak Dinesen, Elspeth Huxley, Neil Sheraton, M. Harding, W. B. Thomas, M. M. Kaye, and C. T. Stoneham there runs a common thread that Brown describes as the "myth of the empty land" (117). As has been argued extensively, Africa's literary canon challenged these colonial fallacies and problematized the racist undertones upon which they were based.[13] I extend this scholarship to demonstrate the ways in which land, landscape, and topography feature in the kind of identity-making that Eastern and Southern Africans quotidianly engage in. In the space between vernacular and official landscapes, I'd categorize the latest round of cultural map-making in Oloitokitok as quasi vernacular. Rob Nixon's *Slow Violence and the Environmentalism of the Poor* (2011) establishes two kinds of landscapes: vernacular and official. Nixon defines vernacular landscapes as characterized by the "historically textured maps that communities have devised over generations, maps replete with names and routes, maps alive to significant ecological and surface geological features" (17). Official landscapes are quite the opposite, consciously ignorant of previous ways of knowing the land. The recent migration of Gĩkũyũ, Kamba, and Chagga speakers into Oloitokitok clashes with previously conceived vernacular landscapes belonging to the Maa-speaking community. New arrivals lack fluency in the Maa language and have lived and farmed on the land for about two generations. They have but shallow roots in this region, compared to pastoralists who've roamed and grazed these lands for several centuries. And yet that does not make the kind of maps and landscapes that newer settlers compose official. Often, land transactions are neither recorded at the appropriate government offices nor are monetary exchanges accompanied by transfer of title. Although newcomers to Oloitokitok adopt an "extraction-driven manner that is often pitilessly instrumental," they are not governmental, nongovernmental, or corporate (17). Contemporary migrants lack the bureaucratic force that accompanies official landscapes, but they also lack the linguistic, temporal, and place-based skills that generate vernacular maps. Of course, some migrants are fluent Maa-speakers, but these are few and far between.

The current wrangles of landscape representation occur during not just an ongoing environmental crisis but also during global health pandemics, entrenched governmental impunity, a retraction of civic participation, and a popularization of both white supremacy and fascism. My goal is to transcend the struggles of the past, even as we learn from the resistance movements in our history. I find a lot of encouragement in Nixon's dissection of the predicament. He divines the point in question as primarily "representational"; in other words, "how to devise arresting stories, images, and symbols adequate to the pervasive but elusive violence of delayed effects" (Nixon 2011, 3). This *slow violence* is double-edged. On the one hand it creates the ecological changes witnessed since the mid-1800s, and on the other it accelerates the decimation of non-Western ontologies. This destruction of knowledges, histories, and cultures in turn speeds up increasingly irreversible changes on the planet. In this cycle, environmental destruction hastens cultural genocide, and vice versa. I contend that Eastern and Southern African writers have in fact been engaged with this dual hegemony, at least over the last fifty years—and arguably for even longer. The region's cultural production—in its attention to the global march of European colonialism and in its depiction of lands and landscapes—already offers us a way to depict "disasters that are slow moving and long in the making, disasters that are anonymous and that star nobody, disasters that are attritional and of indifferent interest to the sensation-driven technologies of our image-world" (3).[14] Previously discussed renderings of land as msichana, or even colonial feminizations of African landscapes, exemplify varied approaches to the challenge of representation. Both, as ecofeminism rightly points out, have been inadequate. My somewhat anachronistic reading extends the biography of that strain of critical intervention currently termed ecofeminism. A *proto* ecofeminism is legible in the kinds of sustained attention that the writers in the main body of this book pay to the ecosystems depicted in their art. Trinh Minh-ha's *Woman, Native, Other: Writing Postcoloniality and Feminism* (1989) captures this sentiment beautifully: "The story as a cure and a protection [that is simultaneously] musical, historical, poetical, ethical, educational, magical, and religious" (140). Aside from deciphering the *why* of representing land and landscapes, I'm also interested in the *how*. What aesthetic choices enable an artist to project a particular ecology into her reader's mind's eye? Literature can conjure the real-but-unseen or even the yet-to-be-real.[15]

I previously laid out Kenyatta's and Paton's summoning of unborn nation spaces and civic identities. Eastern and Southern African writers, amid a self-styled millennium of global British imperialism, imagined liberation movements birthing political sovereignty. Similarly, cultural production exhibits environmental threats that are, if not unseen, largely ignored. Nixon's central argument is that current global climatic disasters are easy to disregard especially when they happen to other people, in distant places. But even when catastrophe strikes close to home, the quotidian demands of our consumer capitalism soon misdirect attention toward sensation-driven living: light on reflection and heavy on addiction. My intervention adopts a postcolonial ecocriticism approach that encapsulates topographical features as agential subjects of study. I invoke Cheryll Glotfelty's (1996) line of questioning: how is nature represented; how does the writer incorporate our ecosphere; what ecological wisdom is advertised; what metaphors of the land are deployed; and how does the artist depict wilderness (xix). *The Disposition of Nature: Environmental Crisis and World Literature* similarly champions the need for "new modes of imagining" (Wenzel 2020, 7). As the author convincingly argues, "Narratives of limitless growth, premised upon access to cheap energy and inexhaustible resources, underwrite the predicaments of the present" (7). There must needs be novel kinds of interactions between humans and nonhuman nature; beyond that, it is only after we've resolved "narrative

problems and problems of the imagination" (7) that Wenzel foresees reju-
venated descriptions of what nature is, and to what ends it is deployed (9).
The nuances and subtleties of art are worth paying attention to. Hence, I
expand our definition of *life* to include nonhuman beings: plants, animals,
and microscopic entities.

DECOLONIAL NARRATIVE TECHNIQUES OF DEPICTING LANDS, LANDSCAPES, AND LANGUAGES

West Africa's forest-savanna in Kissidougou, and the ways in which this
landscape has been (mis)read by residents, urban dwellers, bureaucrats, and
colonial agroforestry experts, is indicative. When ministerial officials from
Conakry visit this southeast Guinea community, a mix of seasonally biased
observations, urban condescension, and monetary self-interest produces a
misreading of the ecosystem as degraded and overused (Fairhead and Leach
1996, 268–69). This follows a practice by colonial foresters who depicted
the autochthons of Kissidougou as "inadequate resource custodians whose
destructive activities [were] in need of regulation and repression" (268). But
the reality is much more complicated.[16] Although previously vilified as environmentally destructive, recent work in Kissidougou starkly demonstrates
that inhabitants have been conscious wardens of the commons. Rather than
destroying forest cover, they have in fact been planting trees and seeding new
foliage. The people of Kissidougou "bluntly reverse policy orthodoxy, representing their landscape as half-filled and filling with forest, not half-emptied
and emptying of it" (2).[17] The competing narratives peddled by natives versus outsiders manufacture misrepresentations of the Kissidougou landscape.
What are seemingly apolitical cycles of plant growth must in fact be examined within the "contexts of local productive relations and wider economic
systems" (Moore 1996, 125). The extraction-focused characteristic of colonial
economies, as well as the clientelist aspect of postindependence Guinea-
Conakry, influence the misperceptions within which Kissidougou is trapped.

     Kissidougou is a prime example of the multidimensional nature of space;
space is not only territorial but also social and cultural (Darian-Smith, Gunner, and Nuttall 1996, 2). This multipronged approach informs my own discussion of how land, landscape, place, and space are depicted across a variety of Eastern and Southern African literary texts. As a dynamic concept,
landscape encompasses historical, "cultural contestations," as well as "mul-

tiple and complex meanings attached to both land and place" (3). If some of the literature I examine is only tangentially interested in space, place, land, and landscape, *Different Shades of Green: African Literature, Environmental Justice, and Political Ecology* nevertheless encourages such study. Byron Caminero-Santangelo (2014, 8) argues that an African canon that highlights the "relationship between anticolonial struggle and the fight against environmentally destructive legacies of colonialism can still be considered environmental and can be more important rhetorically in the struggle against ecologically destructive processes than forms of nature and environmentalist writing that suppresses histories of empire." Caminero-Santangelo privileges the disentangling of connections between colonialism, modernity, empire, and global climate change. I wholly second that view. As previously noted, the parallel destruction of African ontologies has done as much damage to the environment as the rapacious extraction of raw materials from the continent's forests, rivers, oceans, farmlands, and mineral deposits. Caminero-Santangelo's "postcolonial regional particularism" decenters traditional ecocritical approaches, attends to global imperialism, and illuminates not just nonhuman subjects but also human others (9–10). I advance a similar theoretical approach, unlike first-wave ecocriticism that Caminero-Santangelo indicts for its propensity to expunge the history of indigenous communities, their resistance against colonial subjugation, and their patterns of migration, which complicate Western notions of settlement versus wilderness (10). I endorse an inversion of the nature/culture binary on which European views of African lands and landscapes have previously been based. Coherent definitions of space and place enable us to better appreciate the cultural dimension of ongoing environmental crises.[18] Humanists and artists, despite all appearances to the contrary, are vital for a truly global climate revolution. Fully addressing ongoing climatic changes demands combining knowledge areas.[19] Representations of land and landscape in Eastern and Southern African literature are exemplary of relations between humans and their ecology. At its most profound, the current environmental crisis is a matter of how we, as a global community, variously relate to our home planet.

My central argument depends on reading beyond human life—incorporating flora, fauna, and molecular life. A dual-track examination of colonial empires and the presence of nonhuman life demonstrates analogous "treatment by humans of nonhuman others and the way colonialists view[ed] the colonized natives. Similar parallels exist between the way humans treat animals and the manner they treat human minorities" (Mwangi 2019, 2). This conclusion demands renewed appreciation of the agential capacity that non-human life has on the environment. The elephant is a case in point:

> Elephants in the African savannas clear bush, knock over trees and trample paths to waterholes, creating a patchwork of habitats that can support more species of animals and plants than either a grassland or a closed-in woodland. Rainforest elephants, by feeding on fallen fruits and depositing their seeds in piles of nutrient-rich dung, are important regenerators of growth and dispersers of forest trees. (Orenstein 2013, 17)

Our own bias about humanity's superiority in the animal kingdom leads to repeated failure in grasping the capabilities of nonhuman life. More so when flora and fauna are represented in works of art. Our interpretation of such depictions falls short, or merely confirms prejudice in favor of human invincibility. *Naturalizing Africa: Ecological Violence, Agency, and Postcolonial Resistance in African Literature* proposes that "the relationship between humans and other life forms in African literature has significant implications for rethinking questions of agency and resistance in African studies as well as in postcolonial studies" (Iheka 2017, 2). How African writers incorporate plant and animal life in their work influences critical discussions about local and global decolonial activism against imperialism. *Cultivating the Colonies: Colonial States and Their Environmental Legacies* argues that "European rule in the tropical colonies showed the extraordinary impact of humans on the environment and the speed at which they could destroy nature" (Oslund 2011, 2). It was during the colonial era that science and technology were increasingly deployed in interactions between humans and nature since, ultimately, "managing plants and managing people were not, after all, very different from each other" (2). Ecofeminism, especially as constructed by Africanist theorists, exposes slippage between how landscapes and female bodies are imagined. Ayo Coly's *Postcolonial Hauntologies: African Women's Discourses of the Female Body* (2019) delineates "the production of the African female body as a privileged rhetorical element of both colonial and postcolonial discourses about Africa" (11). Black bodies, which happened to be female, were distorted by colonial and postcolonial powers as allegories of place. In the three land transactions described previously, conversations of land in gendered terms resonate with Coly's assertion that "the strong presence of the African female body in the colonial visual archive aligns with the metonymic construction of Africa and the African female body" (24). At the level of everyday speech,

I witnessed that invoking land in metaphoric language portraying women served as an opening formula to these property negotiations. Marjorie O. Macgoye, in her poem "For Miriam," evokes "Mother Africa" as a stand-in for the female persona. Mother Africa remarks that her "fingers are hard and stiff . . . to hoe / the heat-cracked furrow, husk the grain, [and] split pods" (Macgoye 1995, 118). Macgoye's Mother Africa is associated with toil and hard agricultural labor.

African Literature Today: Environmental Transformations positions African ecocriticism as redefining personhood to highlight "shared agency among humans, other life forms, and things" (Iheka and Newell 2020, 5). This is a critique of the African literary corpus that pays attention to flora, fauna, topography, and the ecology at large. What the authors characterize as "powerfully post-human and cross-species imaginations" are indeed a hallmark of the writing we encounter (3). To paraphrase Henri Lefebvre (1991, 39), this kind of literature is produced by artists who "aspire to do [much] more than describe."[20] Catherine Boone's (2012) analysis of land-related tensions in Kenyan elections over the last forty years extends Lefebvre's thesis regarding spatial appropriation. Boone argues that competition for land in Kenya manifests as "struggles to capture or retain state power" (77). This interpretation is particularly poignant regarding bogus civil strife; as Boone contends, "opportunistic [Kenyan] politicians manipulated local issues and fomented violence for electoral gain, but the tensions they manipulated were, to a large extent, land-related and long-standing" (78).[21] Arguing that "human existence requires land for existence" Cezula and Modise (2020, 15) challenges the colonial fallacy of tabula rasa by asking "'Was the land empty, or was the land emptied'" (8)? Emptied, indeed. By adopting the kind of "multifocalization" advocated for in *Geocriticism: Real and Fictional Spaces*, we witness an array of inhabitants who were forced off the land: hunter-gatherers, farmers, pastoralists, fishing communities, nomads, wildlife, migrating fauna, indigenous flora, and much else besides (Westphal 2011b, 114). At the supernatural level, alienating human communities from their forests, valleys, mountains, and so forth meant cutting access to sacred spaces; the result was a loss of spiritual traditions akin to denying worshipers passage to their shrines and temples.

The tripartite alliance of European settler-farmers, evangelizing missionaries, and colonial administrators—while aiming at unique goals—often united in their quest for alienating African lands (Gathogo 2020, 4). Tabitha Kanogo's *Squatters and the Roots of the Mau Mau 1906–63* (1987) examines Gĩkũyũ squatters as a key element in fomenting the anti-British Land and

Freedom movement (derogatively termed Mau Mau). Kanogo discusses cultural and sociopolitical forms of coercion that expressly sought to create a cheap pool of unskilled agricultural labor available for white settler farmers (1–2). For one, European settlers depicted East Africa's savannahs as safari country.[22] Trophy hunters—including Ernest Hemingway and Theodore Roosevelt—alongside tourists, flocked to the Rift Valley, jousting with Maa-speaking communities for the area's sense of freedom. Ole Kulet's *Blossoms of the Savannah* interrogates the ways in which young Maa women's subjecthood is not always aligned to the same ideals of limitless self-fashioning. This perception of space extends beyond the physical senses. Proponents of geocriticism correctly argue that "places are perceived with our eyes, but it seems most appropriate to diversify sensing to include the sounds, smells, tastes, and textures of a place" (Westphal 2011a, xiv). Robert Tally Jr. (2011, 2) notes that geocriticism "explores, seeks, surveys, digs into, reads, and writes a place; it looks at, listens to, touches, smells, and tastes spaces." What I find to be missing from this approach is an acknowledgment that geographies can *also* be perceived from a metaphysical point of view.

UNRAVELING THE FALSE BINARIES OF TIME, PLACE, URBANITY, AND GENDER

Places and spaces evoke memories; they can be routes toward the supernatural. As Fiona Moolla (2016, 1) notes in *Natures of Africa: Ecocriticism and Animal Studies in Contemporary Cultural Forms*, "recognition of the life of animals and the significance of the natural world" is common in various customs and traditions across the African continent. Asking new questions and reading differently, encompassed in how geocriticism encourages us to rethink the "ways that we make sense of our own spaces, of our own mappings" necessarily involves incorporating the supernatural, the beyond-human, and the other-worldly (Tally 2011, 8).[23] Beyond ecofeminism and geocriticism, there's also the burgeoning field of ecomedia—a cross-genre and cross-media examination of the ways in which storytellers invoke the natural world in their narratives. "Working across media as method hues [*sic*] closer to the spirit of interconnection animating the environmental humanities. [In fact,] the fullest scope of ecological relations manifests not only in the interface of geographies and lifeforms but also when various media interact in the environmental humanities" (Iheka 2021, 63). There is a wholesomeness to such African ontologies as *ubuntu* (*ũmũndũ* in Gĩkũyũ, *utu* in Kiswahili), which encompass not only human inhabitants but also the ancestral dead, the unborn, flora, fauna, and varied topographical features.[24] The Cartesian dualism of mind/body is largely inadequate in representing this continuum of life and living beings. Jill E. Kelly (2018, xxxvii) expounds further on this connection, elaborating on how Cape Town's Table Mountain provided "physical and spiritual security" as well as sustenance. Mickias Musiyiwa (2016) explores Shona land mythology, especially as espoused in popular songs; elsewhere, in close readings of poetry by Chenjerai Hove and Musaemura Zimunya, Syned Mthathiwa (2016, 277) proposes that "the presence of animals and other aspects of nature . . . reveals and highlights the Shona people's embeddedness in their ecology, and exposes the relationship between the people, their land, and flora and fauna." Similarly, James Wachira (2016) describes Samburu and Ndorobo ecopoetics as fashioned through animal praise poetry. Kelly, Musiyiwa, Mthathiwa, and Wachira demonstrate that indigenous communities variously expressed human-ecosystem relationships, weaving (hi)stories, imagined or otherwise, that imbue geographies with metaphysical attributes.[25]

The colloquialisms *marching through history* and *penetrating space* demonstrate the ways in which Western thought classifies time vs. space into binary gender categories. This is an apt portrayal of what Edward Soja (2010, 1) terms "spatiality of justice"; geography, Soja argues, "is an integral and formative component of justice itself, a vital part of how justice and injustice are socially constructed and evolve over time." Sylvia Tamale's *Decolonization and Afro-Feminism* explicitly connects ongoing "exploitation of women [to] the degradation of the environment" (2020, 6). As a rejoinder, Tamale offers an Africanist ecofeminism, one that "mimics and recycles" the continent's indigenous knowledge systems in the analysis of how both women and nature have been commoditized by anthropocentrism and capitalist-patriarchy (86). Doreen Massey's *Space, Place, and Gender* notes that "time which is aligned with history, progress, civilization, politics, and transcendence [is] coded masculine"; space, misperceived as "absence or lack," is coded feminine (1994, 6). The relationship between time-space and gender influences depictions of land and landscape; transforming the natural environment through agriculture, industry, or even wildlife conservation is encouraged, often at the expense of indigenous communities.[26] Class prejudice, as well as racism and sexism, influence how variously identified subjects experience their surroundings. Overall, "a fuller recognition of the simultaneous coexistence of others with their own trajectories and their own stories to tell" encourages us to think beyond human inhabitants of a particular ecosystem, incorporating into our awareness not only flora and fauna but also the otherworldly beings with which we cohabit the planet (Massey 1994, 11). It is worth noting, as Cheryl Wu (2016, 142) argues, that "the challenge of locating environmental issues in African literature lies in the fact that they may not look like environmental issues, as addressed or represented in Anglo-American environmental literature." *Global Feminist Politics: Identities in a Changing World* argues for a "reworking of allegiances that cross the divides within the term 'women'" (Ali, Coate, and wa Goro, 2000, 3). The text zeros in on the diverse class, racial, age, disability, and sexuality identities collapsed into the broad category of *women*. Each constituent has unique aspirations.

Oyèrónkẹ́ Oyěwùmí's *The Invention of Women: Making an African Sense of Western Gender Discourses* (1997) argues that the very category "women" deserves reexamining. Oyěwùmí contends that in precolonial Yorùbá culture, "the body was not the basis of social roles, inclusions, or exclusions; it was not the foundation of social thought and identity" (x). Subsequently, colonial and postcolonial directives against women's access to, and ownership of, land must be approached skeptically and with an eye toward ideologies of patriarchy and "biological determinism" (x). Kenyan writer Rebeka Njau, for instance, recounts a story in which a woman—stuck in a land dispute between her brothers and her late father—committed suicide (James and Njau 1990, 104). It is worth noting that there exists a *proto* ecofeminism in women's poetry from the Seventies. Adeola James, in her interviews of African women writers, sketches out an aesthetic impulse that variously encompasses artistic production, socioeconomic justice, and environmental activism. James notes that

> our world will be destroyed unless we do something urgently to save it. In the early 1960s, we denounced colonialism; today, we need to speak out, to join together across the continents to save ourselves, and to begin to prepare a viable future for our children. This is the only way we can arrest the cycle of suffering, poverty and oppression. (1990, 6)

Rebeka Njau (her pen name is Marina Gashe) and Uganda's Assumpta Acam-Oturu explore the backbreaking work associated with plowing the land and subsistence agriculture. Njau's (1995, 117) poem, "The Village," laments that both young and old women

> *Plod up and down the rolling village farms*
> *With loads on their backs*
> *And babies tied to their bellies.*
> *In the fields all day they toil*
> *Stirring up the soil with hands and knives.*

Similarly, "Arise to the Day's Toil" by Acam-Oturu highlights the never-ending nature of rural economic production. The poem's narrator summons the woman:

> *Wake up—it's time to weed the fields*
> *in the distant hills . . . Until the cock crows*
> *And the circle begins again. (1995, 142).*

In both Acam-Oturu's and Njau's work, women are the main forms of labor animating African landscapes and providing sustenance for their families. Micere Githae Mugo's "I Want You to Know" (1972) explores a more equitable interaction between two individuals and the land around them.

> *I watered the tender shoots*
> *you planted*
> *in my little garden*
> *. . . Flowers now adorn the ground*
> *the fruits are ripe. (1995, 128)*

The poem invites an open-ended interpretation of planting, gardening, flowering, and harvesting. There is an undercurrent of sexual intimacy between the persona and the subject addressed in the poem. The open-endedness includes the possibility of same-sex desire coming to fruition.

LINGUISTIC PLURALITY AS A CATALYST FOR ECOLOGICAL DIVERSITY

Mugo, Acam-Oturu, and Njau highlight labor-intensive subsistence agriculture. Women, men defined as landless, and the youth were generally expected to provide most of the work time. Paradoxically, when male black writers describe the Kenyan landscape, they omit the productive energy required to prepare farmlands, plant, weed, harvest, and turn a profit. Ngũgĩ wa Thiongo's *Dreams in a Time of War* (2010) portrays the farming districts of his childhood. Ngũgĩ remembers walking home from school along a path that "went through a series of ridges and valleys, but when listening to a tale, one did not notice the ridge and fields of corn, potatoes, peas, and beans, each field bounded by wattle trees or hedges of kei apple and gray thorny bushes" (5). In visualizing this verdant neighborhood, Ngũgĩ neglects to mention which segments of the local community spend time working the land. Ngũgĩ's rural idyll, unlike Njau's poem, disconnects agricultural productivity from backbreaking activities. As Susan Kiguli (2012, 74) notes, "Ngũgĩ sees real value in connecting and harnessing the power of what he refers to as the African peasantry who are the essential producers of labour"; this recovery, however, accompanies a dismissal of black women's contributions. Beyond agrarian production, land lies at the "basis of social and political power, and therefore at the heart of gender inequalities in the control of resources" (Tsikata and Amanor-Wilks 2009, 1). In Kenya's Nakuru County, for instance, repeated land conflicts over the last three decades have resulted in "violence, leading to deaths, displacements, dislocations, and mistrust among people"; overwhelmingly so, women and children bear the brunt of these clashes (Nyaga et al. 2020, 1). Similarly, Elspeth Huxley's *Flame Trees of Thika: Memoirs of an African Childhood* (1959) views the surrounding vistas with no recognition of Gĩkũyũ female labor. Huxley is obsessed with the soil's "untapped fertility"; she describes this fallowness within the time span of millennia (3, 6). The implicit message in Huxley's description is that indigenous farmers have only to put in the bare minimum of effort for maximum husbandry returns. This assessment, as has been documented by environmental historians, is an erroneous representation of local systems of shift cultivation. Simultaneously, Huxley rhetorically creates space for white settler farmers. If African productivity is premised upon minimal investment, it is only fair that colonial farmers take over and make better use of the land. Grace Musila (2012, 224) brackets this as Kenya's "troubled reliance on a colonial archive of whiteness." Tragically, this phenomenon further manifests in the contemporary postcolonial moment as "grammars of whiteness articulated through white male authority and ownership of land and wildlife" (225).

Indeed, this underlying imperialist rhetoric is one key difference between Ngũgĩ's decolonial texts and the kinds of colonial writing produced by Huxley, Robert Ruark, Isak Dinesen, and others. On the one hand, juxtaposing Ngũgĩ's alongside Huxley's memoirs is contrasting two different forms of storytelling: Huxley's rhetoric of cartography versus Ngũgĩ's indigenous oral narratives performed in the vernacular and rendered in translation. For example, forms of the word "map" appear multiple times in Huxley's text. "Thika in those days . . . was a favorite camp for big-game hunters and beyond it there was only bush and plain. If you went on long enough you would come to mountains and forests no one had mapped and tribes whose languages no one could understand" (Huxley 1959, 1). Even when the young female protagonist is experiencing landscapes in real time, she still invokes the register of cartography to digest the sights and sounds in front of her. Logically, Huxley's perception of languages understood by "no one" and lands mapped by "no one" does not add up. Speakers of said languages understood each other, just as much as inhabitants of said unknown spaces had mental maps of their vicinity. What Huxley really means is that no "white-identifying" person spoke said languages or inhabited said lands. Huxley privileges white body supremacy in her description of unknown tongues and spaces. This violence is multiply depicted in *Flame Trees of Thika*. Huxley's description of a former South African pioneer, Henry Oram, skirts the outer edges of colonialist violence. "Oram was the kind of man who never settled down. He had left a prosperous farm in the Transvaal, and before that in the Free State, and before that in the Cape, to come to B.E.A. . . . and bully into productiveness another patch of bush and veld" (5). Huxley renders Oram's relationship to landscapes initially in Southern Africa and now in British East Africa (B.E.A.) within the realm of physical violence. Bullying the land is especially significant in South African and Kenyan colonial states that spawned racial segregation. Huxley, like Ruark, Dinesen, and other white colonial writers, couches this violence within the language of white supremacy. Huxley describes how "respect was the only protection available to Europeans who lived singly or in scattered families, among thousands of Africans accustomed to constant warfare and armed with spears and poisoned arrows" (9). The text summons fantasies of warring Africans to justify racial violence against colonized peoples.

Ngũgĩ addresses this viciousness, doing so in a way that focuses on the local as opposed to expansive land-grabbing gestures whose intent is colonialist and imperialist. Describing the escape of an armed guerrilla, presumably his older brother Good Wallace, Ngũgĩ states that the forest fighter ran "up the ridge till he disappeared, apparently unharmed, into the European-owned lush green tea plantations" (2010, 7). It is ironic that settler tea plantations provide safety for fleeing guerrillas; in the first place, it is European cash crop agriculture that has occasioned the violence from which Good Wallace and his compatriots are fleeing. Ngũgĩ seizes tea plantations and reorients them within the ecology of decolonization, as opposed to settler instincts of weaponizing the environment. Ngũgĩ's canonical work approaches issues of African land rights from multiple perspectives—especially the influence of neo-postcolonial domination. Here, I not only complicate our understanding of postindependence African nationalism but also extend Ngũgĩ's discussion of postcolonial citizenship by closely examining categories of identity such as class, ethnicity, and gender. There exists a large body of well-deserved critical attention on Ngũgĩ's oeuvre.[27] I extend scholarship by Simon Gikandi, Evan Mwangi, Gĩchingiri Ndĩgĩrĩgĩ, and James Ogude on Ngũgĩ's literature—as well as analysis by Mukoma wa Ngũgĩ on other Makerere writers—to examine Ngũgĩ's female contemporary: Grace Ogot.

Alongside Ngũgĩ's *Weep Not, Child* (1964), *The River Between* (1965), and *A Grain of Wheat* (1967) was Grace Ogot's *The Promised Land* (1966). I perceive similarly anticolonial aesthetics and motifs in Ngũgĩ's and Ogot's texts, and yet Ogot has garnered barely a fraction of Ngũgĩ's literary acclaim. In the first chapter, I provide much needed critical attention to Ogot's writing. As the first female author published in Eastern Africa, Ogot holds a luminary position that helps magnify the region's literary canon. Signe Arnfred and Akosua Adomako Ampofo, in their introduction to *African Feminist Politics of Knowledge: Tensions, Challenges, Possibilities* (2009), propose feminist activism and scholarship as "ultimately about transformation. Visions and hope for a better future are necessary ingredients of feminist knowledge production" (25). Kenya's Akili Dada, a nonprofit focused on girl's education, laments that although African women have robust mentoring traditions "we continue to rely on western epistemological/theoretical models on mentorship, which often do not capture the multiplicities/realities that exist in African socio-political contexts" (Kabira, Nderitu, and Kabira 2020, 4). As Amina Mama (2019, 2) contends, African feminist theorizing and praxis is "a woman-centered radical political philosophy" that continuously renews itself by leveraging the "intellectual labor of sustained reflection."[28] What is noteworthy is the extent to which imperial knowledge systems distorted what were previously wide-ranging accommodations of gender nuances. Ifi Amadiume's (1987) work on gender in precolonial Igbo communities is instructive. Amadiume notes that "the flexibility of Igbo gender construction meant that gender was separate from biological sex. Daughters could become sons and consequently male. Daughters and women in general could be husbands to wives and consequently males in relation to their wives" (15). The mapping of Victorian sensibilities regarding masculinity and femininity onto Igbo society created rupture. Part of the recovery work that African ecofeminists attempt includes reconstruction of the various ways it meant to be "man," "woman," or gender nonconforming. There's an established intellectual genealogy that links gender-based violence with environmental degradation. Patricia Kameri-Mbote's "Access, Control and Ownership: Women and Sustainable Environmental Management in Africa" connects the kinds of man-made ecological changes that Ngũgĩ depicts with feminist politics, identifying a "disjuncture between women's movement and the environment movement in Africa" (2007, 37). South African writer Lindsey Collen argues that her own fiction, especially *The Rape of Sita* (1993), "examines politics, colonialism, and sexual violence as related fronts in women's resistance" (2004, 103). Maria Lugones's (2008, 747) work on decolonial feminism similarly identifies a "complex interaction of economic, racializing, and gendering systems." What Lugones terms the "coloniality of gender" is established on a "dichotomous hierarchy between the human and the nonhuman" (743). Male/female and human/nonhuman have been foundational binary systems in the sociopolitical organization of our world over the last 400–500 years.

SYMBIOTIC RELATIONSHIPS BETWEEN COMMUNITIES AND TOPOGRAPHIES

A three-mile hike on an unpaved Oloitokitok road offers a microcosm of ongoing land transformation. During the long droughts on this leeward side of Mt. Kilimanjaro, dust abounds. Trucks plunge wheels deep into a fine gray powder that blows every which way under a slight breeze. Overhead, there is better evidence of *development*: three electric pylons transmitting power from the Emali-Oloitokitok highway. More evidence of *progress*: a large private development sits between the dusty road and the Kimana Sanctuary. Given its proximity to the wildlife reserve, residents muse that this will likely be a tourist hotel. Those rumors are also based on the architecture: two-story townhouses facing the park. Directives by Kenya's National Environmental Management Authority—that all construction sites clearly display a project description and the names of the proprietor, contractor, and civil engineer—are flouted here. Top Kenyan politicians are whispered in relation to ownership of this hotel; nothing has been confirmed yet. I am deeply intrigued by the various kinds of *time* that flow side by side in this space. Right next to the expansive but mysterious construction site is a patch of young tomato seedlings. Several men are sweating under the noon sun while running water from one *jaruba* to the next. Jarubas are shallow basin-like structures cut from the volcanic Oloitokitok soil. Plants are seeded in the banks of these jarubas and irrigation is directed into the center. Tomatoes (*nyanya* in Gĩkũyũ/Kiswahili) mature in three months. The humid heat in Oloitokitok, plus daily irrigation, pushes the plants from seedlings to flowering to fruits at a brisk pace. Calves, cows, bulls, goats, and sheep graze along the road. The herds cut across and head toward Kimana Sanctuary; they feed alongside its electric fencing. Birdlife follows closely behind—landing on the backs of twitching cattle to pick off insects and ticks. Goats and sheep might give birth twice annually, while young heifers are sold off at the Kimana livestock market at the age of two or three years. Wild herbivores, especially zebras and herds of male Thompson gazelles, are feeding on shrubs not too far away. Zebras love this spot—often rolling in the dust on hot afternoons. Noisy individuals bray out loud; gazelles watch me watch them. I squat in the shade of a thorny bush. They stare right back; it's clear who's invading whose space.

Three hundred meters away, there's a sixty-acre farm owned by Wawerũ, a former trucker from Nebraska. Originally from Wangige, closer to Nairobi, he moved to the United States in the early 2000s and lived in Illinois. Of his many occupations, struggling to attain his American dream, the latest was as a truck driver. He plied the Midwest, on routes I-35 and I-80. When we first met, we reminisced about Nebraska winters. Now, he farms. On his return to Kenya, he bought the sixty-acre farm. He also imported agricultural equipment, packed into shipping containers: used tractors, combines, push lawn mowers, and generators. He dug into the Oloitokitok aquifer and pumps water to irrigate green beans, bell peppers, onions, and tomatoes. Some of his bean crop has been exported via trucks to the port of Mombasa and from there shipped to the Gulf. Oloitokitok's complexity is its presence along competing moments of time and space. Within the Kenyan imaginary, Oloitokitok is far off—hundreds of kilometers from hip urban areas. These off-grid, bush spaces are reserved for backward peasants and tourists: both apparently reveling in reversing developmental time. Nevertheless, given Oloitokitok's position along the highway to Tanzania, there's regional cross-border commerce and migration. Beneath more recent patterns of movement lie indigenous cycles of pastoralism, as well as bird and wildlife migration. There are also plant phases of germination, fruition, death, and decay. Many acacia trees in this region are centuries old, more ancient than the colonial and postindependence governments that have intermittently claimed supreme dominion. There is a fast-food kind of agribusiness in Oloitokitok. It is characterized by flood irrigation; heavy use of fertilizers, pesticides, and herbicides; cutting or at best heavily pruning indigenous Ol Tepes trees; and charcoal production. The thin scrubland that covers the region is hardly able to secure the topsoil against both wind and water erosion. The results are alarming.

Land metamorphosis is tied to, and influences, symbiotic relationships between communities and topographies. The projects listed above unfold simultaneously. Farmers look to the tourist development and envision new markets for their produce. Residents evaluate the buzz of economic activity and celebrate the rise of property values. This increase, in turn, fuels another cycle of land purchase by speculators who, rightly so, point to ongoing entrepreneurial activity to attract buyers and turn a quick profit. Each new land venture affects previous occupants and influences future patterns of settlement. The complexities of contemporary land conversions are added to historical challenges and concerns. And before residents or regional governments have disentangled either the past or the present, the future has arrived. Land has been a key cause of contention in the past. This continues to be the case in the present. And given the effects of population growth, climate change, global flows of capital, and ongoing resistance to patriarchy, land *is* guaranteed to remain at the center of many emerging conflicts, violent or otherwise. Consequently, African writers theorize an expansive, holistic depiction of African lives. When we read Eastern and Southern African literature with a keen eye toward African languages, we cannot help but recognize representations of African lands and landscapes: African tongues and the spaces in which they are spoken are inseparable. African languages are repositories of indigenous knowledge—including aesthetics, spatial representation, and ecological know-how to support diverse kinds of economic and subsistence activities. It is difficult to depict African lands without referring to the languages that animate said spaces.[29] Conversely, it is awkward to discuss African languages without addressing the spaces where respective languages exist. For example, conversations about Sheng must inevitably reference the urban spaces and milieus within which Sheng was birthed. Those include not only flashy middle-class lifestyles but also the informal settlements where survival is tough and luxury is an elusive concept. Such a spatial-analytical approach must not circumscribe the language, rather this inquiry informs a deeper reflection on the nuances behind words, phrases, and other forms of written/oral/nonverbal communication.

To study post-Sixties Eastern and Southern African fiction with an eye on colonial projects launched in the 1800s is, simultaneously, to scrutinize global climatic changes since the onset of the Industrial Revolution. This is not by accident. Simon Gikandi (2005) sees untapped potential in postcolonialism's opposition to empire. Citing the complexity of intertwined societies, Gikandi argues that "emphasis on culture in postcolonial theory hinders the recognition of the global experience as a structural experience" (622). Rethinking "the politics of global time itself" means a willingness to critically engage the historical context within which my chosen texts emerge (619). Additionally, I pay close attention to how authors deploy history in their work. How the past is marshalled—and to what purposes—influences our views about the present. The teleology of global time—often oriented toward Western Europe and North America—is itself worth questioning.[30] We cannot continue with business as usual.[31] Understanding human-induced transformation of the environment depends on transcending the very tools of Western modernity that caused the problem: rational thinking addicted to binary interpretations of the world. These explanations manifest as oppositional classifications: European/Other, man/woman, human/animal, nature/culture, and, of course, civilization/savagery.

Notions about large tracts of arable African land waiting for investors have produced "successive land rushes" since the late nineteenth century (Cotula 2013, 8). To date, this relentless lust for Africa's soil means that "land acquisition in Africa is still driven by the dependence of Western societies on an expanding availability of material good—fuel for our cars, pensions for our future, and a determination to reduce our carbon footprint without fundamentally questioning our consumption patterns" (174). There is a profound disconnect between land as an investment vehicle—as envisioned by domestic/foreign capital—and land as a source of social and cultural ties—as experienced by local communities.[32] Artistic production—such as the literature examined in this book—attends to the key concerns of access, control, and land ownership. Nuances regarding the balance of power emerge as authors represent land and landscape in their writing. For instance, Ngũgĩ's *Petals of Blood* (1977) arrives at the same conclusion as *The Great African Land Grab*: the central issue in discussions about African lands is "control—who should have the authority to shape key decisions and processes" (Cotula 2013, 181). As Abdon Rwegasira's *Land as a Human Right: A History of Land Law and*

Practice in Tanzania (2012, xx) notes, land is not only fundamental to individual/communal existence, subsistence, and livelihoods but also an arena for legal conflicts with losers and winners in the tension between implicit rights and attendant duties. The African continent is currently facing another scramble for land—(mostly) foreign, like previous ones, and intent on rearranging African social and communal life.[33]

These global ventures make my intervention urgent, given contemporary acquisition of African lands and the media coverage surrounding these transactions. Such events include Chinese infrastructural projects in Ethiopia, Kenya, and Nigeria; Malaysian land leases for biofuels in Tanzania (Mesic 2019); Senegalese-Italian sunflower production (Liberti 2013); and Qatari agribusinesses to grow food in Kenya. In addition, there are American, Chinese, and French naval bases in Djibouti, a proposed Russian naval base in Port Sudan, and U.S. unmanned aerial vehicle units in Niger. While these military sites are initially positioned as a bulwark against global terrorism, they are also evidence of an American, Chinese, and Russian arms race. Meanwhile, the European Union is opposed to multinational corporations using expansive tracts of arable lands in West Africa to supply Europe's staple foods. Consequently, smallholder farmers' loss of previously cultivated fields has been adopted by Western media as the political issue of our times— one with easily identifiable culprits (wealthy nations from Asia and the Arab Emirates) and familiar victims (helpless Africans). Evidently, the liberationist mandate laid out in the 1986 African (Banjul) Charter on Human and People's Rights lives on. The Charter asserts Africans' right to "freely dispose of their wealth and natural resources" and also the "right to a general satisfactory environment" (Article 21, 24). A decolonial aspiration to "eradicate all forms of colonialism" must safeguard both aspirations (Preamble).[34] As Marzec (2007, 25) poignantly poses, "What is it about the character of land that has led it to be invoked as the cause of such anxiety and dread?" Land-related inequality is worsening, exacerbated by processes of wealth accumulation whereby corporations and wealthy individuals grab an increasingly disproportionate share of profits (Wegerif anf Guereña 2020). I extend the critical work done in decolonial studies and examine aesthetic representations of land and landscapes.

I advance the historicist interventions embedded in texts such as Crawford Young's *The Postcolonial State in Africa: Fifty Years of Independence, 1960–2010* (2012) and Abiola Irele's *The Cambridge Companion to the African Novel* (2009). While expansive, these books do not explicitly scrutinize the role of land in African politics or of landscape in the continent's literary canon. Likewise, Neil Lazarus's *Cambridge Companion to Postcolonial Literary Studies* omits any mention of lands/landscapes despite the book's aim "to contextualize the emergence and defining trajectories of postcolonial studies in broad socio-historical terms" (2004, 15). In its decolonial thrust, my project redefines time and space. Although I examine texts published in the five decades from 1966 to 2014, my critical discussion is informed by the deep history of Eastern and Southern African community building. I also take into consideration the presence of European commercial, educational, military, and religious agents. My close reading of fiction by Monica Arac de Nyeko, Grace Ogot, Margaret Ogola, Yvonne Owuor, Moyez G. Vassanji, and others is anchored in the 150-year history beginning in the early 1800s. I deliberately chose this approach to problematize the exceptionality through which African postindependence nations are interpreted. Dystopic post-Sixties African regimes are dissected in Western mass media as though having emerged fully grown in 1959. Such reviews rarely tie the impunity of postcolonial governments to the ravages of a colonial state. And even more seldom does such commentary contextualize the millennium of state-formation that precedes nineteenth-century European colonial presence on the African continent. Concomitant to this temporal narrow-mindedness is a fetishistic approach to the political boundaries of contemporary African nation-states. My own intervention, however, repeatedly crosses national frontiers as I trace sociopolitical similarities across ethnic and civic identities. Here, once again, Mama's (1995, 13) commentary on multiplicity is strongly resonant, including her assertions that African lives exist across "several contexts simultaneously." Rather than subsume local idiosyncrasies, my theoretical reading highlights patterns of resistance when communities face colonial or neocolonial hegemonies.

I chose to focus on contiguous nation-states in Eastern Africa because the geographic proximity disguises an ideological complexity. Land has meant something fundamental in the sociocultural history of each country. Those concerns, however, have manifested in varied political events. The range of struggles over land has spawned a multiplicity of literary interventions. While Kenya and Uganda were both British colonies, Kenya's experience of settler land alienation made for a much more violent response against efforts at political independence. Uganda's relatively calm unyoking from the colonial burden, however, led to a tumultuous postindependence, one marked not only by autocratic military regimes and anti-Indian xenophobia in the

1970s but also by civil strife in the 2000s. Given common concerns about land alienation, citizenship, and identity Uganda's and Kenya's divergent political destinies were wholly unpredictable. Tanzania, too, like Kenya and Uganda, resisted British colonial administration—after Germany's defeat in World War 1. In Tanzania's case, long-running concerns about German and British land theft, and eighteenth-century Arab enslavement, manifested as radical revolution in Zanzibar and as Ujamaa, President Mwalimu Julius Nyerere's philosophy of African socialism. By the 1980s, the promise of Ujamaa had turned into bitter ash, despite, or perhaps precisely because of, Tanzania's explicit efforts fighting Portuguese colonialism in Angola and Mozambique, as well as South African apartheid. The contrast to Kenya and Uganda, with whom Tanzania shares Nam Lolwe (Lake Victoria), is stark. Ethiopia's ability to repel European colonial incursions in the nineteenth century gave way to a checkered and dynamic twentieth century. The country's experience was marked by antifascism in the 1930s, Haile Selassie's monarchy until the early 1970s, followed by socialism and military dictatorship until the early 1990s. Each of these moments has influenced the symbolic and literal meanings associated with land. For example, our contemporary reading of Ethiopian landscapes is inevitably tinged with global collective memories of extreme food insecurity and famine in the 1980s. Finally, I have included Zimbabwean texts in this book for comparative purposes. Zimbabwe, like Kenya, Uganda, and Tanzania, was under British colonial administration. Like Kenya, Zimbabwe's struggle for political independence was marked by violence and uniquely prolonged. A settler economy supported a brutal and repressive regime based on white minority rule. And, just like Kenya, Zimbabwe continues to struggle with challenges of land reform, land redistribution, and political pluralism.

CHAPTER SYNOPSIS

In chapter 1, "Settlers, Lands, and Landscapes: Mystical Realism and the Presence of Nonhuman Life," I juxtapose Grace Ogot's *The Promised Land* (1966) with Margaret Ogola's *The River and the Source* (1994). This reading of the two novels foregrounds their rejection of the assumptions on which settler productivity is premised. Such an analytical investment reveals how colonial representations of land and landscape expunged the presence of animal, plant, and supernatural life forms predating human settlement. While settler-produced visual documents—maps, photographs, and pamphlets—betray an ideology that ignored indigenous land rights and simultaneously projected an idealized notion of British imperialism, Ogot and Ogola parody the settlers' mentality and its connection to brutality. Their fiction challenges the aesthetics of realist novels and highlights the violence enacted upon both colonized psyches and landscapes. I argue for a contrarian reading of the Eastern African canon—one that I term mystical realism. Mystical realism, as a narrative technique, decolonizes our reading and highlights the nonhuman and the supernatural in both the fictional and the natural worlds. Ogot, by re-creating the challenging journey of an indigenous family from homeland to foreign land, deconstructs colonial convictions about East Africa's emptiness and the availability of land for European settlement. Similarly, Ogola wields folklore to represent an indigenous landscape that is intricately dependent upon intergenerational custodianship. Akoko, a matriarch and Ogola's protagonist, narrates Luo mythology and matches these fables to the community's autochthony in western Kenya. For example, contemporary spaces such as Gem, Sakwa, and Rachuonyo have identical names to the heroes who people Akoko's stories.

"Land and Landscape in Zimbabwean Narratives of Transcendence," my second chapter, offers a contrapuntal reading of Yvonne Vera's poetic fiction against a backdrop of Zimbabwean novelists who are simultaneously steeped in both realism and nationalism. While Vera privileges a polyphonic and metaphoric narrative style in her writing, her compatriots foreground linearly driven plots. Authors such as Solomon Mutswairo, S. Nyamfukudza, and Charles Mungoshi confront the legacy of Southern African settler colonies via individualist bildungsroman texts that double as crucibles of the Zimbabwean nation-state. In contrast, another group of writers—led by A. Kanengoni and Yvonne Vera—resists Britain's imperial hegemony at the level of storytelling. Kanengoni's and Vera's work features a community of narrative voices. This orchestra of narrators has a womanist gaze on Zimbabwean lands and landscape—a scrutiny that exorcises capitalist, racist patriarchy. By incorporating multiple narrators—who stubbornly share their tales in nonlinear and circular plotlines—both novelists challenge entrenched pastoral visions of Zimbabwe and the heroic versions of Zimbabwean political history. Vera's collection of texts, for instance, midwifes an open and dynamic form of Zimbabwean citizenship. Vera's poetics in *The Stone Virgins* (2002) incorporate the consciousness of an entire community. To depict the heroism of her female protagonists, Vera weaves a tapestry of narrative positions that includes parents, lovers, peasants, wildlife, trees, and veterans of the Second Chimurenga resistance. This is a sense of belonging that resists registers of development, progress, and modernity—whether peddled by early twentieth-century white imperialism or by post-Sixties black nationalism.

Chapter 3, "Belonging and Mobility: Representations of Kenyan and Tanzanian Urban Landscapes" examines city-based fiction by Kenyan Marjorie O. Macgoye and Tanzanian Moyez G. Vassanji to argue that (post)colonial citizens enact belonging through performative acts of transgression and trespassing. My investigation differs from earlier discussions of African urban literature in that it examines the city as a cultural space and, simultaneously, as a geographic space. Town dwellers respond to these two aspects of the postcolonial African metropolis with a particular kind of political resistance: the performativity of agential power—often manifested as trespassing and transgression. This analysis of Marjorie Macgoye's *Coming to Birth* (1986) entails a discussion of female acts of transgressing, trespass, and performance. For instance, Macgoye's protagonist asserts belonging through her performativity as a city dweller; I argue that Nairobians react to social and physical barriers with deviance and disobedience. In this way, they have repeatedly reinserted their presence in the very spaces where it had been previously prohibited. The second half of the chapter features an examination of M. G. Vassanji's *Uhuru Street* (1991). Vassanji's work demands that a comprehensive appraisal of representation of land and landscape must include an appreciation of inhabitation and mobility. I consider, as fiction does, both private and public spaces as political terrains where power struggles are repeatedly played out. Physical terrains shape political conflicts: geographies either provide the subject for or the stage where these skirmishes unfold. Finally, by focusing on the supposed spatial transgressions of East Africa's Indian diaspora, Vassanji brings to fore questions of ethnicity and demonstrates how cultural and political struggles also shape physical spaces.

"African Languages, African Socialisms, and Representations of Lands and Landscapes," the fourth chapter, examines writing by Ethiopia's Berhane M. Sahle Sellassie and Tanzania's Ebrahim Hussein to demonstrate how the politics of African languages and literature influence representations of lands and landscapes. I argue that Sahle Sellassie and Hussein recenter African indigenous languages as sources of ecological expertise. Ebrahim Hussein's *Arusi* (1980) documents the transformation of Tanzania's colonial-era dependence into neocolonial subservience. Hussein's allegorical discussion of landscapes offers commentary on the rise of individualism at the expense of communalist norms. A disavowal of postcolonial African politics can be deduced from B. M. Sahle Sellassie's *The Afersata* (1968). *The Afersata* displays communal benevolence. In the novel, a sagging, crumbling down hut that burns and is "turned into ashes" serves not only as an object of human shelter but also as a metaphor of the Ethiopian landscape (3). Sahle Sellassie's text, like Hussein's, indicts the state for its autocracy and inability to entrench bottom-up socioeconomic reform. Finally, *The Afersata* is seminal in discussions of landscape representations because the text's imagery of creation and destruction invites a comparison to similar language in Ethiopian political rhetoric.

The final chapter investigates how humanity and the ecology influence each other using work by Kenya's Yvonne A. Owuor and Uganda's Monica Arac de Nyeko. "Representations of Lands and Landscapes at the Humanity-Ecology Interface" argues that Owuor's and Nyeko's writing—though disparate in time and place—demonstrates how environmental trauma often accompanies physical violence against women and ethnic minorities. Owuor's *Dust* (2014) depicts the unfolding cycles of life and death in northern Kenya's spaces. The second half of this chapter performs close readings of M. Arac de Nyeko's short stories; the value of this analysis is threefold. Nyeko's oeuvre anchors the female subject in depictions of land and landscape, while also inviting an exploration of why claims of territoriality are often laced with ethnic prejudice. Hence, her short fiction is a powerful cultural artifact and analytical tool for discussions regarding, simultaneously, narrative and its potential for resistance, the pastoral as a literary genre, violence—especially as it is manifested on the female body—and, ultimately, representations of land. Finally, Nyeko's "Banana Eater" (2008) exposes gender and ethnic marginalization vis-à-vis urban landscapes.

In lieu of a conclusion, my coda elaborates on the use of Africa's indigenous languages in knowledge production. I demonstrate the benefits of such an approach, including a deeper engagement with African ontologies and a reversal of contemporary publishing and reading infrastructures that marginalize African languages while subservient to English, French, and other European tongues. I read Peter Hewitt's *Kenya Cowboy: A Police Officer's Account of the Mau Mau Emergency* (1999), Ngũgĩ wa Thiong'o's *Petals of Blood* (1977), as well as Ronjaunee Chatterjee, Alicia M. Christoff, and Amy R. Wong's (2020) "Undisciplining Victorian Studies" (2020). My juxtaposition of these texts argues for decolonial depictions of ecologies—premised on Africa's indigenous languages.

CHAPTER 1

Settlers, Lands, and Landscapes

Mystical Realism and the Presence of Nonhuman Life

To decolonize representation means to decolonize the cultures through which those systems of representation were produced.
—Catherine Hall, *Cultures of Empire: Colonizers in Britain and the Empire in the Nineteenth and Twentieth Centuries*

When I first read Margaret Ogola, I was struck by the similarities between her female characters' life journey and my own family's migrations and movements. Like Ogola's characters, my maternal great-grandmother experimented with Christianity and formal colonial education in attempts to expand her own life horizons. On the other hand, Grace Ogot's depiction of transregional migration resonated with the voyages made by Karūgū, Mariibe, and other members of my father's kin. Guka Kiongo had long been an acquaintance. My father and Njoki wa Kiongo, his eldest daughter, were classmates. His wife, Grace Wanjirū, had known my paternal grandmother, Hannah Njeri, in the 1930s. Their fathers were tight friends. In the early 1990s, Mr. Kiongo was our next-door neighbor, before he relocated his family to Oloitoktok. We're walking around his neighborhood in 2017 and he's explaining how desolate the landscape was when he first moved here. There were no trees, he points out. And there were few residents who identified as Gīkūyū. He describes how a Gīkūyū visitor distinguished a homestead where he could expect a friendly reception. We planted *Mūkindūri* trees at the entrance to the homestead, he says. A home with a Mūkindūri tree growing in the front yard was probably inhabited by a member of the Gīkūyū community, as opposed to the autochthonous Maasai bomas. Such was a residence he could approach comfortably, strike up a conversation with the owner, and quench his traveler's thirst with a cup of tea.

The Kimana Sanctuary is a community-owned conservancy that connects two highly frequented national parks in the Oloitoktok area: Tsavo West and Amboseli. The sanctuary's 600-odd acres provide ample roaming grounds for the elephant herds that migrate annually between Tsavo and Amboseli. Mr. Saitoti, a game warden, describes how to tell which direction the elephants are traveling: those from the Tsavo region are grayish in color, while those from Amboseli are covered in red earth. Elephants spout mud all over their bodies, or simply wallow in swamps, to stay cool on a hot afternoon. Mr. Saitoti talks about how the big herbivores have shaped Kimana's landscape. Elephants tear off acacia bark for its fiber. They also scratch themselves on the tree, bending young shoots that proceed to grow in the most impossible of angles. Giraffes prune the top juicy acacia leaves, clipping the trees to almost uniform height. Warthogs follow in the wake of elephants, hoping to graze on the juicy, fattening acacia pods that fall as the elephants push the trees with their trunks. Mr. Saitoti depicts a landscape that is not only adequately forested but also inhabited by nonhuman agents that mold the ecosystem to suit their needs.

Mr. Kiongo's and Mr. Saitoti's competing and discordant views of the Oloitoktok landscape are exemplary of how land use colors its representation by different individuals. Mr. Saitoti, born and bred in the area, depicts farming as a secondary interest. In his role as a game warden, the land's key function is to provide a haven for the wildlife that attracts tourist dollars. In this scenario, wild animals are both the cause, and result, of conservation. Fauna has influenced the landscape, creating it as it is today, and, conversely, the present state of the landscape determines how elephants, buffalos, giraffes, gazelles, and a variety of carnivores live. Mr. Kiongo's view is geared toward subsistence agriculture. He moved to Oloitoktok to farm maize, beans, potatoes, and peas, and to rear livestock. Unlike Mr. Saitoti, or the discussion in my introduction about elephants as seminal in shaping forests and savannahs, Mr. Kiongo does not see wildlife as an agent of environmental transformation; elephant migratory corridors, one of which previously crossed his five-acre farm, are a nuisance. Mr. Kiongo fenced part of his farm to deter elephants from feeding on his maize crop, damaging banana trees, and uprooting his orchard. Fauna destroys. He represents landscape as purely influenced by human choices. Ethnic and linguistic rivalry between Gĩkũyũ and Maa communities generates incidents of pastoralists trespassing into maize farms. Recent Gĩkũyũ migrants enforce their right to private property by erecting barbed wire and electric fences.

THE NOVEL, FOLKLORE, AND THE PRESENCE OF
NONHUMAN LIFE FORMS

Like Mr. Saitoti, but unlike Mr. Kiongo, I am interested in how representations of Eastern African lands and landscapes depict nonhuman life prior to human settlement, occupation, and land use. How does an acknowledgment of plant, animal, microbiotic, and supernatural life transform our reading of Eastern African literature? The Eastern African canon, including the two novels I examine in this first chapter, seriously contends with the colonial fantasy of emptiness projected onto African lands. The colonial literature produced by Isak Dinesen, Elspeth Huxley, Neil Sheraton, M. Harding, W. B. Thomas, M. M. Kaye, and C. T. Stoneham was one-sided and self-serving. Elspeth Huxley (1959, 1), for instance, hallucinates about unmapped lands and unintelligible tongues. Paradoxically, Grace Ogot's and Margaret Ogola's genre—the novel—endorses the phantasmagoria of an empty Africa by erasing the presence of nonhuman life. In its duty and obeisance toward modernity, the false teleology of progress, and the march of Western civilization, the realist novel sweeps aside ontologies that credit nonhuman beings with agency, potency, and sentience. Depictions of land, landscape, and topography within the realist novel not only exaggerate human activity but also minimize actions by plants, animals, and the supernatural. Huxley is separated from Ogot and Ogola by both race and class. Consequently, unlike the two Kenyan women, she depicts landscapes from a utilitarian perspective, wholly devoid of any metaphysical attributes. I argue for a contrarian reading of the Eastern African canon—one that I term mystical realism. Mystical realism, as I define it, is a narrative technique that decolonizes our reading of Eastern African landscapes and literatures. Mystical realism highlights the nonhuman and the supernatural in both the fictional and the natural worlds.

A 1908 administrative report by a colonial official in Britain's East Africa Protectorate is illustrative. The document paints a fantasy of East African lands as a tabula rasa based on settler productivity:

The highlands of East Africa have for some time now been more or less vaguely described as a white man's country meaning, as it has been used undoubtedly, a country that lent itself to colonization by Europeans. The climate of the highlands is without doubt excellent and from that point of view suitable for European residence, colonization however goes a great deal further than actual residence, it means residence & work plus the bringing into

existence a white race bred & born in the country. . . . some of us who originally expounded the theory have now become convinced that the climate is
not suited for the up-bringing of a vigorous white race. (np)

The bureaucratic paraphernalia of empire, for example colonial treaties,
served as instruments for expunging nonhuman and supernatural life forms
from indigenous landscapes (Touval 1966; Caulker 2009). The extent to which
this administrative report is premised upon racial eugenics is remarkable.
The subtle difference between European residence in Kenya's White Highlands versus the deliberate praxis of a colonial project is predicated upon the
presence of a self-sustaining white community. Evidently, the administrative
official has developed reticence that a robust whiteness can make a permanent
foothold in this region. Such misgivings, however, did not deter white trophy
hunters from adventuring in East African savannahs. Numerous unknown
and little-known safari men and women partook in this colonial ritual, but
perhaps the top two celebrities who adopted this lifestyle were writer Ernest
Hemingway and politician Theodore Roosevelt.

Cultural critics highlight the sinister connection between hegemony and
representation. This linkage is particularly strong in projections of imperial
power across colonized landscapes. Canonical Eastern African writers inter-
vened in anticolonial movements not merely by shattering the aura of colonial power but also by creating a "legacy of environmental writing and rhetoric" (Caminero-Santangelo 2014, 37). There has been, over the last decade, an
increased recognition of the ways in which nature featured in African anticolonial literature of the 1950s and 1960s. While Byron Caminero-Santangelo
traces the environmental aesthetics of writing by Okot p'Bitek and Ngũgĩ
wa Thiong'o, Elleke Boehmer (2005) astutely links the reproduction of the
English garden—in Australia, India, Jamaica, Kenya, and New Zealand—to
the ascendancy of Britain's empire. By the eighteenth and nineteenth centuries, "the British sprinkled across the world, both in text and in fact, a whole
collection of green spots" (51). British settlers encountered, and overturned,
first-comer narratives that enshrined the custodial relationship between
indigenous communities and their environments.

European newcomers constructed authenticity by emphasizing their animal and crop husbandry and the manners in which such farming activity
transformed *wilderness* into *picturesque* landscape. German East African settlers perceived themselves as "protectors of the African natural world [which
they] accused the African population of desecrating" (Steinbach 2011, 57).

Consequently, hunting in colonial Tanganyika was an important "sign of the higher cultural status of the Europeans. [Hunting] served to reinforce the claims of the Germans over the African soil" (60). Farming, gardening, and hunting were critical experiences in European revisioning of the Eastern African lands to which they had migrated. Aside from the economic and subsistence benefits, these experiences were quasi-sacred rituals that helped to underline white supremacy and bolster colonial conquest. Europeanizing colonized landscapes transformed such spaces into healthier, more settler-friendly regions that would properly belong to their new owners; in multiple ways, "notions of pastoral beauty" not only underpinned environmental transformation but also legitimized colonization (Wear 2011, 25, 37). Likewise, Emily Brownell's and Toyin Falola's *Landscape, Environment and Technology in Colonial & Postcolonial Africa* (2013) demonstrates how "environmental control" mirrored "social control" (6) and the role those imperialist technologies played in "constructing colonial narratives of control, access, immersion as well as separation" (7). J. B. Highfield (2012) echoes this sentiment. Highfield's *Imagined Topographies: From Colonial Resource to Postcolonial Homeland* argues that "colonization left a legacy of exploitative land management. Colonies were either wastelands or treasure troves, seen as places to exploit and alter" (6). Anticolonial writing, like Ngũgĩ's, sought first to reverse the separation of culture from the land upon which its people lived; this process involved creating novel ways of seeing the land and imagining the landscapes; it manifested in writing as "a new landscape of liberation" (4, 6). David Maughan-Brown (1985) comprehensively elucidates Ngũgĩ's fiction and its role in historicizing and memorializing the Kenya Land and Freedom Army's desire for land reform. Unlike Maughan-Brown, however, I focus on female authors who, like Ngũgĩ, have devoted their writing toward economic and political decolonization. Moreover, I'm also writing against the continuity of black patriarchy in the face of colonial hegemony. Ultimately, what Leonard Thompson (2000) concludes about the Southern African situation, that "the land issue was intimately bound up with the question of political power" (63), is applicable across space and time. Just like in Southern Africa, in Eastern Africa "land belonged to the community, not to individuals" (23). Historically, this seems to echo back across millennia. Cheikh Anta Diop's (1974) magnus opus in African history documents that in Ancient Egypt, "though the land was the property of the Pharaoh, the people had enough free access to it to continue their economic activity" (210).

African anticolonial writing chronicled land ownership—native land was not empty but had an aboriginal history preceding colonial occupation—in response to colonialism.[1] Where this impulse manifested as a realist novel, the history of lands and landscapes was restricted to the time span of human settlement. This must be why in the same Rift Valley that spawned *Homo sapiens sapiens*, no realist novel seriously features early hominids. In fact, few writers have staged an Eastern African literature that occurs in the millions of years during which the drama of human evolution was the central epic of the region's savannah. Plant and animal life are ignored, and Eastern Africa is rendered empty prior to Bantu, Cushitic, and Nilotic migrations. Grace Ogot's and Margaret Ogola's writings present and critique various conventions of ownership and territoriality—divine bequest, myths of origin, and violence—all meant to safeguard a community's, or an individual's, land possessions. However, by omitting sustained interest in the region's flora and fauna, Ogot and Ogola unwittingly perpetuate the illusion of emptiness.

Unlike the realist novel, folklore has carved out space for nonhuman agency in the physical world. Unsurprisingly, this happens even when this mythology is rendered into literary works. Because both Ogot and Ogola feature orature in their texts, this results in a kind of antagonism within their texts: some sections acknowledge nonhuman life forms, while others erase plants, animals, and the supernatural from the text's setting. This distinction is particularly visible when we adopt a mystical realism reading approach. In this chapter, I examine representations of land and landscape while paying special attention to fantasies of emptiness as expressed in Ogola's and Ogot's novels. These illusions are themselves foundational to the modes of territorial repossession that Ogot and Ogola design—what I call conventions of ownership. Some of these conventions, especially bloodshed, fail repeatedly. Although armed struggle was a key component of anticolonial efforts to oust European settlers, both authors suggest that its effectiveness could not translate into the postindependence era.

Resisting colonial fantasies of emptiness need not have resulted in the erasure of life forms antedating indigenous human presence. Several ways exist of highlighting and representing autochthonous land ownership or custodianship, or both. Ogola and Ogot do in fact demonstrate these alternatives in those sections of their work that depart from the quintessential aesthetics of the realist novel. My reading of these two female authors concludes that the cultural and historical assumptions with which an individual, or a community, approaches land crystallize into a particular view of landscape. One's gaze upon the land not only engenders a particular rationale for ownership but also manifests in the uses to which that landscape will be put. As it turns out, "what kind of thing nature is or is understood to be [influences] how humans arrange, control, and distribute nonhuman nature" (Wenzel 2020, 9). There are often competing explanations as to why *this individual,* or *this community,* lays claim to *this piece of soil.* Rather than isolate one justification over all others, settlers switch and alternate among several conventions of ownership, strategically choosing the tool set that best meets their current needs. Claims of ownership often depend upon assumptions, fantasies even, of emptiness. Present-day Gĩkũyũ migrants into Oloitoktok retell how, on their arrival at such and such location, they found no trees. These anecdotal histories paint a forlorn region on which they were the first to practice forestation. This historiography not only ignores Maa environmental custodianship, but it also hides destructive deforestation and charcoal burning that followed in the wake of newly arrived residents. These are, clearly, one-sided chronicles. They depict a land that was void of flora, and a landscape that had nothing appealing. In this regard, they are reminiscent of the kinds of stories that Ogot and Ogola challenge. What the two novelists featured in this chapter undertake, instead, is a representation of land and landscape anchored in the people's folklore—demonstrating that culture and ecosystem cannot be divorced from each other. Finally, I read Ogot and Ogola alongside Sylvia Tamale's *Decolonization and Afro-Feminism* (2020), which connects "exploitation of women [to] the degradation of the environment" (86). Tamale offers an Africanist ecofeminism that "mimics and recycles" the continent's indigenous knowledge systems in the analysis of how both women and nature have been commoditized by anthropocentrism and capitalist-patriarchy (86).

ANIMAL, PLANT, AND SUPERNATURAL LIFE FORMS

As earlier noted in the family biography, my father's kin trace their roots back to the Ndorobo community. The Ndorobo, like the Mbenga, Mbuti, and Batwa of Central Africa or the Khoe-Sān of Southern Africa, predated Bantu, Cushitic, and Nilotic migrations into Eastern and Southern Africa. Paradoxically, most Eastern African authors limit their fictional explorations of pre-European African societies to the Bantu, Cushitic, and Nilotic exoduses of the last two millennia. I do, however, perceive a deeper historical trajectory in the folklore that Ogot and Ogola feature in their novels.

Grace Ogot's *The Promised Land* (1996) deploys folkloric aesthetics, weav-

ing tales of epic battles between the Luo and the Nandi that enabled the former to claim supremacy and ultimate ownership of arable regions in western
Kenya. Moreover, folklore is important when Luo families migrate to eastern
Tanganyika; in this new homeland, customary storytelling rites and gestures
signal possession of *virgin* land. Unlike the factual and historical Kenya outside her novel, in Ogot's fictional world resistance is enacted through magic.
The effects, however, can prove to be just as fatal for *settlers* who attempt to
dispossess *natives* even though (or perhaps precisely because) the two groups
share the same racial heritage: African. *The Promised Land* uses narrative
to challenge colonial land discourse. On the one hand, communities privilege emptiness and the potential for settler occupation while simultaneously
reproducing tales that foreground communal ownership of ancestral land.
By staging a conflict about settlement between black Africans, Ogot allows
the reader to imagine questions of *otherness* and settlement outside the colonial paradigm. In other words, colonization of land—whether conducted by
Europeans or Africans—is a narrative process.

Ogot's *The Promised Land* is a circular narrative that ends at the exact
place where it began: the protagonist's home. When Ochola hears of territory
available for settlement in Tanganyika, he is intent on emigrating. He ignores
not only his wife's pleas but also those of his family; he takes Nyapol with
him across Lake Victoria in search of fresh farmland. Ochola and Nyapol
do indeed find economic success in their new home. The couple soon stocks
a bumper harvest, and their young family expands. Unfortunately, Ochola,
Nyapol, and other Luo migrants clash with the Zangazi community they now
live among. This angst results in destructive charms aimed at Ochola. He suffers a mysterious ailment that leaves his body covered with porcupine-like
warts. Numerous traditional healers fail to cure Ochola, and he isn't any luck-
ier at a colonial health facility. Magungu, who is much more successful, exacts
a heavy price for his treatment: immediate departure from the Ochola homestead, before nightfall. Ochola's recovery marks the beginning of the return
journey home. However, the protagonist has undergone deep psychological
changes since his departure. On his return, Ochola is extremely distraught at
having left behind his wealth in Tanganyika; he returns empty-handed after
having come so tantalizingly close to accomplishing his quest for wealth.

Ochola's metamorphosis into a porcupine-man clearly complicates a simplistic categorization of Ogot's *The Promised Land* as a realist novel. Critical appraisals of the text have been similarly varied; for instance, Kathleen
Flanagan (1996) highlights Ogot's "blending of [the] supernatural with real-

istic traits" (371). *Urban Obsessions, Urban Fears: The Postcolonial Kenyan Novel*, on the other hand, positions Ogot's work as "strongly anthropological" (Kurtz 1998, 28). Flanagan and Kurtz demonstrate two extremes of the aesthetic spectrum extant in *The Promised Land*. They're both right. And, in some way, they're both wrong. Indisputably, there is a strong presence of nonhuman life in Ogot's novel—especially the sections that lean toward a folkloric aesthetic. In one incident, Ochola dreams that he is sitting by the river, paralyzed, and totally unable to move. "His body did not seem his own and his hair had changed into long white thorns, which made him look like a porcupine" (Ogot 1966, 124). This is a heavy-handed authorial premonition of what will transpire later in the story. When Abiero, Ochola's brother, gets news of the misfortune that has befallen his sister-in-law and her children, he hurries to Tanganyika. When Abiero finally encounters his brother, he too is "paralyzed by fear. The man standing in front of him was half naked; his face and limbs were like that of a human being but his flesh was completely covered in thorn-like warts. [Ochola] looked like a human porcupine" (139). Other appearances of the supernatural include the sound of a night intruder outside Ochola's house, but upon closer inspection no footsteps are visible. Magungu concludes that the invisible prowler is a ghost (148). Aside from the paranormal, actual animals feature often in Ogot's narrative. Nyapol, on a water-fetching trip to the river, observes "fragile-looking tadpoles [wagging] their tails lazily in the shallows, [and] drifting down-stream with the flow of the current" (70). On the first night, per Luo custom, Ochola must sleep alone in their new home. In that darkness, he is assailed by raucous hyena laughter; Nyapol spends a similarly sleepless night as she listens to the "weird human sounding cries of the birds" (82). As the couple settle into their new homestead, Ochola erects a thorny fence, and occasionally builds a big fire to keep wild animals at bay (83). Animals can also be purveyors of the mystical. When Magungu unearths a snake, a tortoise, a rat, and a monkey's paw from underneath Nyapol's hearth, Ogot's readers understand that these animals are charms deployed in the offensive against Ochola and his family (150). The same evil infests one of Nyapol's cockerels with bird claws, thorns identical to Ochola's warts, and human hair (150–51).

As the above chronicle of animal motifs demonstrates, Ogot's *The Promised Land* incorporates folklore within its hybrid structure.[2] The novel deploys these representations toward establishing nonhuman life prior to the arrival of Luo migrants in the Zangazi region of Tanganyika. Though Ochola and his fellow Luo migrants often rehearse the fiction of an uninhabited space—and even that is highly questionable—there is clear presence of nonhuman life prior to Luo occupancy. The frogs, hyenas, forest birds, and snakes that Ochola's family encounter existed on this landscape long before these groups of humans arrived. Ochola and his family, indeed the wider community, never exhibit any sense of remorse for having invaded a territory already peopled by a variety of fauna. This disregard for other forms of life, premised on the supposed supremacy of the human species, disturbingly buys into European Enlightenment theories. This hierarchy of life delineated higher and lower life forms. Plants and animals were designated as lower, disposable, kinds of life. Simultaneously, non-European societies were characterized as closer to animals, and hence labeled expendable—under the guise of the Atlantic slave trade or even settler colonialism in the Americas, Australia, and New Zealand.

Though published three decades after Ogot's work, Margaret Ogola's *The River and the Source* (1994) shares several thematic concerns. Ogola's work won two major literary prizes in 1995: the Jomo Kenyatta Foundation Prize for Literature and the Commonwealth Writers' Prize for Best First Book. Additionally, her work was assigned as part of the Kenya Certificate of Secondary Education curriculum in the late Nineties. It is in this context that I first read, and watched dramatizations of, her novel. On June 12, 2019, which would have been the late Ogola's sixtieth birthday, Google Kenya honored her literary and public health career with a doodle. *The River and the Source* is an intergenerational epic that centers around women's lives. Ogola plots Kenya's metamorphosis from the late 1890s to postindependence. As the sociopolitical atmosphere transitions from British colony to Kenyan self-rule, Ogola follows a dynamic cast of female characters. The matriarch, Akoko Obanda, enjoys the last vestiges of Dholuo precontact society.[3] Her daughter, Maria Nyabera, ignites the family's experiments with colonial modernity: converting to Catholicism, enrolling in formal education, and joining the British World War I campaign. Akoko's spirit lives on in her granddaughter, Elizabeth, a teacher who mothers a new generation of postcolonial Kenyans. Elizabeth represents the nation's efforts to advance economically, especially in her careful tutoring of Akoko's great-grandchildren into respectable professionals. Vera is the epitome of this maturation. She is both an engineer and a member of the Opus Dei; Vera's character combines the civilizing and Christianizing missions that set forth British annexation of Luo territory at the beginning of Ogola's novel.

The River and the Source portrays an Eastern African landscape inhabited by the supernatural long before humans arrived. Mention of a Dholuo deity signals the presence of nonhuman life prior to human settlement. Through Akoko, Ogola offers her readers the following piece of tribal lore: "*Were* is a great spirit. He saw that the world needed more than spirit forms. So he created Ramogi and his brothers who were men. Man has a form which is spiritual" (74; emphasis in original). Humans are directly descended from Were, and, more importantly, the Luo community and their god are spiritually connected. Though not explicitly reversing Enlightenment propositions of the body/soul binary, Ogola's creation story argues that humans are simultaneously endowed with physical and spiritual attributes. Ogola decries the separation of body from soul and does so in a way that empowers non-European ontologies. Ogola's mystical realism philosophy is decolonial in the way it challenges Western thought; *The River and the Source* describes a Luo region where spiritual life forms predated humans—African and European—as well as indigenous ways of knowing that enabled the community to fully comprehend their position in this ecosphere.

MYTHS OF ORIGIN AND COLONIAL FANTASIES OF EMPTINESS

Akoko's myth of Dholuo origin depicts a Luo landscape that is intricately dependent upon familial and intergenerational bloodlines. The caretaker relationship between the land and its people mirrors the caregiver affiliation linking parents to their young ones, or adults to their aging parents. Akoko's tale goes on to say:

> *Were* sent the men he had created to various parts of the world to settle in it. Ramogi he sent to the country around the great lake which was a great favour for he had more spirit than his brothers. The wife whom *Were* gave him was called Nyar Nam who embodied the spirit of the great lake. They had many children including Rachuonyo, Sakwa, Asembo, Yimbo, Gem, Uyoma, Nyakach, Seme and Ugenya among others who settled around the lake, tilling land, taming animals and catching fish. These are the children of Ramogi from whom we all arise. (74)

Ogola's text chronicles indigenous societies and institutions. In addition to retelling history, *The River and the Source* marshals folkloric aesthetic conventions to demonstrate indigenous land occupancy. Ogola achieves this by deploying oral traditions and repeatedly invoking their educational role to pass on communal wisdom from one generation to the next. Within the context of the novel, contemporary Luo occupancy of the land is predicated upon a long lineage—an antecedence so far reaching it stretches all the way back to the time before humans roamed the landscape. Ogola's text thus highlights how the Luo landscape emerges from Luo cultural expression. The naming of Sakwa, Gem, Seme, and so forth reflects Luo identities and practices. In response to European fantasies of an African blank slate, this myth links settlement, occupation, and naming practices (Mũchiri 2019, 249). Earlier members of the Dholuo community named their districts after Ramogi's offspring. The caretaker role that such stories privilege vis-à-vis indigenous communities and the lands they occupy is vastly different from the exploitative intent of colonial map-making. Decades earlier, Kenyan politicians Jomo Kenyatta and Oginga Odinga produced similar writing. Kenyatta's *Facing Mount Kenya* (1962), an anthropological work on Gĩkũyũ culture, and Odinga's *Not Yet Uhuru* (1967), a memoir that also included Luo ethnography, deploy ethnic mythologies toward anticolonial movements. My fourth chapter argues that Ebrahim Hussein's and Berhane M. Sahle Sellassie's writing in African languages demonstrates how this African-centered knowledge production was simultaneously pursued in the literary world.

In this constellation of authors, Ogola's *The River and the Source* is an important rejoinder to a Kenyan canon that has been dominated by male voices. If anthropology has previously been the preserve of her male counterparts, Ogola wades in and redeploys the ethnographic genre in her fiction. Her very creation story invites a gender critique. Why, for instance, does nongendered Were only create men—Ramogi and his brothers? Why are women written out of this story—only appearing offstage as spouses to Ramogi and his kin? Revising this disconnect between a narrative peopled by men, yet retold by a woman, is what criticism on Ogola has termed a "celebration of the spirit of womanhood" (Gikandi and Mwangi 2007, 131). Ogola rehashes Dholuo mythology through the eyes of a female cast. Unlike Kenyatta and Odinga, her account of twentieth-century Luo political history is enacted through female bodies: bodies that must navigate not only precolonial forms of patriarchy but also colonial objectification and neo-postcolonial exploitation.

DIVINE BEQUEST AND REPRESENTATIONS OF FECUNDITY

Like Ogola, one of the tropes that Ogot marshals in response to European delusions about empty African lands and landscapes is the myth of origin.

While minimally successful in challenging British territorial conquest—often marked by hoisting the Union Jack—myths of origin also yield to the very ontologies they purportedly resist. Ogot's version of Dholuo genesis notes that

> when [God] created this land, he must have had a better purpose for it. He must have said that this land, like the land of Canaan, would flow with milk and honey so that its inhabitants could have plenty to eat and drink and live a better life. (17)

This version of Dholuo ethnography privileges human action and ostensibly expunges the presence of nonhuman life in the time before Luo settlement. As noted earlier, such an approach inadvertently endorses a culture/nature binary whereby humans claim supremacy over the rest of the ecosphere. Additionally, Ogot's story represents landscape from a utilitarian perspective. The land is primarily useful in its capacity for animal and crop production. Land is, certainly, a key factor of production. And yet land is often much more than a means for subsistence or agribusiness. This tale disavows land's capacity to generate social ties and a sense of identity—as other sections of *The Promised Land* demonstrate.

Finally, by mobilizing the Christian story of the Israelites escaping from Egypt to Canaan, Ogot ratifies the missionary raison d'être. Deploying Biblical motifs, writing in the novel genre, and the very use of English demonstrate the extent to which colonial projects had entrenched themselves. Simultaneously, of course, Ogot's use of these tools potentially works to undermine the very hegemony from which they manifest. Several fissures appear. Unlike Were, the spiritual form to whom Ogola assigns no gender, Ogot's God is male. This troubles any self-identification that Nyapol might undertake with this deity. Moreover, Ogot phrases God's actions as "must have," suggesting some doubt as to whether this is how events transpired. Ogot stages the very schism between a Luo divine and his subjects that colonial administrators hoped for between their subjects and their ancient traditions. Incidentally, that same chasm is visible between present-day Kenyans and the state. Anecdotally, it is remarkable that as recently as Kenya's 2017 presidential election, Raila Odinga, a leading statesman with a large Luo powerbase, invoked the Canaan motif. Odinga portrayed himself as Joshua, willing and capable to lead his people to the Promised Land (Majanga 2017).

Ogot represents Tanganyika's landscape in the rhetoric of private property. She invokes the imperial fantasy of empty non-European lands through her use of the epistolary form to mimic communication between white settlers and their home. Consider, for instance, the following report that Ochola pens for his sibling back in Kenya:

> To my brother Abiero . . . I should like to tell you that I have arrived safely in the land of Tanganyika. This land is very beautiful. It has many hills and valleys like the land of Seme, and the soil is very fertile. . . . I have fenced in a large area of land for myself. Very few people live here, and those who do are mostly our people. (Ogot 1966, 85)

The letter begins by finding similarities between Seme, Ochola's home, and his newly settled farm. Ochola suggests that although he now lives far from his family and friends, his new locale is *just like home*. Ochola then describes the landscape in glowing terms, much like British propaganda, which sought to encourage more immigration from the United Kingdom to East Africa. Having depicted the geographical acclaims of Tanganyika, Ochola drops the coup de grâce: Tanganyika is either scarcely populated or wholly unoccupied. This is the major difference between Seme and Ochola's new farm in Tanganyika. While the former is overpopulated and its soils have been depleted, the latter is sparsely peopled and its numerous resources await exploitation. This dissimilarity between the two locations is digested through narratives—such as Ochola's letter—that propagate fantasies of Tanganyikan emptiness. More importantly, *just like home* serves as a charm to help ward off, and possibly obscure, the increasing hostility of the Zangazi peoples among whom Ochola has settled. In Ochola's letter, we witness how "descriptions of the new land can betray a great deal of ambivalence over the settlement project as the settler makes mental comparison" to their previous homes (Weaver-Hightower 2011, 128).

VIOLENCE AND THE ERASURE OF HISTORY

As opposed to the aesthetics of folklore—which represent animal, plant, and supernatural life forms that predate human settlement—the realist parts of Ogot's and Ogola's fiction depict landscape as merely the backdrop for human conflict (Mũchiri 2019, 246). *The Promised Land* redramatizes tensions between Christianity and indigenous beliefs during the early part of Kenya's twentieth century. Ochola's brother converts to Christianity and enrolls into a missionary school. As a result:

> Abiero changed. He became so possessed with his faith that the villagers thought he was mad. He stole his father's precious pipe and broke it on a rock outside the village. He was hostile towards any of his younger step-brothers or sisters who sang traditional songs. The teachers at school had said that these were sins, things of darkness . . . even dancing to the throbbing African drums annoyed him. Eager to civilize his brothers and sisters, he sang Christian songs to them with great fervor. (Ogot 1966, 34)

Abiero's cultural transformation is no less bizarre than Ochola's mysterious ailment. While the latter is physically unrecognizable, Abiero has become culturally grotesque. His behavior is explicable to his kin only in the language of demonic possession. The spirit that moves within him—one that is violent, overzealous, and deranged—is unlike anything the neighborhood has ever known. Abiero's hostility, while perpetrated in the name of the Prince of Peace, destroys what is valuable to his siblings. I am especially drawn to the image of the large stone upon which Abiero smashes his father's pipe. Abiero, the new convert, has metaphorically become stone-like. He is wielded by a European civilizing and Christianizing mission to demolish what is read as sinful. Abiero, like his missionary tutors, decries customary practices supposedly engendered by forces of darkness: in other words, most Dholuo ontologies. This rift between Abiero and his family was not accidental. Colonial projects depended upon such communal ruptures to advance. This is precisely why in Kenya, for instance, multiethnic political coalitions were habitually proscribed and driven underground. In the same way Ogot represents Seme as the scenery for an emerging rivalry between Christianity and African spiritualities, the British Colonial Office projected an atavistic tribalism on the region—from which they had saved a mass of grateful natives. Where the reality on the ground did not match this fantasy of precolonial wars, the British East Africa Colony instituted *divide and rule* policies to sow discord. What we now know, of course, is that African "populations were not closed reproducing entities with unchanging cultures" (Thompson 2000, 11). There was, and still is, a remarkable amount of ideological invention and cultural adaptation among communities across the African continent. What European colonials perceived as static societies were more often caricatures reflecting the observers' own anxieties and deficiencies.

On the other hand, Ogola demonstrates that identifying colonial misrepresentation of African cultures does not mean harboring a romanticized history of indigenous communities. *The River and the Source* depicts landscape as a backdrop for gender-based rivalry. Although Ogola does not explicitly blame such conflict on colonial expansionism, her narrative indicates that colonialism exacerbated such issues. After Akoko's husband died, his brother,

> Otieno Kembo, took over the chief's stool with glee and sat on it with heavy arrogance. He appropriated his brother's wealth and tried to grab his widow's personal property as well. . . . [Akoko] knew that as a woman, a widow and a sonless mother, the only male in her direct line being a little baby, she was greatly disadvantaged. . . . She felt the weight of injustice that women have felt since time immemorial in her male-dominated world. (Ogola 1994, 66)

Ogola chooses to discuss the clash between Akoko and her jealous brother-in-law through the lens of a long-running Dholuo patriarchy.[4] Ultimately, Otieno was deposed through the help of a colonial district commissioner. He was dethroned and forced to recompense Akoko for lost private property (84). *The River and the Source* paints a series of misfortunes. Akoko would not be in this predicament if her first born son had not died—a casualty of British-German Tanganyika battles in the Great War. Hence, British colonialism is evidently not the savior of Luo widows it presents itself to be. Simultaneously, Akoko would have no need for a male benefactor if the community was not so steeply patriarchal. The result of all this is that Luo women are hard-pressed to find support within or without their community. This is the kind of patriarchal and (neo)colonial tyranny that Sylvia Tamale (2020) addresses through the lens of radical African feminisms. In my third chapter, I read Marjorie Oludhe Macgoye's fiction to demonstrate the ways in which women, unsuccessfully, sought respite in colonial urban areas. Ogola and Ogot depict female "subjectivity as multiple, dynamic, and continuously produced in the course of social relations that are themselves changing and at times contradictory" (Mama 1995, 2). A great deal of this energy emerges through creative representations. As Mshai Mwangola (2008) argues in "Performing Our Stories, Performing Ourselves: In Search of Kenya's Uhuru Generation," "artistic performance [is] the primary site of knowledge production, consumption and transmission on the African continent" (6). In other words, "writing weaves into language the complex relations of a subject caught between the problems of race and gender" (Minh-ha 1989, 6).

 The Promised Land also reimagines intraethnic and interethnic violence. Ogot not only represents the Luo landscape as a stage for political supremacy, but she also demonstrates how violence erases any history embedded on the land. In the first case, *The Promised Land* hints at intra-Luo rivalry; the Seme community fought against their kinfolk from Gem. Essentially, Gem wanted to conquer Seme and steal their land (Ogot 1966, 42). Aside from such Luo fratricide, Ogot's novel also discusses an ancient war between the Luo and their Nandi neighbors. This much earlier conflict was won by the Luo; they drove the Nandi off the land and settled on it (23). The intergenerational stories that Ochola's people tell are simultaneously cathartic and noxious. By suggesting a teleology that begins with Nandi persecution by the Luo and ends with Luo hegemony and settlement on these lands, the narratives erase the preceding history of Nandi influence on the landscape (Mũchiri 2019, 247). Beyond that, of course, these tales of epic battle embellish human prominence on the land. The stories erase nonhuman presence on the land, including the plants and animals shaping this region before Nandi, Luo, or any other human habitation. Luo historical amnesia buttresses various fantasies of emptiness. The phantasm of an uninhabited landscape is untenable unless preceded by the hegemonic work of expunging a people's history. This applies not just to Nandi lives before the arrival of the Dholuo but also to animal, plant, and supernatural life forms antedating the Nandi. British colonialism instituted a similarly dual tracked genocide—not just the decimation of indigenous communities but also corruption of their cultural, religious, and spiritual practices. This intricate, and intimate, oppression made for a particularly bitter anticolonial struggle. The kind of reading praxis I advocate for under the title "mystical realism" performs the recovery labor vis-à-vis presettlement nonhuman and supernatural life forms.

Ogola represents a late colonial landscape populated by traumatized African bodies. Her portrayal of anticolonial resistance by the Kenya Land and Freedom Army (Mau Mau) sketches a landscape that is dying, "shot, maimed, killed" or uprooted at the whim of British armed forces (Ogola, 157). Unlike Frantz Fanon (1963, 94) who argues that "violence is a cleansing force," and thus elaborates on the benefits of anti-imperial warfare, Ogola is ambivalent about bloodshed in anticolonial politics. She does not foreground the cathartic quality of extreme acrimony. Instead, Ogola's depiction invites disturbing questions regarding revenge and how it hinders national reappraisal of key questions about inequity. "The Kikuyu especially suffered greatly. . . . They returned atrocity for atrocity and blood flowed—both black and white" (Ogola, 157). Even as Ogola highlights Gĩkũyũ suffering during colonial Kenya—as exhibited by the random violence that could be enacted on them—she also seeks to flatten indigenous cultural differences under the rubric *black*. On the one hand, she deploys *black* as a category that encompasses *all* African experiences at the hands of their colonial masters, yet she is forced to emphasize the Gĩkũyũ community's involvement as atypical of what other black Kenyans experienced. It appears that Gĩkũyũs are *blacker* than other black Kenyans and hence the recipients of especially heinous acts under British colonial policies.[5]

Ogola's discussion reflects a dilemma that has plagued historiographical projects in Kenya since independence. Endeavors at memorializing anticolonial politics often result in depictions that, like Ogola's, foreground both Gĩkũyũ exclusivity and exceptionality—twin effects of the unique violence that the colonial state enacted on central Kenya. Such ideas have been co-opted for the purposes of ethnic chauvinism: After ousting British colonialism, to whom should the country or land, or both, belong? Should it not belong predominantly to the Gĩkũyũ who bore the brunt of British oppression rather than collective ownership by the Kenyan nation? What is left unsaid by Ogola's phrase "the Gĩkũyũ suffered greatly" is that other communities grieved, too. Frequently, however, the corollary to Ogola's statement is assumed to be *no one else suffered*. Furthermore, even if Gĩkũyũ interests reign supreme will these be managed by the *loyalist* section of the community—that which collaborated with British policies—or will these people be marginalized? While Ogola's use of Gĩkũyũ suggests a homogenous community with similar experiences at the hands of colonial officers, nothing could be further from the truth. The very titles *loyalists* and *Mau Mau* express the various camps that Gĩkũyũ families sought to align themselves with during the anti-British peasants' uprising. As it was understood by the Kenyan population—and as historical evidence demonstrates—loyalist families collaborated to safeguard British imperialism and were rewarded with land grants and their children with formal education. On the other hand, Kenya Land and Freedom Army sympathizers were often relocated from their ancestral land, corralled into densely populated villages, and forced to eke out a living under extremely harsh conditions. Often, as Ngũgĩ's *Dreams in a Time of War: A Childhood Memoir* (2010) demonstrates, a single family would split into two camps: each vehemently opposed to the other.

In its overall trajectory, Ogola's text is linear—setting out from late precolonial Luo-land, journeying through colonial Kenya, and terminating in the postindependence nation. The eponymous river is an apt metaphor for this beeline movement: beginning at the source, ending at the sea. I find this troubling for two reasons. First, in her representations of landscape Ogola overlooks the trauma experienced by plants and animals during British anti-Mau Mau campaigns. Bombing raids on Land and Freedom Army hideouts in Mt. Kenya and the Aberdare ranges, the ancestral homes of the Ndorobo and Gĩkũyũ communities, destroyed foliage in attempts to deny the guerrillas forest cover (Maina 1977, 70). Despite strong forays into folklore, *The River and the Source* is, after all, a human-centered drama. The adverse environmental effects of settler cash crop farming or even of forced villagization do not feature. Second, Ogola seems to unwittingly equate the sociopolitical systems that anchor late precolonial Dholuo society, Britain's Kenya colony, and the postcolonial nation-state that secures flag independence. Concerns regarding equity, social justice, redistribution of wealth, and the fallacy of modernization are subsumed in a teleology that marches forward, ever forward. This aesthetic move mirrors the political decisions made by Kenya's *founding fathers* to adopt, almost wholesale, the colonial state they had previously fought so hard to dismantle. Supposedly, a black leader at the head of such a cannibalistic state could manipulate it for the good of his people. As numerous polities soon discovered, however, that was wishful thinking. Political sovereignty would have better served the people if there had been a deep revision of the basic tenets between the state and its people, and between the people and their ecosphere. By embracing Western terms of modernity, civilization, and progress, newly independent African states were unknowingly overseeing a system that perpetuated wealth transfer to the Global North.[6] In turn, these flows of global finance further impoverished communities that had barely transcended decades of brutally extractive colonial policies.

Ogot's writing is somewhat different in this regard. In addition to featuring animal, plant, and supernatural life forms and challenging assumptions of human supremacy, the plotline is circular. Ogot's tale ends where it began: at Ochola's home. The circular plotline travels thousands of miles only to return where it started. Ogot's *The Promised Land* goes further than Ogola's work in questioning the circumstances of its production, calling attention to its adoption of aesthetics from the Western realist novel, and signaling the dangers of an aborted decolonial politics, in Kenya and across the African continent. I fundamentally believe that defying colonial fantasies of emptiness need not have resulted in the erasure of nonhuman life forms antedating indigenous communities. Adopting what I termed a mystical realism mode of reading recovers nonhuman and supernatural life forms predating human settlement. There exist numerous genres that highlight and represent autochthonous land ownership or custodianship, or both. As I'll demonstrate in the next chapter, Zimbabwean decolonial writing adopted circular narratives to challenge registers of progress and development, underpinned by Western modernity. Writers such as Yvonne Vera and Alex Kanengoni problematize the teleology of advancing civilizations as caricatured in Ogola. Two important aspects of Vera's and Kanengoni's nonlinear stories are a narrative technique based on mystical realism and the use of polyphony. Both authors gather a multitude of voices as the storyline unfolds; consequently, their texts unsettle the hegemonic omniscient third-person narrator—and the patriarchal voice of capitalist, Christian, white supremacy that hides behind it.

CHAPTER 2

Land and Landscape in Zimbabwean Narratives of Transcendence

"millions of [Africans] torn from their gods, their land, their habits, their life"
—Aimé Césaire, *Discourse on Colonialism*

Colonial incursions in the late 1920s partly explain my ancestors' treks away from natal lands in Gachie, Waithaka, Rirūta, Thogoto, and Manguo. Each of these voyages was in search of *waramu*—literally, expansive spaces where both they and their livestock could multiply in plenty. In addition, Karūgū and Mariibe migrated in response to Eastern African colonial demands for semiskilled labor on coffee plantations and dairy farms. This is the kind of economic competition that Tabitha Kanogo expounds upon in *Squatters and the Roots of Mau Mau, 1906–63* (1987). Around the same time, but much farther south, the forceful colonial conjoining of Zimbabwean cultural, economic, and social production to the global flows of imperialist finance traumatically impacted how communities related to their environments.[1] The 1930 Land Apportionment Act further commodified land in colonial Zimbabwe, subsequently leading white settlers to acutely fetishize it (Ranger 2010, 64). Surprisingly, Timothy Burke's seminal study on Zimbabwean consumerism, *Lifebouy Men, Lux Women: Commodification, Consumption, and Cleanliness in Modern Zimbabwe* (1996) does not examine land as a commodity. Prior forms of household agriculture by indigenous Zimbabweans were now competing against cash crop farming lorded over by European settlers. Maria Mies and Vandana Shiva (1993) contrast the vernacular materialism and subsistence that most women in the Global South perform to the malevolent materialism of commodified capitalism and mechanized Marxism. These critics' conceptualization of ecofeminism is predicated not only upon a sacredness of all life forms but also a decolonial perception of free-dom "different from that used since the Enlightenment" (18, 6). Central to this theoretical work is undermining dichotomies of man versus nature, man versus woman, and spirit versus matter (5, 17).[2] Similarly, Byron Caminero-Santangelo and Garth Myers (2011, 6) propose a postcolonial ecocriticism that concludes that "environmental representation is *always* shaped by social history" (emphasis in original). How Pax Britannica portrayed Zimbabwe's natural resources was driven by an extraction economy and the search for African markets to absorb European manufactured goods.

Refuting such utilitarian views of the Zimbabwean landscape is an important—though by no means the only—theoretical intervention that Alex Kanengoni's and Yvonne Vera's fiction achieves. *Environment at the Margin: Literary and Environmental Studies in Africa* (2011) extends such decolonial approaches by challenging colonial ideologies that

> depict African environments as places of wilderness in which nature is iden-tical with, absent of, or threatened by Africans themselves. This vision rein-forces binaries of nature and culture, wilderness and civilization, and the human and nonhuman that encourage an instrumentalist approach to both places and people. Such colonial narratives and their postcolonial permuta-tions have had damaging effects and have led to ineffective efforts at environ-mental protection or regeneration. (Caminero-Santangelo and Myers 2011, 14)

Colonial ordering of space is visible in Bulawayo between the 1890s and the 1960s. In response to segregationist land policies, Zimbabweans deployed the bicycle not only as a "prestige object" but also as "an essential tool with which Africans were able to create and maintain alternative landscapes" (Ranger 2010, 80). The policing of space in colonial Zimbabwe was anchored on a cleaving of the countryside from the township. There was similar intent in Kenyan colonial urban planning, about which I will speak at greater length in chapter 3. Here, I focus on Vera's and Kanengoni's decolonial representa-tions of the Zimbabwean ecosystem—and their use of mystical realism as a narrative technique. An important aspect of that recuperative work involves empowering a multitude of voices to reconfigure a postcolonial nation build-ing project that largely excluded women, the economically disenfranchised, and nonhuman life forms.

Following Mies, Shiva, Caminero-Santangelo, Myers, and Ranger, I closely examine the aesthetics of polyphony and the poetics of nonlinear narratives. I am especially interested in deciphering how polyphony and circular narratives influence representations of trauma-shaped lands and landscapes. Petina Gappah's *Out of Darkness, Shining Light* (2019) joined an established Zimbabwean literary canon that incessantly challenges the basic premises of empire. Dambudzo Marechera's *The House of Hunger* (1978) wrestles with the English language as it portrays life in colonial Rhodesia. Marechera's experimental aesthetics were adopted by later writers who explored the traumas of imperialism. Tsitsi Dangarembga's *Nervous Conditions* (1988) and *The Book of Knot* (2006) address the psychological turmoil of colonization from a young woman's viewpoint. Chenjerai Hove's *Bones* (1988) also features a female protagonist and is told by multiple first-person narrators. Hove's *Ancestors* (1996), on the other hand, complicates any attempts to return to a precolonial society. The diasporic journey in Marechera's *The House of Hunger* is further developed in Noviolet Bulawayo's *We Need New Names* (2013).

Aside from language and trauma, another visible strand in Zimbabwean fiction is representation of land and landscape. Hence, in S. Nyamfukudza's *The Non-Believer's Journey* (1980), land is paradoxically a source of strength for anticolonial forces while also proving to be quite injurious toward the rest of the indigenous community. Charles Mungoshi's *Waiting for the Rain* (1975) opens on an ominous note. The ecosystem is undergoing significant changes—trembling air, "roaring thunder," grumbling earth, and "shrieking lighting"—all of which terrify the people (1). Mungoshi paints physical landscapes that are deathlike and that cause intense fear in his characters. Written in the aftermath of Zimbabwe's independence, Solomon Mutswairo's *Mapondera: Soldier of Zimbabwe* (1983) rhetorically deploys wildlife's sovereignty, describing the people as "free and independent" (61). The author's description of post-European life is filled with horror. Instead of chorusing birds and galloping herbivores, we now get "scarecrows," "cane rats," and "white cobras" (61). These three images of ruin populate the new lives of the eponymous Mapondera and his kin; their world has been overturned.

My previous chapter argued that Ogola's and Ogot's fiction demonstrate the unbreakable bonds between cultures and their nurturing ecosystems. I established that mystical realism, a narrative technique that decolonizes our reading, highlights the nonhuman and the supernatural in Eastern African fictional and natural worlds. In this second chapter, I shift my analysis toward the metaphysical and the supernatural aspects of local topographies. The texts I examine feature an ensemble of narrative voices. This orchestra of narrators exorcises capitalist, racist patriarchy through a womanist gaze on Zimbabwean lands and landscape.[3] By incorporating multiple narrators—who stubbornly share their tales in nonlinear and circular plotlines—Yvonne Vera and Alex Kanengoni challenge entrenched pastoral visions of Zimbabwe and the heroic versions of Zimbabwean political history. I extend my critical intervention across Vera's entire oeuvre, whereas Ranger's scholarship in *Bulawayo Burning: The Social History of a Southern African City, 1893–1960* (2010) revolves around Vera's *Butterfly Burning* (1998). And although Kanengoni's *Echoing Silences* (1997) has not garnered as much critical acclaim as Vera's work, I read it as an important complement to the political activism of Zimbabwean literature in the late 1990s. Zimbabwe gained political independence about twenty years later than most African nations. Within that time, the dystopia of black self-rule had set in; the misgivings hinted at by Grace Ogot and Margaret Ogola in my preceding chapter now appear full-blown in Zimbabwean writing of the 1980s and 1990s. Twenty-odd years of African sovereignty had demonstrated that the nation-state, parliamentary democracy, and similar trappings of Western modernity did not take root on African soil. Wholly adopting the colonial state and tinkering superficially with who appeared as its titular head, or even in its ministerial and administrative positions, did not bear what the masses envisioned as they shouted *Uhuru!* (Freedom!) in Kenya, Uganda, and Tanzania, *Indépendance!* (Independence!) in Congo-Kinshasa, or *Kwacha!* (New Dawn!) in Zambia. Cursory manipulations were simply not radical enough, period. Among other achievements, Vera and Kanengoni—through the use of mystical realism—unseat assumptions of human supremacy by deliberately sharing their literary canvas with nonhuman life forms.

Alex Kanengoni's and fellow Zimbabwean Yvonne Vera's representations of land, landscape, and the wider ecosystem create space for nonhuman ontologies by including animal speech. Alex Kanengoni's *Echoing Silences* is replete with animals. Munashe, the protagonist, shares space with buffalo, elephants, hyenas, lions, an eagle, and even a baboon spirit (1997, 10, 12, 76). Yvonne Vera's writing is similarly full of animal motifs. Vera's *Nehanda* (1993) features anteaters, crabs, snakes, millipedes, featherless birds, beetles, ants, chickens, dead cattle, caterpillars, charms made from lion and leopard skins, insects unknown to Linnaean taxonomy, vultures, locusts, ostrich feathers, black crows, crickets, spiders, chameleons, horses, and bats (1993, 1, 6, 16, 21, 26, 30, 35, 39, 41, 47, 50, 58, 60, 62, 74, 75, 81, 90). In *The Stone Virgins*

(2002), Vera describes wingless insects attempting flight, a cannibal spider, and dreaming herbivores (35, 84, 90). What differentiates these literary depictions of animals from those we explored in chapter 1 is that, unlike Grace Ogot and Margaret Ogola, Kanengoni and Vera give individual voice to the animals featured in their work. Distinct animals are audible in Kanengoni's and Vera's fiction. There are real dangers to writers incorporating, perhaps even co-opting, animal speech. Evan Mwangi's *The Postcolonial Animal: African Literature and Posthuman Ethics* (2019) argues that the presence of animal characters capable of speech provides "strong support for the belief that animals and humans are incarnations of each other" (97). Although animals are not human, the similarities between them make the animal/human boundary a lot more porous than Western modernity lets on (16).

Alex Kanengoni and Yvonne Vera are particularly interested in breaching the borders separating animals from humans, and nature from culture. These two writers include speaking animals in their novels; and they also craft circular narratives that are characterized by polyphony. Both Kanengoni and Vera weave a multitude of voices into their tales—not only animals but also speech from a wide range of human subjects. This rupture enables Kanengoni and Vera to undermine the omniscient third-person or first-person narration often associated with the novel. Vera and Kanengoni contest the supposed teleology of Western civilization and its attendant concerns of progress and development in the Global South. They do so by composing narratives that are decidedly nonlinear. These circular plotlines are polyphonic, refuting the discursive dominance customarily practiced by patriarchy, capitalism, Christianity, and white supremacy. Vera and Kanengoni are at the forefront of artists who championed a truly radical African liberation, and their work can be read against other Zimbabwean writers. Vera and Kanengoni, unlike their counterparts, desired a decisive break from what Robrecht DeClerq (2020) terms utopias of white Southern Africa. For instance, Charles Mungoshi, S. Nyamfukudza, and Solomon Mutswairo—unlike Kanengoni and Vera—invest in unidirectional plotlines. Mungoshi's, Nyamfukudza's, and Mutswairo's narratives double as historiographies of nation building. Their writing uncritically endorses the forward march of history and foregrounds an omnipotent narrator who symbolically embodies the entire community's political potency, biography, and voice. However, such an aesthetic choice erases all forms of agency except those that are explicitly male and elite. Kanengoni's and Vera's writings deliberately recuperate space in the public imaginary for marginalized voices—not just human ones, such as women, youths, the aged, and the differently abled, but also animal, plant, and supernatural life forms.

There are thematic and aesthetic continuities between a subset of Zimbabwean fiction and the writing we explored in the first chapter. Yvonne Vera and Alex Kanengoni challenge the Grand Narrative of Empire at the level of storytelling. If empire self-presents as omnipresent and eternal—nonexistent on day one, fully evolved on day two—Vera and Kanengoni slow down the retelling of stories about imperialism. Their work focuses not on the large sweep of history, though they're clearly very aware of that, but on individual lives. This is the very material that empire seeks to ignore. Imperialism happened one life at a time, one fallen community after another, from one conquered society to the next. There were lots of setbacks, and resistance has been part of this history from the get-go. As Sekgothe Mokgoatšana and Goodenough Mashego (2020) document, "dispossession not only uproots communities but destroys their livelihood and indigenous resources for food security" (1).

The Grand Narrative of Empire thrives on a solitary voice; in contrast, Vera and Kanengoni weave inclusive narratives that incorporate not only marginalized human subjects but also nonhuman voices. These multiple voices further support the ecological diversity of the lands across which empire sought to establish itself. There were savannahs, forests, mountains, deserts, rivers, lakes, oceans, islands, and much else besides. Including a diverse cast in their novels rejects the policing, surveillance, and atomization of African cultures by colonial ethnographic *experts*. Vera and Kanengoni deliberately include mystical elements in their books. This results in a kind of mystical realism, an aesthetic that is deeply embedded in their writing. Mystical realism goes beyond folklore. It is coherently integrated; it is not featured as an anomaly, an illustration of primitive African art; and it is not italicized as a foil to the rest of the novel. Instead, mystical realism questions the very foundations of Western ontologies and the emergent projects of modernity. Lived reality and the supernatural, bifurcated in Western ontologies, coexist side-by-side in Vera's and Kanengoni's worlds. In combining mysticism and realism, I mean not the binary either/or but rather a continuum. The spiritual and the material are merely two extremes—in between is a spectrum on which all life forms subsist. Elsewhere, Besi Brillian Muhonja (2020, 22) terms this a "holistic environmentalism that is rooted in radical utu."

NONHUMAN LIFE FORMS IN REPRESENTATIONS OF LAND AND LANDSCAPE

Yvonne Vera's *Nehanda* is based on the biography of Nehanda Nyakasikana, a freedom fighter who led the 1890s Chimurenga—the liberation war against the British South African Company . The historical Nehanda did not live to see her quest for freedom fulfilled. We follow Vera's Nehanda, the eponymous protagonist, from birth to death. Her childhood is filled with enough auspicious omens to signal that she will grow to be a seer for her people. In the Chimurenga against the British South African Company, Nehanda was joined by Kaguvi, who also features in Vera's rendition. In *Nehanda*, Kaguvi first appears as a butler to a white colonial administrator. He suffers humiliating work conditions, and it is this disconnect from his ethnic heritage that supposedly radicalizes him enough to lead the insurrection. Kaguvi's employee, Mr. Browning, and his British compatriot, Mr. Smith, are caricatures of white settler life. They not only espouse racial theories grounded upon white supremacy but also courageously attempt to shoulder the White Man's Burden in this forlorn colonial outpost. At the end, it is Browning and a Catholic priest who oversee Nehanda's and Kaguvi's hanging—the inevitable demise for natives, supposedly, too savage to appreciate Her Majesty's expansive cultural and political dominion. Beyond that, the mysticism that Vera weaves throughout the story foreshadows a second Chimurenga, one that culminates in the 1980 downfall of Zimbabwe's white minority government.

In *Nehanda*, Vera focuses on animal sentience and agency. Vera's representation of land and landscape foregrounds interspecies interactions that border on the mystical. Humans and nonhumans coexist on the same plane, often peacefully, but liable to conflict. Animals and supernatural life forms, especially animals that serve as conduits to the supernatural world, are represented in a form of realism that also deeply incorporates the mystical. By doing so, she deftly sidesteps the pitfall of appropriating animal voices. Birds, for instance, are more than powerful symbols—their presence troubles characters' psyches. A young Nehanda hallucinates about birds

> flying freely without their bodies. The[ir] large swooping wings disappear and the bodies of the birds return and they are naked without any wings or feathers. Look, [Nehanda cries,] the black crows have returned to the sky. There are black crows in the sky, so many of them that they block the sun from the earth. (Vera 1993, 26)

This daytime vision terribly agitates Nehanda. She is physically distraught, suffering from insomnia, and finally in need of *nanga*, a medicine man who provides relief. The birds' nudity, and their uncanny ability to crowd out the sun, combine to portend great malevolence. Even more disturbing is a dream that Nehanda's mother had prior to this. In the nightmare, "black feathers fall from the sky and bury her daughter. . . . [Mother] runs through the feathers, which grow around her until she is completely lost, and can no longer find her child" (17). There is a compounding of evil in this portrayal of black fowls. On the one hand, I read these birds as a far-sighted premonition of the aerial weapons of war ultimately turned against the Zimbabwean resistance in the 1960s and 1970s. Vera, however, is interested in the birds not as mere literary symbols, but precisely as birds. In their flight between the skies and the land, these feathered creatures mediate between the spirit world and world of the living. Birds are intermediaries who constantly remind Nehanda's community that ancestral *mhondoro* and *mudzimu*, a core part of the supernatural, are omnipresent. Toward the end of her life, as Nehanda grapples with the defeat of her people's resistance, she is once again visited by a bird. She is hiding in a grotto.

> On the opposite side of the cave, hovering above her in the darkness, sits a large bird. She does not see it, yet she can feel its presence. Its eyes move over her body, waiting to destroy her. Then she hears the flapping of heavy wings, and the air inside moves. She listens intently for the bird to move once more, so that she will know where to direct her scorn. (68)

Nehanda's relationship to this unseen bird is antagonistic. She is not afraid of its animality; rather, she is acutely aware of its capacity to kill her. The bird is a worthy, if unwelcome, opponent. There exists more familiarity between Nehanda and this ominous bird-figure than there does between her and the Catholic priest who invades the privacy of her incarceration on the eve of her execution. This unnamed priest's presence at Nehanda's last moments is totally unlike the efforts taken by "progressive missionaries to facilitate land-ownership by Africans in the context of dispossession" (Kumalo 2020, 4). Mwangi's (2019, 6) assertion that colonized subjects used animals "as allies against the violence of colonialism without animalizing the colonizer to justify causing harm to the animals used as avatars of the colonizer" is quite relevant here. The cave bird is much more than a stand-in for a murderous colonial state. The bird is, also, simply a bird. It is one among many other dangers that Nehanda has previously faced and vanquished.

Across her entire oeuvre, Vera expertly combines mysticism with realism. For this reason, her work is often described as poetic fiction. Vera's "novels rival the master narrative of 'official' history by exploding its appropriation of 'the land' under the auspices of cultural nationalism" (Graham 2009, 135). One important way she achieves this is by chronicling the dense networks that manifest on landscape. While colonial and black bourgeois master narratives limit such linkages to human agency, Vera expands her representations of the ecosystem to include not only marginalized human subgroups but also animals and the supernatural. It is in this way that, as Kwame Anthony Appiah (1991, 353) notes, Vera's writings "reject not only the Western *imperium* but also the nationalist project of the postcolonial bourgeoisie" (emphasis in original). In "Re-Mapping the Colonial Space: Yvonne Vera's *Nehanda*," Khome Mangwanda (2002, 141, 143) argues that land constitutes the nation's "cultural consciousness"; colonial invasion is a crisis because it jeopardizes communion between the living, the living-dead, the ancestors, and the unborn. As we just saw, birds serve as intermediaries between these parallel, and often porous, cosmologies.

Alex Kanengoni's *Echoing Silences* similarly deploys mysticism to explore the supernatural. At the most basic, however, this is a war story. The narrative technique is rhizomic. Kanengoni's text opens with the protagonist at work, in an office. Suddenly, however, the reader accompanies the main character in a review of his time serving with anticolonial guerrillas in Southern African jungles. The author's description of how this posttraumatic episode disturbs Munashe's tranquility demonstrates how invested the text is in a stream-of-consciousness narrative arc. Munashe's actions—he "staggered," "wobbled," "flung open" a door, and "shouted breathlessly"—suggest a psychological experience not easily rendered into neat cause-and-effect patterns (1). Munashe's perception of a long-past tragedy—he bludgeoned a young mother and her child to death, using a garden hoe, under orders from his superiors—is visceral and real. Standing in his manager's office, he can hear the baby's shrieking and see the woman's terrified eyes, just as though it were happening right now. For Kanengoni to write that "the walls of Munashe's mind had already fallen in" is to highlight the extent to which rationality and the presumed forward trajectory of history have both failed (1). Instead, the past finds its way back to the present, repeatedly haunting the lives of those who survived. The rest of the novel follows Munashe's attempts to reconcile himself with this past trauma. This, however, cannot be an individual undertaking. For instance, his family, and even his neighbors, are present at a séance event that seeks to placate the ghost of the young female murder victim. And at the end of the novel, Munashe, dead and in heaven, participates in a political rally. He recognizes Zimbabwean heroes, long fallen, as well as the woman he murdered. They all forgive his heinous act.

In a way that doesn't merely mimic verbal speech, animals converse with humans. Kanengoni depicts interspecies dialogues that underline how multiple life forms have always shared the same ecosystem. As a guerrilla, injured and hiding from enemy forces, Munashe encounters a lion. Munashe is drawing water from a pond when a splash startles him; he is frightened, even more so when he recognizes the lion's mane and locks eyes with the animal (12). Gazing into the lion triggers recollection of his totemic animal spirit. Munashe had previously seen the animal from a distance. But

> he had not known the animal had such an awesome presence. . . . he saw the lion as huge, etched in the bright white afternoon sun, then he understood the feeling of greatness that his people derived from being associated with such an animal. . . . the animal watched him closely and Munashe saw the fierce light in its eyes. Then it grunted, as if in recognition, and walked majestically away. Munashe was mesmerized. The lions usually made their way to the water hole as the sun went down. What then was this one doing in the heat of the day? Was it a messenger from his ancestral spirits? (12)

Munashe interprets the lion's odd behavior as the overture to a conversation. In this two-way interaction, the lion makes sounds and it is left to Munashe to decipher what those audible signs mean. What appears to Munashe as "recognition" may indeed be a whole range of other responses, including fear, puzzlement, or indifference.

Kanengoni chooses to preserve the lion's psychic sovereignty. He does not burrow into the lion's mind process to enlighten his readers on what the lion makes of this moment. Munashe's fear, however, clearly turns out to be unfounded. The lion does not harm him. When the lion turns back, Munashe responds by clapping his hands, acknowledging in Shona that he has seen the lion (13). Munashe perceives the beast before him in multiple ways. First, this is a dangerous carnivore that may easily kill him; it is sensible for him to act cautiously, and to stay calm. Although he bolts his rifle, he neither aims nor fires at the lion. Second, the lion is an extension of the perils he has escaped as a rebel fighter. The lion's jaws and sharp claws may do him as much bodily harm as the enemy's bullets or mortar shells. Finally, however, the lion as a totemic spirit animal is Munashe's kin. After Munashe claps and chants in Shona, the lion pauses, looks back, and grunts one last time before heading into the scrub (13). Their conversation has ended; each has been recognized by the other. That Munashe reacts to all three perceptions, simultaneously, drives home this landscape's dynamism. The land is multiply populated not only by humans but also by their animal and supernatural kin. The three life forms are incessantly in proximity.

I perceive a similarity between the mysticism depicted in Munashe's totemic relationship to the lion and Vera's portrayal of a lion-figure just before Kaguvi's execution. At this point in *Nehanda*, Kaguvi has been arrested, imprisoned, and pressured by a priest to accept a Catholic baptism. As he awaits the hangman's noose, Kaguvi is aware of

> the lion which is now crouched at the opposite side of the room, its mane raised angrily until its brown and yellow hairs touch the roof. The lion crouches, ready to attack him. . . . Kaguvi keeps the voracious eyes of the beast close to his own, and they send mysteries to each other, mysteries that can no longer unite them. All the promises have been broken, and Kaguvi's spirit is naked to his creator, his ruling spirit manifest in the animal. The lion has arrived to prepare him for the next life which he will enter carried in the safety of its belly. He will travel in the belly of the beast for many days, then he will be freed to join his ancestors who have prayed for him from the earth. The lion will outlive him with new lives. (Vera 1993, 88)

Kaguvi's lion exists both as an apparition and as a physical reality. Weakened by torture at the hands of his captors, Kaguvi's mind no longer has a firm grip on reality. He is fast approaching the world of the living-dead, and in preparation his soul is looking for a new vessel to hold it. The lion, as his spirit animal, fulfills this purpose. On a physical level, his pain and bodily discomfort translate into the lion's supposed anger. This antagonism between Kaguvi and the animal captures the fear, the bitterness, and the violence between Chimurenga fighters and their British opponents. The lion, after all, was a symbol of the British Crown. But Kaguvi and his community do not wholly abandon the lion as a mystical figure. The fact that lions still walk in the Zimbabwean savannah, but not on the British Isles, enables Kaguvi's community to reclaim what would otherwise be a symbol of their oppression. Deep Shona ecological knowledge, plus the porosity of physical versus spiritual realms, enable Vera to depict an all-encompassing landscape. As in Kanengoni's representation above, Vera demonstrates that human, animal, and supernatural realms are always contiguous.

Echoing Silences, like *Nehanda*, also features a bird motif that troubles the protagonist. Munashe gazes at a bateleur eagle, fascinated that the bird of prey spends an entire day "sitting motionless"; he thinks the bird is lonely and feels empathetic (Kanengoni 1997, 13). After he reverses his line of thought, however, he begins to wonder whether it might not be the eagle feeling sorry for him; this thought brings Munashe to tears (13). Munashe and his fellow combatants cannot agree on whether the bird signifies malevolence or benevolence. Vera's and Kanengoni's depictions of eagles, lions, and crows anchor representations of land and landscape from the perspective of nonhuman life. When Munashe introspects on what the eagle makes of his hiding in a cave, he is attuning himself to an avian way of viewing the world. This decentering of human experiences in the environment questions human contempt for other species except ourselves. Vera's and Kanengoni's uses of animal motifs challenge the human/animal binary. As I argue in the next section, there merely exists a porous border between the human world and the animal world; moreover, there are spiritual diviners with the power to successfully straddle both spheres of existence.

Inexplicably, there has been a rather bifurcated history of critical engagement with Kanengoni's work. While Zimbabwean and South African-based scholars regularly study Kanengoni, the Africana literary branch of North American academia does not. As a result, in the last fifteen years, barely any scholarship on Kanengoni has appeared in the top peer-reviewed journals: *African Literature Today, Journal of the African Literature Association, Research in African Literatures*, or even the *African Studies Review*. It seems that while Kanengoni has a niche following among academics in Southern Africa, that appeal barely extends to Africanist departments in the United States. Expanding the perceived African canon in North America is, on its own, a worthy justification for including Kanengoni in this chapter. More importantly, however, I believe that Kanengoni's concerns regarding anticolonial wars, trauma, and how these affect physical and psychological landscapes would resonate deeply with scholars of African literature in Canada, the United States, and Western Europe.

I extend critical discussions of Kanengoni's writing beyond his depictions of trauma, to focus on his representations of land and landscape. Stephen Chan and Ranka Primorac (2004, 70) describe *Echoing Silences* as "critically neglected"; they explore Munashe's quest for "moral redemption," and astutely map out how Chimurenga veterans upset Zimbabwe's delicate political balance in the early 2000s. Kanengoni's protagonist expresses a bitterness quite like what the Zimbabwe Liberation War Veterans Association possessed. Elsewhere, Chan (2005, 373) argues that Kanengoni's novel has "one of the most powerful scenes in Zimbabwean literature." I think this hyperbole is well deserved, though I would award that prize to Yvonne Vera. Chan is spot on that Kanengoni is interested in depicting "war and its aftermath, death followed by death, and conditional healing poised between a personal world that has been shattered and a public world that wills itself against healing" (380). In contrast, Eleni Coundouriotis (2014) reads Kanengoni to explore how Zimbabwean literature challenges hagiographies of national heroes and the extent to which such narratives have been deployed politically. Kanengoni, unlike many of his compatriot post-Chimurenga writers, presents a deeply flawed hero. As Terence Ranger (1999, 696) argues, *Echoing Silences* is one of the "most intense expression of horror and disillusionment with the war yet to be published in Zimbabwe." Munashe not only commits suicide at the end of the novel—jumping off the edge of a gully to his death—but his postwar life is decidedly troubling and traumatized. Munashe in no way contributes to the kind of nation building that liberation songs idolized. If anything, Munashe's mental distress constantly prevents his immediate family from fulfilling their civic duties. The tragedy, of course, is that Munashe bears little choice—assailed as he is by the trauma of a heroic, but also atrocious, Second Chimurenga.

THE POLYPHONY OF MBIRA AESTHETICS

Kanengoni's and Vera's re-creations of Mbira music encapsulate the polyphony that permeates their work. The presence of multiple voices provides narrative space not only to nonhuman life but also to marginalized human subjects. As I will show in the second half of this chapter, nonlinear narratives are the most expedient way for Kanengoni and Vera to reconcile a polyphony based on both mysticism and realism. Consequently, both writers depict a Zimbabwean landscape that has been scarred by trauma.

At an exorcism ceremony to cleanse Munashe of the haunting from his murder victim, Kanengoni lays out the intricate relationship between Mbira music and the supernatural. Added to this is communion with nature, in the form of thunderstorms, lightning, and rains. Overnight, the spirit medium vaNyagadzi wrestles with the storm; she crashes into the fierce rains, is swept off her feet, and tossed into the air (Kanengoni 1997, 47). To accompany her duel, a Mbira drummer "rolled his hand over the drum once, twice, thrice [while] the lead Mbira player hit his riff keys" (47). The entire ritual is anchored on the Mbira *Tondobayana* war song. vaNyagadzi takes center stage; vocal and instrumental accompaniments are merely supportive. The metamorphosis vaNyagadzi undergoes is otherworldly. In trance, she is now a lioness.

> The lioness growled, its canines flashed in the gloom. The storm reared. Outside, the eastern sky began to yellow and the cocks in the neighborhood crowed alternately: the ancient spirits were on the prowl. Inside, the lioness continued to roar. The music throbbed. And above the music, the hesitant voice of Munashe's father could be heard chanting the praises of Shumba, the lioness, the totem of his people. (48)

Kanengoni expertly combines the aesthetics of mysticism with realism; Munashe's mind is simultaneously processing the Mbira music, the séance, and his past trauma. This is especially visible when, completely overtaken by the music and dancing, he "asked for a walking stick and held it as if it was an AK rifle and he pointed it at imaginary enemies and began to shoot from the hip" (50). Munashe is reliving the terrible fear he experienced as a guerrilla fighter. The spirit medium guides him through the ghostly spaces of his damaged psyche, back into the present.

> The lioness roared, wrestling with the storm, rolling on the floor and the music throbbed and pulsated. And then the lioness pinned the storm to the ground and the sky flashed and tore apart and there was thunder and Munashe thought it was enemy artillery at Mount Selinda bombarding their positions across the border at Espungabeira. (50)

Munashe's past is still very much with him. Kanengoni paints a metaphysics whereby the past and the present are conjoined and extremely permeable. So too are human and nonhuman worlds. In her role as diviner, vaNyagazi crosses and recrosses that metaphysical barrier. To accomplish this, vaNyagadzi takes on the totemic spirit of the lioness. She roars and rolls like a lioness. The audience interprets her actions as those of the largest cat in the bush. However, vaNyagadzi's is only one of several mystical transformations. Kanengoni describes how

> even the drummer could not keep the drum under control, and he lurched as he desperately tried to stop it from running away with the song. Then the song crashed into the ravine that the drum had unsuccessfully tried to avoid, and died. (50)

The song and the drum have become agential subjects; they too are key actors in Munashe's spiritual reawakening. The Mbira alchemy that turns inanimate objects into living beings similarly transforms human bodies into animal figures. During this deeply mystical moment "the song coughed as if it was choking and died away. The lioness continued to roar" (57). The song and drum are anthropomorphic. Kanengoni's writing has entered the realm of the poetic and nothing is merely what it appears to be. Panashe Chigumadzi (2018, 14) argues that "the mbira is dangerous—a mouth through which spirits stir up their people."

This instant of polyphony comprises drumming, the sounds of the Mbira, the chanting, singing, and dancing, but also *so much more.* This duality is similarly demonstrated by vaNyagadzi—simultaneously older woman, spirit medium, and incarnation of a lioness. The ceremony engenders two additional otherworldly transformations. In the vicinity, attendants hear a "booming howl, hoom hoom hoom," announcing the arrival of Mberere, vaShekede's embodiment of a baboon (Kanengoni 1997, 76). The lioness and the baboon avatars, personified by vaNyagadzi and vaShekede, respectively, interact as animal-figures. The lioness growls and bares its canines at the baboon; the baboon reacts with fear: whimpering, sniveling, and scuttling away to safety atop a Musasa tree (77). Inexplicable events in *Echoing Silences* challenge readers' sense of disbelief. Within Kanengoni's world, the real and the imagined constantly intermingle. As Maurice Vambe (2002, 127) argues elsewhere, spirit "possession celebrates the myth of eternal return and regeneration." What readers experience is a continuous circle of life. Mbira music facilitates communication "between people of this world and that other beyond the sky" (Kanengoni 1997, 76). After Munashe's exorcism, villagers are perplexed at the "discovery of lion footprints around the village. Where had the lions come from? Surely not from the overcrowded, barren communal areas where even finding a hare was considered a miracle?" (78) The ecological ruin wrought on the ecosystem around Munashe's home has wiped out previous nonhuman inhabitants. Large carnivores have disappeared, unable to feed on the few remaining rodents. The absence of lions, the inhabitants' totemic spirit, signals a disconnect between their spiritual lives and the ecosystem on which they now subsist. For this reason, sighting lion paw tracks is an auspicious occasion. Evidently, "attributing agentic abilities to these nonhuman forms moves them away from the category of mere objects to be exploited and discarded. This move recognizes the otherwise 'inert' objects as life forces worthy of consideration" (Iheka and Newell 2020, 7). *Echoing Silences* strongly suggests it is not coincidental that this happens at the same time as vaNyagadzi's spiritual experience.

vaNyagadzi's success as a mystic spawns Munashe's metamorphosis into Rudo, the young mother he killed during the war. Speaking in a high-pitched voice, adopting the mannerisms of a shy female guest, Munashe rocks an imaginary bundle in his arms and begs *"a moment's rest under the shade of the musasa tree in the middle of the home to breast-feed my baby"* (Kanengoni 1997, 76; emphasis in original). Munashe's foray into the depths of his memory leads his family to the young woman's kin. Her family has long since despaired of ever finding out what befell their daughter. At this point in the story, Munashe the killer becomes Rudo the victim.

> Munashe fell into convulsions, frothing at the corners of his dry mouth, and then he suddenly sat up and looked at the people gathered. "It's been such a long, long journey. I am glad I have finally arrived home. I haven't seen Mother yet, where is she? Mother, your daughter Rudo has finally come home from the war. . . . Father, I have not returned from the war empty-handed. I have brought you a small gift. . . . Your grandchild's name is Hondo. He is my gift to you. All the time I spent out there was not spent in vain. . . . After so much pain, isn't this good news?" (83)

Kanengoni leaves it unexplained how Munashe finally learned that the woman and her baby were Rudo and Hondo. Perhaps this is some repressed memory that Munashe finally unlocks?

This plot twist is remarkable. Kanengoni's first sentence in the novel states "as always, it began with the cry of a baby somewhere" (1). The mother and baby who appear here at the very start of the narrative are not named until page eighty-three of this ninety-page novel. This is an astonishing authorial choice. Rudo and Hondo haunt Munashe's existence throughout the text, and yet Kanengoni purposefully withholds their names until much later in the plotline: after the séance. Moreover, once revealed, the names hold deeper significance. Rudo is the Shona word for love, while Hondo means war. Kanengoni plays on the patriotic love with which guerrillas marched to the front, only to be recompensed not merely by death and sacrifice but also by greed, political self-aggrandizement, and the betrayal of their decolonial dreams.

Rudo is back. Rudo is dead. This seeing-double cannot mask the all-encompassing tragedy. While Rudo's family may finally gain closure, this comes at the cost of giving up all hope that their missing child and grand-child may yet return home. There is no longer any possibility of a miraculous reunion. Rudo's family indicts the entire Second Chimurenga as a moment of loss and suffering. Their reaction is the complete opposite of the hagiography with which postwar historiographic projects chronicled this part of Zimbabwean history. Rudo's mother asks:

> Is this you Rudo, my daughter? Is this how you have decided to come back to your mother? Is this the grandchild that you promised you would bear for me a long time ago when you were still at school? . . . Is this our harvest for all our effort during the war? Is this the harvest we are reaping after all our pain and sacrifice? Is this our reward for sleepless nights, and all the shooting and the dying in the dark? (84)

Rudo's parent suggests that a disproportionate amount of sorrow has been exacted on the community and there have been no commensurate returns. The physical and psychological agony has all been in vain. Opening each question with "is this," Rudo's mother rhythmically sings her misery. Phrasing the refrain in present tense highlights the passage of time—especially the extent to which the past has forcefully, irrevocably leapt into the present. This woman's bitterness indicts the senselessness of the war experience. Whom, Rudo's mother asks, "got anything out of the war" (85)? Presumably, the plush political posts garnered by Robert Mugabe and his club have not been beneficial for the community. These people are in limbo: previously ravaged by a colonial force and now largely betrayed by the postindependence regime. After two decades of struggle for political sovereignty, they are rudely awakened to the fact that the resistance must continue, albeit on a different battleground.[4] A similar critique of the postindependence dystopia is textually palpable in Yvonne Owuor's and Monica Arac de Nyeko's fiction, which I discuss in chapter 5.

SOUNDS, MUSIC, AND POLYPHONY

Kanengoni's *Echoing Silences* is a powerful portrayal of trauma. The novel's success hinges on transcending the "limitations of the protagonist's memory" and instead channeling an entire community's history (Coundouriotis 2014, 175). This happens because Kanengoni weaves together multiple voices: the lioness, the baboon, Rudo. Earlier in the plot, Munashe remembers Christmas family gatherings. Cattle was slaughtered to feed the crowd and Munashe was distressed witnessing the "slow arching swing of the axe aimed somewhere between the ears of the animal, the fatal piercing crack and the doomed bellow of the ox as it slumped to the ground" (Kanengoni 1997, 29). This "doomed bellow" adds to what is already a long list of sounds that accompany death and anguish. Similarly, as guerrilla fighters attack a village harboring suspected collaborators, Munashe perceives the "plaintive cry of the baby ahead of the doomed crying of the old man torched and flaming" (25). As previously noted, Hondo and his mother have been with Munashe ever since their tragic end. Hondo's cries now accompany the suffering of others. *Echoing Silences*, like several of Vera's novels, has "causal and temporal links between episodes [that] are often not explicitly stated, nor are the episodes themselves ordered chronologically" (Chan and Primorac 2004, 75). While depicting human trauma, Kanengoni and Vera mimic the freely associative mind of someone struggling with post-traumatic stress disorder. Munashe not only witnessed horrible acts of war but he also perpetrated some of these heinous crimes. His is a haunted life. The real and the otherworldly constantly clash in his mind; in fact, the boundary between these two spheres of existence is extremely porous.

Yvonne Vera's poetic fiction is infused with music. There is rhythm in her word choice. In both *Butterfly Burning* and *Nehanda*, Vera uses her language of cadence to depict scenes overflowing with song and dance. Vera deploys indigenous musical genres—Mbira and Kwela—to represent not only ecological diversity but also the human toll of European imperialism. Kaguvi, Nehanda's co-conspirator in the anti-British campaign, is depicted as a truly gifted performer. Music is an important tool in transcending communal inertia and channeling it toward political activism. At the onset of the resistance, Kaguvi uses music and divination to prepare his people for the battles ahead. Kaguvi

dances the forest that surrounds them, dances the hills and the plateaus, dances until the sounds of the birds become their own war-songs, dances until the strength of the lion is in their limbs, the flight of the eagle is the speed of their feet, the cry of the jackal surrounds them, and their spirits soar. (Vera 1993, 60)

This séance is simultaneously a lesson for political cadres and a celebration of the region's ecological diversity. Kaguvi and his community are only one species among many who call this ecosphere home. Kaguvi's people channel the varied attributes of the fauna around them to increase their martial resolve and their chances of success on the battlefield.[5] If the birds, lions, and jackals are not physically present in battles against the British South Africa Company, they are very much attendant in spirit. I see this as an extension of the custodial relationship between the Shona and their land. The community are caretakers; they must preserve this landscape not only for their descendants but also for the flora and fauna that surrounds them.[6] Edward Said is categorical that "the main battle in imperialism is over land" (1993, xii–xiii). Said positions the battles over ownership, rights of settlement, demarcation, and redistribution of land not in physical violence but in narrative. This is spot on. The kind of "radical dispossession" that constitutes colonialism stole not just indigenous Zimbabwean lands but also their labor, their culture, and their histories (Deane 1990, 10). As we saw previously in chapter 1, the presence of supernatural life forms is an important rejoinder to colonial fallacies of emptiness.

Vera's depiction of Mbira music grounds the existence of ancestral spirits within the musical performances of the Shona. Genealogical voices are a key addition to the expansive history that her works narrate. In *Nehanda*, Mother arranges a divination ceremony after the eponymous protagonist suffers from inexplicable hallucinations. During the event, Mbira artists

send quivering mournful sounds through the air, reminding one of birth, of death and of the serene presences of the departed. The *mbira* is the sound of water falling on rock, and of water flowing along secret and diverse streams. It is the weeping of those who inhabit the earth. (27–28, emphasis in original)

Vera anchors the spectators' experience of this music as more than melodic. There is history intertwined in the sounds of the Mbira. There is belonging, identity, and memories of the living-dead. Aside from the spiritual, there is also the material: water. Vera metaphorically invokes water, a life-giving element, in her description of Mbira music. I interpret this to mean that Mbira is fundamental in a way that entertainment and leisure do not capture. The music is much more than about pleasure; in the way it connects the community to its cultural and political past, it is integral to their way of being.[7] What Vera portrays resonates deeply with Emily McGiffin's (2019, 7) description of the Izibongo poetic genre from South Africa; within Izibongo, the "spirit that inspires the poet to speech, moves from the landscape through the body of the poet, and into the air." This analysis perfectly encapsulates the mystical element of Mbira music. Both Izibongo and Mbira

> disrupt notions of space and time, progress and development, possession and distribution that have advanced alongside the rise of the printed word and an increasingly global capitalism. In doing so, they make present and visible more ancient ways of relating to time, language, and landscape and draw listeners' focus to the implacable natural forces that ultimately organize human lives. (7)

KWELA MUSIC: TRANSCENDENCE IN URBAN LANDSCAPES

In *Butterfly Burning*, we see Vera provide a convincing response to the unbearable toll that imperialism took on African lives. Township life in colonial Bulawayo during the mid-1940s was harsh. Black lives were largely characterized by squalid living conditions, low wages, chronic unemployment, as well as racial segregation. Vera maps out how black residents of Bulawayo turned to Kwela music for the spiritual and psychological rejuvenation that earlier generations had received from Mbira ceremonies. *Butterfly Burning* ends in the protagonist's self-immolation. Phephelaphi has just discovered she's pregnant again and knows that her maternal condition has ruined any chances of getting accepted into nursing school. She is devastated. Cohabiting with Fumbatha, her lover, has been eventful, though not personally fulfilling. Fumbatha and Phephelaphi choreograph their quasi marriage into a series of silences and intimacies. They each bear childhood trauma that haunts their adult lives: Phephelaphi was abandoned by her mother at birth, while Fumbatha grew up in the shadow of his father's execution. Navigating such personal histories, while surviving British colonialism, has been psychologically burdening.

In Vera's writing, Kwela music is refuge. It is the artistic response of a colonized community. Black Bulawayo transforms pain into brilliant notes and sounds, repression into melodies.

> Kwela music brings a symphony of understanding . . . Kwela strips you naked. Anything that reminds of pride can be forgotten in the emptiness introduced. A claim abandoned. A lover lost. It is the body addressed in its least of possible heights. A stone thrust. The knees down and the baton falls across the neck and shoulders. Kwela. Climb on. Move. Turn or twist or . . . move. No pause is allowed, and no expectation of grace. Kwela. Cut, pull, bend. It is necessary to sing. (Vera 1998, 7)

Kwela is the response of a downtrodden people who seek to reclaim their dignity. Rhythm and melody are vital antidotes to the everyday acts of prejudice that black Bulawayo endures. Lizzy Attree (2002, 73) sees in Kwela music a "metaphor for the transformative power of language." This township-grown genre provides courage to survive another day. Kwela "in daylight is incessantly bold"; and so are its participants (Vera 1998, 8). Kwela is an important form of release, surrender, and transcendence. Bulawayo is bursting with energy, creative or not. Amid all this turmoil, Kwela offers "a joy that is free, that has no other urgency but the sheer truth of living, the not-being-here of this here-place" (86). Attending a Kwela performance feels like savoring a moment of peace stolen from an otherwise unforgiving city.

Kwela's power transforms the physical body. Kwela is mighty precisely because it moves the body. Doing so influences how a person relates to their inner and outer environments. Phephelaphi and Fumbatha attend and watch an evening performance.

> Two agile dancers pull their white cotton skirts with blue dots high up and hold them way over their swinging waists then collide with the music, rounded hips twisting, the body rocks with one full spasm and the neck a pillar smoothed with the bright light, their eyes close in a free caress, an evocation, their slim bodies rock back and forth, and waiting lips tremble with the desire for unborn moments, and the music is a dream too true to enter so they enter it, enter with hope . . . the ground is too near, the harmony too beautiful, the ground too inviting so the song pulls the body up again and swings it sideways because the songs swells a fine pitch where all is deep water, plain and clear (87)

Vera's prose seduces us to ignore that this is, in grammatical terms, a run-on sentence. The words shimmer off the page, getting us to overlook comma splices. Contravening rules of standard grammar is itself an authorial choice that questions linguistic hierarchies instituted by colonial policies.

This is a subtle reminder that these performers, Fumbatha and Phephelaphi included, are themselves suspended in between languages and translation. Though speakers of Shona, isiNdebele, or other Southern African tongues, they are now forced to interact with a colonial hegemony that fetishizes facility with English.

Kwela rises above lyrics and tunes. Vera tells us that this music births a "dream," one that participants approach with "hope." The moment of transformation certainly begins with dance steps; however, it morphs into political aspirations about the future of the nation. In the short span of Kwela choreography, we jump from celebration to liberation. The songs bear a long history, illustrated by Vera's description of "deep water, plain and clear." This harks back to my earlier discussion of Mbira, which Vera similarly described as the sound of flowing water. In the present instant, Kwela results in "laughter and joyful rest," a pause from the daily struggle to survive (87). It is clear, however, that the music simultaneously extends its reach far into the past and into the future. Kwela, though so far in this chapter only discussed in the urban (Bulawayo) context, is a quintessential product of the entire Zimbabwean landscape—urban, rural, and the in-between. Kwela archives, compiles, curates, and adapts myriad notes from animals—domesticated or not—as well as topographical features and flora.

The two female bodies that Vera highlights in this passage are representative of women's agency—often erased when retelling the history of empire. Black women, living in urban landscapes, were troubling to both colonial administrators and indigenous political entities. Black female labor, skilled or unskilled, challenged both homegrown and colonial patriarchy. Racist and sexist beliefs obsessed about black women's sexual looseness (Ranger 2010, 71). Urban spaces were deemed corrupting to African women, whom both black and white men fantasized about shackling in the countryside. Vera's female dancers bust this misogyny. In response to men's attempts to control their bodies, these women swing their waists, swirl their hips, and delight in the sensuality of their lips, eyes, and knees. Vera implicitly intimates at the women's sexuality and the liberated way they wield it. Terminating her pregnancy, as Phephelaphi does, is itself an act of wrestling women's productive labor away from men's control. *Butterfly Burning* recuperates the kind of marginalized history that imperialism and patriarchy often ignore. In *Making Freedom: Apartheid, Squatter Politics, and the Struggle for Home* (Makhulu 2015), a similar phenomenon is captioned as a history of battles for access to the city for and on behalf of African migrants, of their combining of work and domestic life, and of a broad array of everyday practices that ultimately transformed the geography and demography . . . and, eventually, forced changes to apartheid law itself. Africans, by sheer presence . . . would change the course of history. (5)

Though documenting Cape Town, key elements of this analysis apply to Bulawayo, especially if we keep in mind the shared history of racial segregation between both spaces.

The impulse to recover lost narratives extends to Vera's representation of urban landscapes in *The Stone Virgins* (2002). *The Stone Virgins* spans the years 1950 to 1986. It follows the lives of two sisters, Thenjiwe and Nonceba. Alternating between urban Bulawayo and the rural hamlet of Kezi, the plot reveals how these two women are affected by the Second Chimurenga for Zimbabwe's independence. Tragedy abounds. Thenjiwe is assaulted and her head cut off. The assailant, Sibaso, is a former guerrilla fighter, psychologically scarred from skirmishes with Rhodesia's colonial forces. Sibaso returns and mutilates Nonceba's face. By the end, Nonceba's home in Kezi is terribly unsafe; she relocates to Bulawayo.

Vera contrasts the spaces occupied by white versus black residents of Bulawayo. The luscious and expansive space accorded white settlers is best exemplified by Selbourne Avenue.

> Selborne Avenue in Bulawayo cuts from Fort Street (at Charter House), across to Jameson Road (of the Jameson Raid), through to Main Street, to Grey Street, to Abercorn Street, to Fife Street, to Rhodes Street, to Borrow Street, out into the lush Centenary Gardens with their fusion of dahlias, petunias, asters, red salvia, and mauve petrea bushes, onward to the National Museum, on the left side. On the right side, and directly opposite the museum, is a fountain, cooling the air; water flows out over the arms of two large mermaids. A plaque rests in front of the fountain on a raised platform, recalling those who died in the Wilson Patrol. Wilson Street. Farther down the road is a host of eucalyptus trees, redolent, their aroma euphoric. Selburne Avenue is a straight, unwavering road, proud of its magnificence. (3)

Vera's catalogue of white settler culture in Bulawayo—Selbourne, Jameson, Grey, Abercorn, Fife, Rhodes, Borrow, and the Centenary Gardens—displays the extent to which this landscape has been reshaped by colonial culture. Bulawayo is a space wherein settler colonialism has thrived, so much so that it has displaced and ejected indigenous Shona and Ndebele societies. After approximately a century of occupation, Europeans pride themselves on having established a legacy that is "straight, unwavering" and "proud of its magnificence." This heritage has had several strands to it: historiography, architecture, and gardening. The medley of dahlias, petunias, and aster shrubs transfers the English country garden from the British Isles to Bulawayo. The Centenary Gardens, mermaid fountain, National Museum, Charter House, and the Wilson Patrol plaque are architectural objects designed to support imperial historiography. Bulawayo's elite spaces are not only reserved for white residents but also marked by settler tastes, desires, and sensibilities.

In contrast, the oppressed nature of African presence in the city is aptly demonstrated by *ekoneni*, a vernacular coinage to describe the space at the corner of a building. A shallow existence at the edges of Bulawayo's edifices is all that Africans enjoy. Nothing could more symbolically signify black political and economic marginalization. These angled spots offer but a flimsy toehold in the city. Colonial Bulawayo is self-consciously hostile to its black population, despite its addictive dependence on their labor, taxes, and capital.

> *Ekoneni* is a rendezvous, a place to meet. You cannot meet inside any of the buildings because this city is divided; entry is forbidden to black men and women; you meet outside buildings, not at doorways, entries, foyers, not beneath arched windows, not under graceful colonnades, balustrades, and cornices, but *ekoneni*. (11)

Ekoneni is the preserve of those whom empire discards. Vera's writing, in contrast, shines a light on these liminal spaces to highlight the fraught existence of marginalized subjects. She deliberately drags these otherwise ignored bodies and voices back into history—both imperial and Zimbabwean. Vera's work, like Kanengoni's, features a community of narrative voices. By incorporating multiple narrators—who stubbornly share their tales in nonlinear and circular plotlines—both novelists challenge the entrenched heroic version/vision of Zimbabwean political history. Vera's collection of texts midwifes an open and dynamic form of Zimbabwean citizenship. Vera's poetics in *Nehanda* and *Butterfly Burning* incorporate the consciousness of an entire community. To depict the heroism of her female protagonists, Vera weaves a tapestry of narrative positions that includes parents, lovers, peasants, and veterans of the

Chimurenga resistance. This is a sense of belonging that resists registers of development, progress, and modernity—whether peddled by early twentieth-century white imperialism or by post-Sixties black nationalism. The fraught nature of colonial existence in Vera's Bulawayo echoes Anne-Maria Makhulu's (2015) observations of Cape Town. Makhulu argues that we must read Southern African cities for a history marked by "the fact of homes here and there, in the city and in the country, and in doing so [index] a much longer history of migration and displacement" (2).

NONLINEAR NARRATION AND REJECTING NATIONALISM

Echoing Silences tasks readers with distinguishing when narration morphs from one setting to another, or when a different character takes over the storyline. The omniscient narrator is not indispensable to the plot. Rather, the narrator plays a supporting role, occasionally filling in gaps, but never taking center stage. This technique underlies a paradigm shift in how history and social justice unfold. Kanengoni is not beholden to a Big Man sense of history. In a recent Zimbabwean historiography that is self-consciously inclusive as opposed to exclusionary, Panashe Chigumadzi (2018, 19) confesses that she "must lower [her] eyes from the heights of Big Men who have created a history that does not know little people, let alone little women." There is no alternative but for us to reorient our historical gaze. For one, Munashe is a flawed hero. Moreover, the very action in the novel proceeds at the direction of an orchestra of voices. This outlook not only revises previous omissions regarding the heavy casualties of independence wars—physical torture, murder, psychological trauma—but also consciously includes the efforts of women and children—whose acts of resistance are often overshadowed by those of male guerrilla fighters and political leaders.

At the end of *Echoing Silences*, Alex Kanengoni depicts a political rally attended by the dead: in heaven. Speakers at the meeting strongly indict postindependence Zimbabwean governments. Kanengoni challenges hegemonic Zimbabwean nationalism, and, by extension, the Grand Narrative of Empire that nationalism supposedly dethroned. Kanengoni argues that the hypothetical expulsion of imperialism did not actually take place.[8] The birth of a decolonial nation was prematurely aborted. Jason Moyo, founder of the Zimbabwe People's Revolutionary Army, takes center stage at this mass gathering. Moyo was assassinated in 1977, likely by Rhodesian armed forces (Sunday News 2016). Moyo's political analysis questions why "the wealth and the economy of the entire country was slowly becoming synonymous with the names of less than a dozen people" (Kanengoni 1997, 87). What he describes is a kleptocracy that entirely betrays the social justice ideals of the First and Second Chimurenga.

This selling out occurred subtly, aided by the acquiescence of those in power. Moyo specifically decries how Zimbabwean history has been perverted. Historiographic projects have mangled the nation's past, replacing truth with phantoms that frighten the people into blind obedience:

> It all began with silence. We deliberately kept silent about some truths, no matter how small, because some of us felt that we would compromise our power. This was how the lies began because when we came to tell the history of the country and the history of the struggle, our silence distorted the story and made it defective. Then the silence spilled into the everyday lives of our people and translated itself into fear which they believe is the only protection that they have against imaginary enemies whom we have taught them to see standing behind their shoulders. They are no longer able to say what they want. Neither are they able to say what they think because they have become a nation of silent performers, miming their monotonous roles before an empty theatre. And behind the stage, we, their leaders, expend our energy, coining high-sounding words—indigenization, empowerment, smart-partnerships, affirmative action—with which we will silence them forever. We owe the people an explanation. The struggle continues. (87–88)

This is a clarion call for a renewed struggle. As Moyo states, "the struggle continues." This echoes the Mozambican chant "La Luta Continua," which was shouted in support of anti-Portuguese resistance. Moyo's, and by extension Kanengoni's, conclusion is that the work of radical decolonial liberation is far from over.[9] The catalogue of eponymous silences that Moyo outlines do indeed echo louder than the sharpest sounds. It is these political and ideological compromises that have devoured the dream of economic decolonization and Pan-African unification.

Listening to Jason Moyo, however, is not the first time that Munashe has experienced a disconnect from Zimbabwean nationalism. We get a sense of Kanengoni's political skepticism much earlier, about halfway through the novel. While a guerrilla fighter, Munashe overheard a "tedious" and uninspiring political commissar lecture on the collective bitterness that led the black man to take up arms and fight the white man: he who came in 1890 and pushed the black man into the dry and arid parts of the country blah, blah, blah and Munashe thought what an over-beaten path! Shit. (52)

Munashe's irreverent reaction to this political indoctrination highlights a grave disconnect between the movement's lofty ideals and the daily compromises for survival. Moreover, this version of Zimbabwean resistance erases Nehanda Nyakasikana, the prophetic seer who marshaled the First Chimurenga. Expunging Nehanda is an astonishingly sexist act—one that handicaps the second quest for liberation by ignoring previous successes and lessons learned. I read Kanengoni's portrayal of Rudo as a direct challenge to historiographic projects that have omitted women from the struggle. Rudo stands in for numerous women—fighters and noncombatants—who also lost much in Zimbabwe's march toward political sovereignty. In my next section, I conclude this chapter by examining how Vera and Kanengoni represent land and landscape in their writing. Having served as the backdrop for indigenous resistance against British imperialism, this region's ecosystem is scarred by trauma. Those wounds are visible in literary depictions of land and landscape.

REPRESENTATIONS OF TRAUMATIZED LANDS AND LANDSCAPES

Kanengoni's *Echoing Silences* frequently approaches Zimbabwean landscapes with an eye for metaphoric connections between humans and the land. This kind of aesthetic is best demonstrated in Vera's poetic prose. Nevertheless, Kanengoni is a key inflection point in this transformation. For example, while discussing Munashe's mental health at the end of the Second Chimurenga, Kanengoni resorts to a description of the sky. Munashe imagines that he and a dead female combatant are floating, "drifting between the clouds, softly touching the woolen edges and then tearing the clouds apart and tossing the fleecy pieces into the air around them and watching the wind push the pieces away" (70). Colloquially, Munashe's head is in the clouds. Moreover, like the skies he fantasizes about, his mind disintegrated because of trauma. Munashe is suffering from PTSD, and his family must subsequently help him recover and bring the pieces of his life—and his mind—back together. Kanengoni deploys fog and mist to depict the mental anguish that Munashe endures.

At other instances, Kanengoni's representation of the land highlights the absence of plant and animal species. There is an ecological disaster unfolding. We, as readers, are primed to experience this loss of biomass with sadness. The death of plants and animals is, in and of itself, wretched and melancholic. Munashe examines the postconflict terrain and notes the absence of various flora and fauna. After the war, the land, like the Zimbabwean people, is missing *limbs* and loved ones. There is a general sense of loss as Munashe looks at the horizon:

> He wondered what had happened to the bruised land. It lay on its side looking visibly sick. Where had the false-medlar, the ebony and the spiny-leaved monkey orange trees gone? Where the masked weavers with their intricate nests overlooking silent pools? Where were the song thrushes perched on swaying lucky-bean branches? Where was their chorus of funereal song? Where were the silent kingfishers watching the rolling world from the top of a branch? Where was the ugly, primordial candelabra tree that his grandfather had told him was the staple of the equally primordial rhinoceros? (72)

The land lays prone, injured, and "bruised." These are the effects of almost a century of resisting British colonial settlement. The lack of foliage is reminiscent of the disappeared lives—soldiers, guerrillas, and civilians. Munashe speaks often of friends he'd made in the anticolonial resistance who are now dead. In the way he repeatedly asks "where" in relation to plants and birds, he is simultaneously grieving the death of fellow rebels. He mourns the demise of his compatriots by focusing on environmental destruction. Each tree lost reminds him of a friend who succumbed to bombs, grenades, or bullets. In this book's conclusion, I will expound on similar environmental destruction linked to British militarism and its efforts to preserve the Kenyan colony.

Unsurprisingly, in the same way Kanengoni maps human suffering onto the environment, he also matches recovery and human transcendence of pain onto depictions of the landscape. As Munashe laments the death of Kudzai—a female soldier he fell in love with—he reimagines her as a rocky promontory. There are two stony outcrops overlooking Munashe's village; he named "the smaller boulder Kudzai and the bigger one, himself. Each sunset, he climbed up the hill and sat on the bigger boulder, and felt Kudzai beside him" (72). Kudzai's presence has been transferred onto the stone. It is not that the stone is feminized, rather that it embodies Kudzai's spirit. The stone monument becomes Kudzai, a companion with whom Munashe can watch dusk envelop the settlement below. Furthermore, Munashe sees Kudzai in the grassland around him, "picking ripe ebony fruit, mischievously biting off the peel and offering him the juicy flesh" (73). Kudzai's supernatural existence in rocks, the veld, and even on an ancient Musasa tree signify not possession—of female characters by Kanengoni's protagonist—but rather a oneness between what is human and what is landscape. The Musasa tree becomes a symbol of peace and transcending violence. The large plant serves not only as protection from the harsh sun but also as respite from the ravages of brutality. The Musasa is shelter; it personifies the communal care that a person expects from friends and family.

Kanengoni depicts not just natural landscapes but also spaces of human settlement and agriculture. As argued in *Beyond Nature Writing: Expanding the Boundaries of Ecocriticism* (Armbruster and Wallace 2001, 4), the "environment also includes cultivated and built landscapes, the natural elements and aspects of those landscapes, and cultural interactions with those natural elements." Kanengoni's (1997) representations of European versus African crop and animal husbandry illuminate the racial segregation of colonial Zimbabwe. The varying landscapes are exemplary of bigoted economic policy. The white agricultural town of Beatrice is described as

> occupied by highly mechanized farms whose homesteads with their satellite dishes showed through the last butterflied bauhinia flowers, flouncing purple bells of a profusion of jacarandas, and the bright red of a few early flamboyant, and swaying blue gums. Across the Mupfure River . . . the rolling landscape was punctuated by monstrous combine harvesters steam-rolling across a field and a cheese-making factory on a dairy farm. (40)

Productive as these white spaces may be, they are still an anomaly. They do not exist symbiotically with the local environment. The author's description includes innuendo of abnormality, encapsulated in the words "highly mechanized," "steam-rolling," and "monstrous." Although colors attract the viewers' (and the readers') attention, it is the sinister automation of this landscape that leaves a lasting impression. The march of progress, emblematized by a capital-intensive agribusiness, is unstoppable. Not even a guerrilla war perturbs this settler community. Life continues, despite indigenous resistance to colonial occupation. Beatrice town is untroubled. In truth, however, while the Grand Narrative of Empire projects this omnipotent facade, the imperial project is in jeopardy. We know this from the vast financial and military resources that the Rhodesian state expended to defeat Zimbabwe's struggle for political independence. Another reason why we can be skeptical about this veneer of colonial opulence is that this prosperity is racially segregated.

The wealth in Beatrice is only surpassed by the extreme poverty in the surrounding indigenous locations. Just twenty kilometers from Beatrice, the countryside is afflicted by "neglect and deterioration" (40). The destitution of the neighboring villages "showed in the road's state of disrepair: the corrugated ridges zigzagging across the road, the deep mounds of dangerous sand at the edges and the narrow, hanging, derelict bridges" (40–41). Munashe witnesses the economic plunder of his people. Despite paying taxes, contributing to the nation's wealth, and providing labor for Zimbabwe's agribusiness, mining, and manufacturing industries, indigenous communities never received an equitable share of the nation's gross domestic production. For example, white farmers had access to affordable credit, subsidized seeds and fertilizers, and extension services that black farmers never got. In such an unlevel playing field, it was easy for white farmers to outperform their black counterparts. Instead, African farmers were herded into "overgrazed pastures, and depleted forests whose remains lay in small heaps of firewood along the road"; this is "tired communal land" that exposes "denuded and barren earth" (41). The extent of economic devastation is matched by ecological destruction. Colonial interference with indigenous relationships to the ecosystem has been deadly. Curtailing and criminalizing such activities as shift cultivation and nomadic forms of pastoralism had resulted in overuse of existing resources. Unable to recover, the landscape is suffering. Munashe observes that the "sun burned fiercely. Nothing spoke of promise. The tired villages stretched into the distance, limp and motionless, as if they too had given up living a long time ago" (41). The community's hopelessness is reflected on their landscape. A solitary "dust-devil spiraling from the naked land" calls to mind not only the physical attributes of the land but also its spiritual significance to the community (41). Land is much more than flower gardens, combine harvesters, and large herds of cattle.[10] Precisely because land holds spiritual importance, the decolonial process of land reform needed to be much more expansive than it was. Earlier, we read Moyo's indictment of the postindependence kleptocracy. A big part of this has to do with Zimbabwe's inability to inclusively address the land question.[11] That failure has come to haunt the country well into the twenty-first century, almost four decades since flag independence.

MAPPING GEOGRAPHIC FEATURES

One remarkable contribution to the Zimbabwean *land question* is Yvonne Vera's poetic prose and her mapping of geographic features onto human bodies.[12] The titular heroine in Vera's *Nehanda* (1993) observes her hands and notes that "rivers and trees cover [my] palms; the trees are lifeless and the rivers dry" (1). In a text that repeatedly collapses the passage of time, the statement above foreshadows the protagonist's demise by the end of the book. Vera mines the real-life Nehanda's late nineteenth-century biography to construct a story that frequently meanders from the present, the past, and the future. "Lifeless trees" immediately foretell Nehanda's hanging by the colonial administration. Her death is similarly prefigured by the "dry rivers"—an imagination of her blood no longer moving through her body after she succumbs to the noose. Aside from supporting these prophecies, the topographical features that Nehanda sees on her hands are real. Nehanda experiences her own body as a true extension of the environment around her. And in the same way, she experiences the ecosystem as an appendage of her own physical body. These connections are as vital as those between a tree and its branches, or those between a river and its tributaries. The projection of environmental features onto human bodies is counterbalanced by natural elements that take on human agency. For instance, shadows "melt," the sun swallows the earth, and the wind "whirls and waits" (36). Aside from creating a circular logic to her poetics—whereby attributes are multidimensional—Vera is also deeply interested in locating the environment as an *actioning* entity. The landscape in Vera's fiction is not merely a backdrop where the characters' actions take place; rather, her ecosystem is alive, frequently acting upon and influencing its human, animal, and plant inhabitants. By extension, it is impossible to own land, simply because "land does not belong to the living" (36). To sell the land is incomprehensible.

Vera depicts a Zimbabwean landscape that is dynamic and agential. Contrast this with historic colonial assertions that the land was abject—while paradoxically profiting from the plunder of Zimbabwe's natural resources. Mr. Browning, a British administrator, describes the vistas he sees as "monotonous since the horizon is always before one's eyes, without any distracting landmarks to obscure vision" (45). The kind of infrastructural location markers that Browning desires—bridges, highways, railroad tracks, police stations, schools, hospitals—are lacking. Hence his expressed intent to modernize and civilize these *empty* spaces. Yet nothing could be further from the truth. What Browning sees as emptiness is very much alive—if examined from an indigenous perspective. For one, the geographic features can speak. The community has learnt to listen to the voices that come "from the cave, from below the earth, and from the roots of trees" (68). Unsurprisingly, these kinds of landscape-based sounds make their way into the people's music. As we saw earlier, Kaguvi channels his immediate ecosystem and "dances the forest that surrounds them, dances the hills and the plateaus" (60). Both Kwela and Mbira emerge from Zimbabwean physical and psychological landscapes. Evidently, there is nothing monotonous about forests and plateaus; they serve as musical inspiration. In this instance, geographical features take on metaphysical significance.

Vera's landscapes are alive and vibrant. Her characters interact with the terrain as though it were a living relative. Both African nationalisms and European colonial projects were premised on the perceived fecundity—under the *right* circumstances—of African lands. It was as the self-appointed guardians of these spheres of productivity that both black and white men aspired for leadership and political control. However, this was a flatly utilitarian view of land and landscape.[13] Vera and Kanengoni, like Grace Ogot and Margaret Ogola, reject this simplistic view of the region's ecosystem. The reason for deep-seated concern about colonial alienation was a recognition that land not only served as an economic resource—enabling agriculture, hunting, and animal husbandry—but that the landscape also served as a spiritual connection to the ancestors, the living-dead, and the unborn. Elsewhere, Vera (2002, 38) writes, "The land does not belong to us. We keep the land for the departed. . . . How can something so vast and mysterious belong to anyone." The land was an all-encompassing entity that meant life—in the fullest sense of the word—to the indigenous inhabitants. Vera and Kanengoni underscore a custodial relationship to land that is vastly at odds with the possessive nature of colonial expansionism. In the next chapter, I examine representations of Kenyan and Tanzanian urban landscapes that deconstruct both colonial control and state surveillance. Marjorie O. Macgoye and Moyez G. Vassanji create characters who enact strategic trespassing and disobedience.

CHAPTER 3

Belonging and Mobility

Representations of Kenyan and Tanzanian Urban Landscapes

And what's a legend, if not someone who tries to get into the flow of history, out of the mud of the past?
—Lindsey Collen, *The Rape of Sita*

URBAN CULTURAL ARTIFACTS

On November 19, 1954, Margaret Wanjirū received Kikuyu, Embu and Meru passbook number F5510 from the Colony and Protectorate of Kenya. Margaret was twenty years old and worked as a filing clerk in Nairobi. She was my maternal grandmother. Between 1954 and June 1955, she rented a room at Plot 174 in Makadara. The residence permit lists her work address as Domestic and Hotel Workers Union, Box 5171, Nairobi. Grandma then moved house, living at Kariokor House 308 between 1956 and 1958. Kariokor was a mangling of the words Carrier Corps, referring to the African porters who served in Britain's World War 1 campaign against German Tanganyika. On April 2, 1957, Grandma was issued with a movement permit allowing her to travel between Nairobi and Kiambu every weekend, to visit her family. From January 2 to December 11, 1958, while still at Kariokor, she was employed as a receptionist at the Nairobi Driving School. On October 3, 1959, Margaret applied for a movement permit in preparation for a business trip. On the next day, she traveled to Machakos, about sixty kilometers away. She was tasked with opening a local branch of the Transport and Allied Workers Union, her employer since leaving the Nairobi Driving School. Colonial surveillance of my grandmother's movements extended to her siblings. Under the "Special Endorsements" page in her passbook is an entry for Edwin Njoroge, her younger brother. In November 1957, he'd been allowed fourteen days to visit Nairobi and seek gainful employment. Since he was living with his older sister, he was automatically added to her passbook. Two years later, Edwin received a travel permit to attend Jeans School for an industrial relations course in November 1959. To say that the colonial city produced novel forms of social control is an understatement.

Passbooks. Poll tax receipts. Employment cards. These are just some of the bureaucratic inventions Britain deployed in monitoring a colonized population. Muthoni Likimani's semiautobiographical work *Passbook Number F.47927: Women and Mau Mau in Kenya* (1985) recounts the evasive maneuvers women performed to survive in Kenya during the tumultuous 1950s. Civil disobedience was another response to this oppression, as was armed resistance—epitomized by the Kenya Land and Freedom Army (Mau Mau) uprising. To avoid disproportionate punishment, the marginalized often resort to low level acts of insubordination. While such rebellious exploits do not defeat the overarching structures that enforce tyranny, they give a semblance of agency. Undercover resistance sustains hope that fundamental revolution will yet come to fruition. Often, these unspoken desires for social and political transformation are bracketed within the arts. In 1950s Nairobi, communities responded with artistic inventions that digested their new reality. In this regard, African cities have a long history as vital sites for new social formations. Like chapter 1, this chapter looks at Kenya and Tanzania. However, unlike that previous discussion of rural-to-rural migration, this current section surveys literary representations of Dar es Salaam's and Nairobi's urban landscapes. I argue that novels set in colonial Dar es Salaam and Nairobi chronicle performative acts of transgression and trespassing. Transgressing and trespassing challenge the settler colonial and capitalist balkanization of land and landscape instituted through a fallacious rural/urban divide.

To comprehensively lay out my argument, I must needs incorporate urban-spawned art forms. Yvonne Vera's poetic and polyphonic fiction in my previous chapter anchors Kwela music within Bulawayo's urbanity. This new music genre thrived in a dense cultural milieu. Kwela gave voice to a city-based yearning that earlier musical forms could not aptly express. Urban spaces serve as fertile ground for the (re)invention of culture. Novel cultural artifacts redesign the aesthetic underpinnings of Africa's metropolitan artistic production. In the 1960s and 1970s, for instance, readers in Accra, Lagos, Nairobi, and Johannesburg helped create and sustain the publication of photo novels in South African-based *Drum* magazine. A hybrid of James Bond and similar Hollywood crime dramas, the photo novel *African Film* was a home-grown action thriller that entertained readers across the continent.[1] Nairobi's cityscape has spawned a literary tradition best represented by the gritty and visceral 1970s urban fiction of Meja Mwangi, David Maillu, and Leonard Kibera. Furthermore, there exists a vibrant Nairobi music scene. Twist and Rumba dominated the airwaves after independence. More recent popular hits use Sheng, the sassy and combative vernacular of Nairobi's inner suburbs made from English, Kiswahili, Gĩkũyũ, Hindi, French, and Dholuo vocabulary. Nameless, Size-8, and Nonini have released albums in Sheng, while Mũrimi wa-Kahalf, Queen Jane, and Kĩgũtha are representative of artists working with an indigenous language: Gĩkũyũ. Nairobi's soundtrack is a medley, featuring Dholuo, Kamba, Somali, reggae, dancehall, and Taarab musicians.

The Kenyan capital's transportation network has also produced its own cultural praxis—*matatu*(ism)—named for the shared taxis that ferry passengers regionally. These practices are a collection of hip styles, informal employment, and the repeated subversion of authority—including the *policing* of language.[2] The transgression of language rules as exemplified by Sheng is synonymous with how the matatu often contravenes traffic laws—and is consequently viewed as a menace on Kenyan roads. A February 19, 2013 article in Kenya's leading newspaper, the *Daily Nation*, castigates Sheng, and by extension matatu-ism, as "vile and useless" (Muganda 2013). This linguistic transgression is a vital source of Sheng. The hipness is shared across the border in Tanzania, where artists such as Lady Jaydee and Diamond produce music that is self-aware in its novelty and modernity. What these cultural phenomena have in common is sustained interest in the use of *performance* to disturb established power dynamics. These art forms inspire my reading of fictional urban landscapes.

Literature by Marjorie O. Macgoye and Moyez G. Vassanji carries similar concerns. These two writers have imagined Nairobi and Dar es Salaam, respectively, as locations that problematize discussions of public/private spaces, place, and landscape. Mike Davis (2004) eloquently argues that metropolitan destitution is linked to loss of a rural sense of belonging. In *Planet of Slums*, Davis urges a reconsideration of urban squalor and the extent to which this is intertwined with land politics in the countryside. Davis expands the definition of urbanization "as structural transformation along, and intensified interaction between, every point of an urban-rural continuum" (7). The formation of African cities is complex. Urbanization is often characterized by a "hermaphroditic countryside," one that is half-urban, half-rural (7). While land refers to the physical terrain—the geography on which cities are built—space gestures toward the metaphysical architecture that emerges and how citizens navigate it. To better comprehend the phenomenon of "partially urbanized" geographies, we must marshal both land and space as concepts through which to discuss African cityscapes (7). Hence, we can speak of communal/public space versus private space. While privileging space in my discussion of urban landscapes, it is imperative to fully acknowledge the gender, migrant, and ethnic complications—challenges often overlooked by nationalist and nativist approaches. Space is an acutely scarce commodity in cities around the world, and more so in the Global South. After the onslaught of International Monetary Fund and World Bank neoliberal policies in the 1990s, there was a rapid increase in urban populations, and it is estimated that more than three-quarters of city dwellers in the developing world occupy space *illegally* (15). This is a consequence of Bretton Woods' structural adjustment programs that not only accelerated the migration of excess labor to informal settlements but also reversed any "urban bias" in postcolonial social welfare policies (10, 18). Subsequently, cities have become key stages for disenfranchised urban dwellers on which they improvise varied forms of ownership—or belonging—to compensate for the lack of actual land tenure.

EASTERN AFRICA'S URBAN LANDSCAPES

Rashmi Varma's (2012, 95) work has identified two primary metaphors through which Kenya's capital is signified: as a "parasite on the body of the nation and Nairobi as a prostitute, a degraded body in itself." African postcolonial writers depict cities suffering from "stinking back alleys, ramshackle dwelling, jobless youth, floating waste, corrupt officials, alcoholism, thievery and juvenile delinquency"; this narrative approach is described as "excrement vision" (95). In Kenya, Meja Mwangi's visceral fiction from the 1970s is an apt representation of this aesthetic. Nationalism has been unable to resolve the challenges of urban poverty due to its contamination with either patriarchal feudal-like "clientelism" or "ethno-religious" bigotry (Davis 2004, 29).[3] To understand literary representations of urban landscapes necessitates a critical lens that includes claims to space in the city in terms of belonging and mobility. Urban areas serve as crucibles for the renegotiation of power, hierarchy, and subjectivity. My investigation extends previous discussions of African urban literature by examining the city as a cultural space and, simultaneously, as a geographical space. Urban dwellers respond to these two aspects of the postcolonial African metropolis with a particular kind of political resistance: reassertion of their agential power. This is often manifested as trespassing and transgressing.

The analysis of Marjorie Macgoye's *Coming to Birth* (1986) in the first half of this chapter entails depictions of Nairobi's landscape. I do so by magnifying characters' acts of transgression, trespass, and performance. For instance, Macgoye's female protagonist reacts to social and physical barriers that seek to keep her out of certain spaces with deviance and disobedience. Unlike fiction encountered in chapters 1 and 2, Macgoye portrays urban landscapes in textual descriptions that mimic photography. Furthermore, she deploys women's artistic production to demonstrate the value of city-dwelling women forging spaces—whether cultural, political, or physical—for themselves. Critical scholarship has dissected the ways Macgoye addresses women's concerns as they pertain to postcolonial systems of wealth inequity. I wish to read her fiction with an eye for the aesthetic choices Macgoye makes as she (re)creates and represents Nairobi's cityscape and landscape. In critiquing the narrow, sexist viewpoints of masculine patriarchal nationalism—which imagines the nation as either "loose" woman or motherland—Varma offers a "postcolonial feminist citizenship that is drawn from the gendered labor of obtaining the right to inhabit the city as a political subject, and to be represented as such in the cultural work of postcolonial fictions" (2). *Coming to Birth* has already garnered a national audience since publication. In the late 2000s, the text was assigned to students sitting for the Kenya Certificate of Secondary Education exams. In addition, dramatizations have helped disseminate the text to wide public readership. Although Ngũgĩ wa Thiong'o has more international acclaim, Macgoye's writing is equally well regarded nationally.[4]

The second half of my chapter features an examination of Moyez G. Vassanji's *Uhuru Street* (1991). He too represents urban landscapes—in Dar es Salaam—via the twin lenses of trespassing and transgression. Vassanji's work demands that we consider both private and public spaces as political terrains where power struggles are repeatedly played out. Physical terrains also shape political conflicts. Geographies either provide the subject for rivalries or become the space in which these skirmishes happen. Finally, by focusing on the plight of East Africa's Indian diaspora, Vassanji foregrounds questions of ethnicity; he demonstrates how cultural and political struggles could also potentially shape physical landscapes. Studies of Vassanji's collection of stories have been interested in his depiction of East Africa's Indian diaspora. Writing about twenty-five years into the era of African self-rule, Macgoye and Vassanji demonstrate how literature recovers lost histories.

MOBILITY AND TRESPASSING: INTERACTIONS WITH THE BUILT ENVIRONMENT

Coming to Birth is a narrative about the rural-urban migration of Paulina, a young woman from the shores of Nam Lolwe (Lake Victoria). She initially moves to Kenya's colonial capital at the height of anti-British politics in the mid-Fifties. The tense political situation is reflected in the novel by Paulina's numerous encounters with the anti-independence efforts of British colonialism, including barbed wire, police patrols, and home searches by belligerent security personnel. Her exodus, however, is not unidirectional. She returns to her natal village either to bring in the harvest or simply to create some space between herself and Martin—her husband—with whom relations swing from friendly to violent as his temper dictates. Macgoye's text traces Paulina's life alongside Kenyan political history and there are strong allusions that the two are often intertwined—for example, when Paulina loses her only son during public riots that historically occurred during President Mzee Jomo Kenyatta's visit to the lake-side town of Kisumu. Furthermore, there is a strong sense that Paulina's maturity—from a wide-eyed sixteen-year-old bride to a cosmopolitan urban citizen—is mirrored by Kenya's own political coming of age. The story ends with much hope that Paulina—and Kenya, metaphorically—will "come to birth" and send forth much-awaited progeny.

Critical attention on Macgoye's narrative examines how gender intersects with the politics of space. Every step of Paulina's journey in Nairobi is made in the face of patriarchal opposition. Critics have foregrounded how *Coming to Birth* invites a discussion of women's exclusion from urban areas; the city is presumed to be a male space (Barasa 2009, 79, 157). If women in Macgoye's text eventually discover the urban as a space for emancipation, they do so against men who connive to create a "dichotomy between public and private spaces," aimed at coercing women into silence (59, 81). Central to such tensions between the status of the rural and urban spheres are assumptions that depict the rural as the space of immaturity or backwardness, or both. This is in addition to colonial privileging of the urban over the rural. In a critical afterword to Macgoye's novel, Valerie Kibera (1987, 159, 163) points out that the "chaotic new world" of towns and cities into which Paulina ventures was multiply a "literal, psychological, and symbolic" fracture from her customary norms; this migration deposited her into a limbo that catalyzed either empowerment or disenfranchisement. Paulina's maturity has significance outside her own personhood—her growth is indicative of wider sociopolitical transformations—a sentiment echoed by none other than Ngũgĩ wa Thiong'o on the back cover of *Coming to Birth*.

Joseph Slaughter (2004) attends to the demarcation of space in Nairobi from an urban planning perspective. Colonial infrastructure was aimed toward the belief that urban planning could play an instrumental role in the "development of a civil [African] subject" (37). This manner of planning colonial cities suggests that "Nairobi's urban *geo*graphy becomes Paulina's personal *bio*graphy" (Slaughter 2005, 129; emphasis in original). Slaughter's discovery of the ways in which the urban Kenyan was "expected to be a tinged copy of the urban Englishman" comes as no surprise; to this end Nairobi underwent a "modernist arrangement of space" (Slaughter 2004, 39). Colonial cities, as *performance* spaces, were built to accommodate the "drama . . . of individualism, of discrimination, of differentiation, and civic affiliation"; British tutelage did not aspire toward a colonial citizen who could determine the course of her own urbanization but rather preplanned Nairobi and sought to mold the colonial citizen so she could fit in (Slaughter 2004, 44). Paulina navigates through Nairobi. Simultaneously, Macgoye redeploys the bildungsroman genre to create space for black female agency. Paulina resists the colonial city's impulse to produce apolitical subjects—civilized and yet docile, temporary visitors—just as much as Macgoye challenges the bildungsroman's complicity as an imperialist tool for producing coherent subjectivities.

In British East Africa it was accepted that land—especially under the control of European urban development—held the potential to alter (African/indigenous) individualities. Macgoye's representation of Nairobi questions "gendered (post)colonial urbanism" and challenges the racialized experiences of "full stinking latrine blocks, and the stale air of housing complexes," both of which are starkly opposed to "European order and affluence" (Varma 2012, 108, 112). The colonial city—organized around the marginalization and abjection of black people—was designed to produce certain forms of subjectivity. Urban centers were founded upon racial hierarchies, which assigned political power accordingly. As we saw previously in Bulawayo, Europeans were perched at the top and Africans relegated to the bottom. Nairobi emerged as a space "where the easy distinctions of city and country, tribe and citizen, [or] sexual and wage work" are deeply revised; furthermore, class divisions unraveled as Nairobians consumed the products of a capitalist economy—one key step in becoming a "modern citizen" (113, 115). The colonial city, however, did not manufacture the African subjectivities it desired. The effects of urbanization were chaotic, complex, and bred new subjects who resisted colonialism.

HOW DO CHARACTERS RELATE TO THEIR ARCHITECTURAL SURROUNDINGS?

Macgoye presents the reader with picture-like vistas—or verbal pictures—of Nairobi's city center and central business district, its posh and leafy suburbs, its transportation network, and its informal suburbs with underserved infrastructure where the colonial government shepherded black workers. These panoramas—through their cinematographic depictions of how characters behave—demonstrate a subject's ability to navigate Nairobi, to defy colonial prejudice and occupy urban spaces, and to create their own style in response to colonial modernity. Finally, we see residents' capacity to shape the city, just as urban infrastructure dictates social interactions. Evan Mwangi's (2009) definition of "verbal pictures" highlights Macgoye's textual, yet uncannily photographic representations that display the author's investment in how characters navigate, occupy, and inhabit the colonial city (171). Macgoye's aesthetics of photography demonstrate the novel's interest in depictions of Nairobi not only through the phenomena of trespassing but also using the motif of performance. Mwangi's notion of visual representation in African letters is anchored to his discussion of metafiction—an aesthetic practice he describes as "that form of African literature that is self-conscious, self-reflexive, and self-referential" (6). Similarly, *Coming to Birth* demands that its audience pay attention to its disruptive use of the European novel, as well as its characters' self-awareness in the colonial urban landscape.[5] Macgoye's work uses photographic representational techniques while also foregrounding space; her fiction is especially useful for its capacity to "defamiliarize" and "demystify" (15, 16). Furthermore, by invoking photography, Macgoye demands that we bear in mind the circulation of photographic representations of African cities—either created and deployed by colonial bodies or produced by postcolonial artists. The visibility from Macgoye's use of the photographic indicates that *Coming to Birth* represents urban landscapes through metaphoric trespassing.

Acts of transgression and trespassing form a dual assault on colonial efforts to circumscribe indigenous freedom through law and urban planning. To "trespass" has connotations of unlawful or uninvited entry into land/property that belongs to another (OED). This sort of intrusion is particularly severe in relation to private versus public spaces. Similarly, "transgression" suggests the willful violation of legal boundaries, or infringement of an authoritative order (OED). Together, these two forms of protest transform the African into a haunting presence in the European colonial mind. The colonizer has always to monitor the colonized to ensure they overcome neither social codes nor physical barricades—which seek to demarcate the oppressed from the oppressor.[6] As Paulina's first solitary tour of the city demonstrates, there is much "to be frightened of in Nairobi," and Africans must exercise subtle transgression of urban space (Macgoye 1986, 17). As a newcomer from rural Kenya, Paulina does not yet possess the city dweller's knowledge of how to navigate without overtly contravening (un)spoken laws about Nairobi's segregated spaces. The author describes Paulina's walk from the King George's Hospital where she was admitted, after a miscarriage, to her husband's rented house:

> From the railway line she came to an open space which was the site for the Baptist Centre and from there a line of solid brick houses bordered the road down the valley up and down again, with the more ragged outline of Pumwani beyond. . . . At the top of the hill the other side looked more familiar, not like homes exactly, the buildings were too big and close together for that, but like a market in the country with a petrol pump, a shoe repairer, but further along the barbed wire reappeared and the notices on which one could always make out the big letters, KEM, KEM. (17)

Although the drive to the hospital only took Paulina and her husband a few minutes, her return journey lasts several days because she repeatedly gets lost. Macgoye, however, means more than Paulina losing her sense of direction when she notes that the protagonist "knew for certain now that she was on the wrong road" (14). The road that "bordered" brick residences in the passage above, in addition to the barbed wire, displays the ominous side of Nairobi to Paulina: barriers restricting one's movement. Increasingly, she is becoming aware of the fact that "all Nairobi in those days was full of barbed wire . . . [and] everything was designed to keep you out" (14). The KEM billboards she sees on her walk-about complement the barbed wire and act as visual reminders—mostly to members of the Kikuyu, Embu, and Meru communities, but generally to all Africans—that Nairobi was under siege.

The city demands a lot of know-how from its black residents. Paulina—at the onset of her residence in Nairobi—is still very ignorant. What the novel suggests is that spatial illiteracy acts as a barrier. In other words, Nairobi is a collection of symbols that she has not learnt how to decipher. For one, she could not fathom the sheer size of the colonial capital, much less "imagine that it would take a day to walk across from edge to edge" and be practically "impossible" to recall all she witnessed along the way (11). Ignorant of the magnitude of the space she must navigate, Paulina is emblematic of rural folks who are yet to learn "the town capacity of moving from one place to the next without returning home" (13). Her countryside innocence is clearly legible on her face. For instance, on her train journey from Kisumu she was easy prey for hawkers and pickpockets, and once in the city she is mistaken for a fugitive and locked up in a police cell (6, 19). Later, when Paulina suggests selling vegetables at the market, her husband's barb—that she'd get herself "marched off to police again or to mission again or to bloody holy brothers and sisters again before . . . [she got] ten cents for a twenty-five cent bunch of carrots"—while unfair, seems an apt description of Paulina's "middling ability," closer to that of a Class Eight pupil than of the urbanized wife Martin desires (25, 26).

There is much for Paulina to learn before she, too, can comfortably weave in and out of colonial mechanisms of control and truly claim Nairobi as her own. Although she achieves this by the end of the text, she is initially quite oblivious when compared to Martin and other men who have picked up vital skills to guarantee themselves safe residence in the city. For one, her husband is noted as possessing a "mastery" of the city that was sure to overwhelm Paulina (2). This expertise can also be seen in a group of bus drivers who during their nightly walks from work "deliberately talked loudly in Swahili to show that they were on lawful business, with passes, and had nothing to hide" (9). The colonial directives that had—early in Britain's occupation of Kenya—created exclusively European rural areas known as the White Highlands were later mirrored in the period leading up to independence. The second time round, these commands attempted to re-create the city as a largely white space. As a result, black bodies were repeatedly evacuated from Nairobi especially through police swoops—after which anyone arrested without an employment pass was returned to their home area—but also occasionally through trespass laws.[7] Successful resistance against this legislation depended upon the resident's knowledge. In *Coming to Birth* we accompany the protagonist as she acquires the necessary know-how and becomes more comfortable in the city.

Paulina's growing aptitude is demonstrated in a trip she and Martin take to some of Nairobi's cultural spaces:

> They went to the museum on a Sunday afternoon and saw real leopards and giraffes, only dead and standing up, and birds and butterflies and implements from different tribes. She enjoyed it and begged to go again. They also strolled through the town gazing into the windows of the big shops, where a dress could cost more than a month's wages and a man's suit half a year's. They went out to Ruaraka by bus to visit a friend who lived at the Breweries, and she got a feel of a country district different from their own. They walked in City Park and out among the big houses where people like Martin's employers lived and ladies strolled in soft tissues scandalously bare at the waist. (29)

There is a common thread of enjoyment that Paulina demonstrates as she alternately occupies various urban spaces: the museum, clothing emporiums on the city's streets, and the park. In each of these locations, she adds to her know-how of the city This weekend trip epitomizes the text's representation of urban landscapes; there is, simultaneously, transgression of social norms and the presence of black bodies in forbidden spaces. The city museum, in its association with colonial forms of collecting knowledge—anthropologically classifying it and recording it for posterity—was a space that relied on African absence. In Macgoye's passage above, Africans were more often imagined as sharing space with "real leopards and giraffes"—part of the spectacle—rather than as members of the audience viewing this fauna. Furthermore, the couple's window-shopping experience, as well as their hike to City Park, suggests the kind of leisure that was a preserve of European settlers in Kenya, not their black domestic and farm laborers.

Macgoye foregrounds Paulina's comfort within the cityscape by depicting her emotional response on another visit to Nairobi. A decade and a half after her original journey, we see Paulina marveling both at the urban infrastructure and how sophisticated the city had become. "There was something of the same excitement now that she had felt fifteen years before on seeing the city for the first time—the pleasant sunshine, the continuous change of spectacle, the bustle and the hard-learned possibility of belonging" (90). The writer's mention of Paulina's "marvel" and "excitement" is quite apart from the discomfort she felt on her first trip to the city; back then, there was nothing "pleasant" about Nairobi, and if Paulina noticed the capital's hustle and bustle it was with much trepidation. In the time since, Paulina has matured into a woman who *enjoys* being in the city, despite—or perhaps precisely because of—colonial regulations that make such movements transgressive.

NAIROBI'S CITYSCAPE AS A CULTURAL MILIEU

In addition to the physical trespassing that we see above, *Coming to Birth* is equally interested in moments—both in time and place—when characters enact cultural transgression. Macgoye deploys verbal pictures to represent parts of Nairobi where residents have cobbled together a novel culture from multiple ethnic strands. This cultural borrowing and sharing, much in contrast to colonial efforts to sanitize white from both black and brown, enables characters to further stake their claims to the city. Paulina nervously enjoys visiting Cross Street, a section of Macgoye's imaginary Nairobi where pedestrians see "every little shop front spawning new business, enterprises taking shape on the pavements, [and] the young and strong thronging corners, seeking a way to employ their overflowing energy" (130). This is a district that is itching to expand; it has much vigor, talent, and time to expend on its various economic pursuits and the participants of its business activities are targeting growth. We can easily imagine these small-scale traders overrunning the rest of the city in a frenzy of selling and buying their "gobbets of raw meat, the repetitive rows of the same watches, the same transistor radios, the same suitcases and schoolbags" (130). Furthermore, we get a description of "letters stenciled, here and there reversed, on the insides of shop windows, shirts flung open to the waist, babies' tasseled berets or cut-down ladies' felt hats on bejeweled young men, platform soles and wedges strapped like fetters on girls' feet," all of which immerse the reader in the space (130). Cross Street serves as the cultural equivalent of the blacksmith's forge—it is where new forms are created, inspired by Kenya's ethnic heritage. This "open-ended, polyvalent, dialogic, noncentralized, and improvisational" characteristic makes Cross Street adept at importing cultures from elsewhere (Phillips 2006, xxi). The Cross Street soundscape is composed of Hindi tunes, Congolese music, and the multilingual dialogues Paulina overhears while strolling past shop fronts (Macgoye 1986, 130). This space is unrecognizable as the orderly colonial city that Britain's colonial project sought to conjure several decades before this.

Cross Street shares very little with the "good order of the residential districts, where . . . a servant's shack under the trees, a shrub in flower or the high painted gates of an embassy" betray the very demarcations of black vs. white and rich vs. poor that Cross Street decries (130). Even as the author is interested in the smells, sounds, and tastes of Cross Street, she clearly privileges the visual. Hence the whistles that call after Paulina as she walks along suggest the omniscient male gaze reacting to her, or another woman's body; at the same time, "the ochre-haired moran or cloaked Turkana watchmen with their intricate ear-rings who were always gazing haughtily into windows of electric torches or striped socks" indicate that Cross Street is not wholly transparent—it is not openly visible to everyone (131). The fringe on which both the Maasai and Turkana morans find themselves in relation to the rest of Cross Street is like the periphery that Paulina, Martin, and their friends reside in—in relation to the colonial cityscape.

Physical and cultural transgressions aside, Macgoye uses visual (re)presentations to underscore landscape through the idea of performance. The writer paints *scenes* in which her characters *perform* various civic duties, and it is these very actions that help to accentuate characters' claims to Nairobi. Paulina's interaction with government bureaucracy is a good example of this motif:

> She had learned how to deal with the big city shops. Government offices in the old provincial style were familiar to her—sentries more or less on guard outside the old colonial buildings, whitened stones, trees, long, cool staircases, desks set in ordinary rooms with high ceilings and green or brown paint like a schoolroom in town or a police station, files that were a long time coming and receipts written tediously by hand. (120)

In the passage above, state offices are represented in language that foregrounds the positional relationship between objects and subjects. The list of objects that make up colonial bureaucracy—stones, trees, staircases, desks, ordinary rooms, files, and receipts—evokes the set directions for a play. Macgoye's description, though detailed, suggests that the items are not significant on their own; rather, they are only important due to what they enable occupants to do. I find the anticipation that emanates from this sketch quite like the expectation that a playwright's directions produce in a theater. With the dramatic stage set, Macgoye proceeds to inform the reader of the various parts each of her character's play: Paulina acts with familiarity, while government clerks are charged with being slow and working "tediously." Each character excels at what they do, suggesting that they have long rehearsed and learnt their respective roles. Through words such as "familiar," "tediously," "frighten," "glimpsed," "collecting," and "delivering," we get the sense that this *picture* captures a routine that Paulina has executed before. She is in her element, as it were, despite the basic ominous characteristic of the colonial state machinery. Subsequently, we can read Paulina's appointments with various government departments as performativity of her citizenship; she is *more* Kenyan by going to the bank, passport office, or any other government building. Her transgressive actions, as well as her presence in financial and bureaucratic spaces, underscore her own space in the colonial city. Paulina's actions underscore "everyday experiences and everyday methods of problem solving in everyday spaces" (Phillips 2006, xx). Hers is a vernacular mode of *being* aggregated from her rural, urban, cultural, and professional experiences as a housewife and nanny. To echo Anne-Maria Makhulu (2015, xiv,) black female Nairobians enact a "politics of presence"; "by their sheer presence [women like Paulina changed] the course of history" (5). Urban areas in Macgoye's text have unique attributes that homogenous rural areas lack.

Coming to Birth advocates for the city's plurality over the countryside's insularity and chauvinism. In relation to Paulina's father and his occupation, *Coming to Birth* notes that he

> never seemed to make much money out of this tedious work, month after month, with few stories or excitement to tell about when he came home on leave. It sounded to be a bleak place, close-built, mean little houses, one shop on the plantation, church services in the rudimentary school-room, now and then a wandering musician to gather the Luo people together, nodding to the song and throwing pennies, or Kambas gathering for their mysterious, exhausting dance, up and down, up and down, up and down, with football whistles endlessly screaming. (61)

The unnamed rural district above offers a measly life; it is "bleak," "mean," and "rudimentary." In contrast to the stage that Macgoye presented in Cross Street, Paulina's father's workplace has little vibrancy and the employees' attempts at music and festivity are not rewarding. Hence, it lacks the very thing that makes Cross Street a beneficial location: cultural blending. It is clear from the passage that Luos and Kambas have not merged; each holds onto their own customary heritage without any cross-pollination and the possibility of novel cultural artifacts. Small wonder that Luo music, so far away from home, sounds dour and lacks life and even the musician who has risked much by venturing to entertain his compatriots is rewarded with nothing but passive nods and pennies. At the same time, Kamba traditions remain opaque to Luo speakers; the dances are an emblem of senselessness. Even though they continue for what seems an eternity, they remain "mysterious" and offer nothing to the homesick Luos but screams and inexplicable "up and down" movements. Cultural narrow-mindedness is a principal element of rural colonial spaces—whether in the White Highlands or in regions primarily designated for indigenous communities. In fact, it is this rural idyll that my fifth chapter on Yvonne Owuor and Monica Arac de Nyeko critiques in their pastoral-challenging fiction. Towns and cities, however, provide the colonized population with opportunities to battle prejudice.

Marjorie Macgoye's *Coming to Birth* represents urban landscapes through symbolic acts of transgression, trespass, and performance. Nairobi's residents reacted to social and physical barriers that sought to keep them out of certain spaces with deviance and disobedience. Macgoye's characters repeatedly reinserted their presence in the very spaces where it had earlier been prohibited. Furthermore, through acts of cultural transgression, Macgoye's Nairobians challenge the kind of cultural policing—colonial and postcolonial—that is founded upon gender, class, or ethnic boundaries. Often, such barriers complement physical ones that restrict characters' movements. It is possible to demonstrate ways in which the cityscape has influenced its residents' personality. In reverse, one could also map instances when the people have left an impact on the city, its infrastructure, its scenery, and so forth.

DIASPORA COMMUNITIES AND THE URBAN LANDSCAPE

Moyez G. Vassanji's *Uhuru Street* (1991) also explores Dar es Salaam through symbolic acts of transgression and trespassing. Vassanji complicates representations of urban landscapes by foregrounding the Indian diaspora's propensity for migration and *double migration*. The presence of Indian migrants in Eastern Africa vexed the simplistic racial binary established by colonial powers in relation to citizenship, mobility, and belonging. Indian subjects were not only *too black* to be *white* but also *too white* to be *black*; they simultaneously spanned the dual categories of settler and native. *Uhuru Street* is a collection of sixteen pieces of short fiction that memorialize Tanzania's

Dar es Salaam as it looked in the 1950s through the early 1980s—serving as a fruitful juxtaposition to Macgoye's *Coming to Birth*. Vassanji focuses not only on the political changes that the city and the nation undergo but also on how these alterations are reflected in the daily lives of his characters. In Vassanji's text, characters appear in more than one story—especially the child narrator, whose family configuration morphs as the stories progress. The short story cycle enables a see-saw reworking of complex ideas and serves as an apt metaphor for the (re)negotiation of identities (Davis 1999, 8). Finally, there is a great sense of characters occupying Dar es Salaam—offering a crucial link to Macgoye's text. Vassanji's fictional Dar es Salaam dismantles colonial vigilance and security devices. Ultimately, the eponymous Uhuru Street becomes an urban enclave where residents experiment with multiple (and novel) subjectivities.

Given Vassanji's interest in the fate of Indian migrants to Kenya, Uganda, and Tanzania, scholarly attention has also, rightly, often begun with this historical event. In addition to centuries of trade and economic exchange across the Indian Ocean world, non-African peoples were present during the early colonial period in East Africa. Archaeological evidence has shown the presence of Indian Ocean trade routes that took advantage of the annual monsoon winds to traverse from present-day Mozambique, Tanzania, Kenya, and Somalia to India's western coast. In Zanzibar, Omani Arabs established their headquarters to better monitor trade in enslaved people and ivory coming from the interior. This lucrative commerce was a big cause of contention when European influence expanded in Africa—starting with Portuguese expeditions in the 1490s to British occupation in the last half of the nineteenth century. By the 1900s, the region had received tens of thousands of Christian Goans, Gujarati Jains, and Bohra Muslims, among others. For many, the railway line from Mombasa to Kampala was their main occupation. They would soon set up trade in the frontier towns and emerging cities. By the early 1960s, East Africa had just over 350, 000 Africans of South Asian origin (Younger 2009, 201). South Asian immigrants formed close-knit communities based on a shared cultural heritage. This self-segregation was especially visible in the numerous religious establishments that served segments of this large Desi community. The diaspora's desire for insularity produced tension in Nairobi and Dar es Salaam—postcolonial cities that were both redefining themselves as essentially plural. *Uhuru Street* chronicles a unique cosmopolitanism, as related elsewhere in *Diaspora and Nation in the Indian Ocean: Transnational Histories of Race and Urban Space in Tanzania* (Bertz

2015). This cultural medley of Africans, Arabs, and Indians in the port of Dar es Salaam offered the "awareness of a deeply interconnected history ... [amid changing] ideas about difference and belonging" (35).

Vassanji's oeuvre opposes exclusionary stories of belonging in the African (post)colony. For one, his fiction rejects colonial policies of *divide and rule* that sowed discord among various subjugated people. In addition, Vassanji indicts post-Sixties nationalisms that advanced *African-ness* based on racial criteria. Finally, the author disavows contemporary forms of Western imperialism that portray Africa(ns) in the unitary light of poverty, war, and disease. *Uhuru Street* is about Vassanji's desire to chronicle; the book expresses his belief that Africans "need to tell their stories" (Nasta 2004, 72). The author challenges prejudiced views of the continent as one "homogenous" entity (Desai 2011, 195). Overall, Moyez Vassanji is clearly interested in who gets to (re)tell African narratives. He expresses his frustration at the repeated "hijacking" of histories (Simatei 2000, 29).[8] The writer wields as critical a pen in response to postcolonial nation building by African states and the way they handled the *Asian question*. Furthermore, Vassanji's work with the history of the Indian diaspora and his contribution to their memorialization is reminiscent of the use of folklore in chapter 1 of this book—in Ogot's *The Promised land* and Ogola's *The River and the Source*—where oral narratives have been deployed to stake a community's belonging and claim to space. Hence, writing is not only a "process of remembrance" (Gifford 2010, 177) but also an endeavor to recover "histories of resistance" (Simatei 2011, 56).[9]

MEMORY AND NOSTALGIA ON UHURU STREET

There is a segment of critical work on Vassanji that has examined his illustration of East Africa's sociopolitical context. I wish to extend that scholarship to discuss the author's depiction of Dar es Salaam's built and natural environments and how his characters relate to both. Vassanji himself invites commentary on how the Uhuru Street he writes about is both a metaphorical and geographical space. Uhuru Street, named for the Kiswahili word meaning freedom, is simultaneously real and a "construct with imaginative life" for Vassanji's characters; the space functions doubly as "social structure and a configuration of consciousness and memory" for residents, emigrants, and returnees (Davis 1999, 10, 11). There are two ways of looking at urban space: one is in the relationship between real material space and its symbolic life in the minds of its inhabitants. The second is the question of a diaspora writer's relationship to a place he left—one that is also a space of/for memory and nostalgia for a whole community. Both iterations complicate an ethnic minority's relationship to an African cityscape. In the diaspora's typical longing for home, Uhuru Street morphs into a multiply significant zone for the realization of dreams—either those of the migrants who arrive in Dar es Salaam from the Indian subcontinent or those of the second and third generation who return after brief sojourns in Western Europe and North America.

That Dar es Salaam's Indians are foreigners gets repeated attention in *Uhuru Street*. There are certain locations in the city, and on Uhuru Street in particular, where they are unwelcome. In response to this socially sanctioned exclusion, members of this group constantly venture into and trespass invisible yet taut social barriers. Mnazi Moja grounds are one such space. Though "quite lively" during the day, and occasionally festive—for example during Eid or football matches—Mnazi Moja also had the potential to be ominous; as the narrator in "The Sounds of the Night" points out, during the early hours of dawn "an oppressive and sinister darkness lay over it. The ground at our feet dropped off into blackness at every step, soft breezes like cold fingers of evil brushed past our cheeks" (Vassanji 1991, 68). Evidently, there is "evil" lurking at Mnazi Moja and it is associated with that which is black/dark. Unsurprisingly, in "The Beggar," a homeless black male remembers how he bullied Indian men "walking home nervously across Mnazi Moja Grounds" (31). The nervous men are reacting to their transgression of the unspoken racial barrier that vetoes Indian presence on Mnazi Moja. As the characters' emotional tension displays, Mnazi Moja is not amenable to desegregation. The interpretation of *Uhuru Street* as interested in ideas of light and dark has also been discussed in relation to Vassanji's depiction of darkness in ominous terms, and especially in reference to African vagrants. Dan Ojwang (2000, 52) reads darkness as the depiction of an Africa that is "ready for cultural enlightenment," or as a region that "resists all such attempts to illuminate it." Alternatively, light and darkness help the text "provide a [sharper] contrast between an alleged African aggression and Indian victimhood" (53). The short story collection focuses on Mnazi Moja, which serves as a "cordon sanitaire" between African districts and those where Europeans and Asians lived (44).

Equally illegible is African presence in Dar es Salaam as a colonial city. African residence in the urban area, in the face of colonial regulations that demand all unemployed Africans return home to the reserve, is fraught with danger. *Uhuru Street* describes how at regular intervals green government trucks suddenly appeared in the main streets at night and a general chase ensued, policemen jumping out and checking African pedestrians for their cards. Those who couldn't produce them were carted off to the police station, and if not claimed by their employers the following day were sent off to their villages. (Vassanji 1991, 30)

It is clear in this story that black bodies in urban Tanganyika are under constant scrutiny from the British government.[10] Moreover, these Africans are only permitted to live in the city as long as they are gainfully employed, lacking which they should hastily depart. The use of identity cards, rather than underlining the characters' claim to Tanganyikan citizenship, makes them more vulnerable: without them, they can be forcibly relocated. In this general melee, Uhuru Street becomes a stage where oppressor and oppressed play a game of hide-and-seek. Within this binary, Indian Tanganyikans are simultaneously cast as colonizer and colonized; they occupy a middling ground that is threatened from both sides. Evidently, the "construction of Tanganyikan and Tanzanian society was a process that always flowed over borders" (Bertz 2015, 19). Vassanji depicts a power differential in which the presence of one group in a space they should not visit is reconciled through the handover of some token—money in the case of the beggar who accosts Indians on Mnazi Moja, and ID cards in the case of government soldiers chasing after African workers. Furthermore, that such campaigns occur at night, under the cover of darkness, adds to the threatening aura that all things dark/black hold for the city's Indian diaspora. Hence, the diasporan community operates under siege conditions; the Indianized Uhuru Street is the refuge from which Asians alternately engage in—or retreat from—the wider urban political struggle.

Indigenous animal and plant life challenges Indian migration and the fundamental tenets of racial segregation in Dar es Salaam. When the narrator in "Leaving" moves from Uhuru Street with his family to a different part of Dar, it is implied that this household has strayed far from its comfort zone, surrounded by other Indians, in Uhuru Street. The narrator's description of the new district, Upanga, is filled with apprehension:

After the bustle of Uhuru Street, our new neighbourhood seemed quiet. Instead of the racket of buses, bicycles and cars on the road, we now heard the croaking of frogs and chirping of insects. Nights were haunting, lonely and desolate and took some getting used to. Upanga Road emptied after seven in the evening and the sidestreets became pitch dark, with no illumination.

> Much of the area was as yet uninhabited and behind the housing develop-
> ment there were overgrown bushes, large, scary baobab trees, and mango and
> coconut groves. (Vassanji 1991, 71)

This relocation of the domestic sphere from Uhuru Street to Upanga comes
at a great cost. The continued threat that darkness portends is palpable in
the loneliness and desolation of the nights in Upanga. While the nocturnal
activities registered by transport infrastructure—public transit and bikes—
demonstrate the presence of culture, frogs croaking and insects chirping
point to culture's absence. The flora, too, is disturbing—ergo the "overgrown
bushes" and the "large, scary baobab trees." The lighting produced by motor
vehicles is contrasted to the dense darkness of the shrubs and thickets, just
as that which is African (nature) is opposed to that which is Indian (culture).
This description of Dar es Salaam's peri-urban region indicates that there
exist more absolute racial hierarchies in semirural settings. The mixing and
contestation that accompanies cultural transgression in urban areas is wholly
lacking in the countryside; in this regard, Vassanji raises an argument quite
like Macgoye's in the latter's depiction of Nairobi's Cross Street.

There are times when interior spaces can be just as ominous as those outside the home. Extreme danger often lurks within the domestic scene. The
first-person narrator describes following a character named Ahmed

> into the cave that was their flat. I had never been behind those doors before
> and I did so then with some trepidation. I looked behind me nervously as I
> entered. Inside, it was strangely quiet, and dark. The windows there, except
> for one or two of them, were always kept closed. Some of them boarded up
> with boxtops and plywood. The curtains were drawn that afternoon and light
> was barely visible through them. (41)

In this incident, the skulking danger that has pursued Vassanji's Indian diaspora from Mnazi Moja through to Uhuru Street and the Upanga quarters has
found its way home. This evil, as it is referred to elsewhere, is represented by
the darkness in Ahmed's apartment. It elicits the same nervous reaction displayed by Indian men paying their passage across Mnazi Moja. This gloomy
interior signifies the intrusion of the outside world into the inner sanctum
of Vassanji's Indian community. Vassanji upholds a race/gender hierarchy
whereby brown triumphs over black, just as male conquers female. In the
power contest between black and Indian men, the female Indian body is dis-

puted territory—war booty available to whoever emerges victorious. Conversely, Dar es Salaam—read metaphorically as Mother Africa—is the site for black vs. Indian male struggles for supremacy. Answers to crucial questions about belonging—Who is Tanzanian? Who is African? Who is an outsider?—dictate which men get to allegorically copulate with Africa's (female) body and be productive. Symbolic female bodies are the violated terrain on which conflicts between men are resolved. However, Vassanji's short stories also disrupt such a reading. The text suggests that depictions of women in the Indian diaspora as weak—as they are portrayed by their families and friends—ignores the complexity of their personalities.

STREET-LEVEL POLITICS, ON-THE-GROUND DYNAMICS

I would like to argue that performance emerges as a fundamental tool through which Vassanji's Indian diaspora exerts its claims on Dar es Salaam. There are several examples throughout the text when residents of Uhuru Street perform their interest in spaces—interior and exterior, private and public. Such moments invite the reader to reexamine the nature of *Uhuru Street*, especially its connection to the sociopolitical milieu from which it emerges. An unnamed girl offers one such example of performativity. More importantly, she exerts her own claims regarding public space in a way that challenges women's depiction as helpless bodies on which masculinity—Indian or otherwise—may project its authority, as the narrator in "For a Shilling" notes:

> She swept in through the doorway, trailed by her two youngest siblings, making emphatic gestures with her fat arms, thumping along from wall to wall, glaring at us. Then she came and stood in front of me, arms akimbo, eyes fiery. The message was clear: this was her territory. (38)

It is important that the author describes the incident in the language of land occupation; both "trails" and "territory" suggest and allude to the register with which African spaces were discussed half a century prior during Europe's Scramble for Africa. Ultimately, this domestic scene, and the gender conflicts enacted therein, demonstrate how conflicts for space—the need to inhabit, practice mobility, and belong—unroll in public and private spaces. Vassanji's work not only suggests that a comprehensive look at representations of urban landscapes must include an appreciation of inhabitation and mobility but that we should also consider, as fiction does, both private and public spaces as political terrains where power conflicts are repeatedly played out. As Emily Brownell (2020, 3–4) documents in *Gone to Ground: A History of Environment and Infrastructure in Dar es Salaam*, "When first the Germans and later the British made [Dar es Salaam] their colonial capital, both administrations entrenched racially segregated neighborhoods into urban planning law." *Uhuru Street* comments on issues of race, public space, and, ultimately, literary depictions of urban spaces.

Vassanji demonstrates the Indian vs. African struggles for supremacy in his depictions of a public auction on Uhuru Street. The writer deploys narrative techniques that privilege the visual aspects of the city as well as his characters' capacity to perform their multiple identities on the streets, and sidewalks, of Dar es Salaam. In describing the Mnada—the Kiswahili word for auction—the narrator in "The Relief from Drill" notes:

> It was a square bustling with activity, uproarious with catcalls and jeers and bargains being struck, festooned with brightly-coloured cloth and lit up in the night with the yellow light of kerosene lamps. It was packed in on three sides by rows of mud houses and accessible on the fourth by a short alley. (Vassanji 1991, 43)

Mnada is the stage par excellence: not only because of its "uproarious catcalls and jeers" but also due to its "brightly-coloured cloth" and being "lit up" at dusk by numerous kerosene lamps. Such a description seems equally befitting the space for a theatrical production. Readers get a clear sense of the expanse and beehive activity that takes place at the Mnada; there is evidently much trade going on and high volumes of goods and services exchanged. On the other hand, "catcalls and jeers" suggest ways in which female bodies are on display—if not explicitly on sale—in Dar's commercial spaces. By mentioning that "the Mnada was not a respectable place to shop in because of the type of people believed to hang around there—jobless Africans from the districts, and thieves"—the narrator betrays antiblack prejudice against the auction space (44). The Mnada's association with Africans, and its location in the poor part of the city, make it a dubious site to shop; for the Indian diaspora that does venture out here, there is a performativity to which they must be attuned, least of all being the capacity to bargain and haggle prices down. Such acts of trespass must also take caution in "missing potholes, avoiding banana and orange peels and other rubbish, [and] giving right of way to carts of fruit and other wares pulled by men with impatient voices and straining backs" (43). While the Indian diaspora seeks to assert its presence on a land that is decidedly African—and that has yet to welcome its South Asian "Other"—indigenous Tanganyikans are preoccupied in their attempts at legal residence in a colonial city that scrutinizes their business activities in the hopes of uncovering presumed theft and other forms of crime. Moreover, the African cast must negotiate their racial classification and newly found "Otherness" in relation to the colonial settler. All these, as the vista above notes, make for a cacophony of sounds and sights, during which routines are imagined, rehearsed, performed, and perhaps duplicated, modified, or discarded. And, to be sure, these processes take place at a dizzying speed as *characters* try on novel masks, roles, and identities.

Like all theatrical platforms, Vassanji's backstage also has a backdrop: Uhuru Street. This emerges as the border along which the Indian diaspora's novel urban experiences are played out. Uhuru Street serves to demarcate not only the *safe zones* in Dar es Salaam but also the *cultured* areas. Outside of the protective cordon laid out by Uhuru Street the Indian diaspora is impotent—either because of the ominous black/dark presence that haunts the entire text or due to lack of common cultural currency with which characters may establish their worth. Amid the diaspora's outsider status and general dis-enfranchisement in Dar es Salaam, Uhuru Street is a space the community can claim ownership of. Furthermore, the space becomes a pilgrim's path for those who emigrate momentarily to Europe and North America; when they return, it is almost with religious reverence that they revisit the same streets they previously walked.

It is easy to see how Uhuru Street becomes larger than life in the minds of those who frequent it. The space functions as shorthand for multiple cultural exchanges, each of which has the potential to undermine earlier forms of self-identification. This famous street is described thus:

> The acacia-lined avenue cut a thin margin at the edge of town, it looked out at the ocean a short block away, black and rust red steamers just visible ply-ing in and out of the harbor. Behind it was crammed the old town, a maze of short dirty sidestreets feeding into the long and busy Uhuru Street, which then opened like a funnel back into the avenue. From here Uhuru Street went down, past downtown and the Mnazi Moja grounds into the interior: the

hinterland of squat African settlements, the mainroad Indian stores, the Arab corner stores. (104)

Even as Uhuru Street seeks to mark the margins and edges past which certain elements of Dar es Salaam should not creep, it also brings together a cultural plurality steeped in African, Arab, and Indian influences.[11] Additionally, there is the sense that a global *out there* exists, as indicated by the steamers moving to and from the harbor. Each of these seafaring vessels holds its own unique addition to the cultural space that is Uhuru Street, further complicating the simultaneous policing of boundaries and inevitable mixing that ensues. Mention of the "ocean," the "old town," and "recent roots," however, points toward a history that citizens of Dar es Salaam may wish to forget.

In the same way that the Indian diaspora in East Africa has been accused of conniving with the European colonial project, the Arab diaspora has been accused of benefiting from the sale of African bodies in the slave trade. The old Arab towns in cities like Mombasa, Malindi, Dar es Salaam, and Lamu hold much of this history that, understandably, many of the residents attempt to wish away. The vibrant "black" and "rust red" colors on the horizon, however, suggest that this will not be so. The blood spilt at such spots as Bwagamoyo in Tanzania—the loading dock for enslaved persons captured in the Tanzania/Congo hinterland—seems to reemerge. So too do the black bodies to whom this blood belonged. Selective suppression of memory and the past will not succeed here, Vassanji seems to suggest; rather, residents should be prepared to make inroads—as deep as Uhuru Street itself—into this city's past. And, in the process, the city's residents must reevaluate what each community has contributed to Dar's cultural soup. The narrator's walk down Uhuru Street, past downtown and into the interior, sounds like a rehearsal of the cultural catalogue that such historiographic projects of Dar es Salaam will uncover.

PERFORMANCE AND THE URBAN LANDSCAPE

As the global sociopolitical scene morphs, Uhuru Street is now assaulted by new influences. Cultural importation comes in the guise of returning students, on holiday from various European capitals. These youngsters—eager to distance themselves from the provinciality of Dar es Salaam and their parents, in favor of the metropolitan's elegance—import and display cosmopolitan values. From Vassanji, the reader receives a heady mixture of the urbane in the guise of performativity and a *photograph in words*:

> We still went back for holidays then and we formed a rambunctious group whose presence was hard to miss about town. We were the London-Returned. For two or three joyously carefree months the city became a stage for us and we would strut up and down its dusty pavements parading overseas fashions. . . . We sported flashy bell-bottoms, Oxford shirts and bright summer dresses. And fat pinkish-brown thighs below the colourful mini-skirts of our female companions teased the famished adolescent eyes of our hometown. Come Saturday morning, we would gather at a prearranged rendezvous and conscious of every eye upon us, set off in one large and rowdy group towards Independence Avenue. There to stroll along its pavements a few times over, amidst fun and laughter, exchanging jokes and relating incidences in clipped, finished accents. (104)

In these bell-bottomed and miniskirted teenagers we meet the cast that performs in front of the acacia-lined backdrop discussed previously. *Uhuru Street* notes that the students consciously came "to watch and to be seen," and armed with this knowledge, these young men and women promenade about town intent on catching other people's attention (105). That the students are on display, especially to show off their tastes in fashion, is highly reminiscent of capitalist consumption, in line with the metropolitan ethos they have picked up. Indeed, in storefronts along Independence Avenue "imported goods were displayed in all their glory" (105). What is more, the students' audience is jealous of their outfits as well as their diction, two attributes of their style that set them apart from those who have yet to taste the cultural sweetness of the mother colony. The imagined value of visiting London enables Tanzanians of Indian origin to occupy, inhabit, and perform in spaces that would previously have been off-limits. These *been-to*'s are on Uhuru Street precisely to act out their newly found metropolitan identities and they successfully do so by calling to bear cultural capital acquired from brief sojourns in Europe.

Paradoxically, of course, the students' journeys to and from Europe simultaneously mark them as *less* African. For one, their performance hinges on the rural-urban contrast. It seeks to echo the idea that rural spaces, unlike towns and cities, have little culture. Rather, it is urban areas where one can view communities expressing their creativity, be it in commerce, fashion, speech, weekend leisure, and so forth. Underlying this supposition is the idea that the African generally occupies the countryside, while the diasporic Indian reigns supreme in the cities. Because of this prejudice, Dan Ojwang argues that the typical Vassanji hero has much psychological angst about both himself and his ethnic group. His description, keyed in as it is on the issues of social acceptance and emotional security, is worth reproducing in full. Vassanji's hero is "the man who embarks on a humanist, cosmopolitan quest for an existence much more expansive than his own narrow upbringing in traditional surroundings . . . he hopes to join a wider community of human beings who would act as a recompense for his loss" (Ojwang 2012, 540). As the critic notes, the Indian diaspora in Vassanji's work is steeped in "narrow" definitions of self, gender, and community. It is no surprise that progressive members repeatedly find themselves on the margins and inevitably leave the herd to form a new family. Tragically, however, their own upbringing—as well as the national spaces from which they emerge—makes it difficult to find common ground with individuals outside their cultural spheres. Consequently, it is with "deep nostalgia" that the hero/ine returns to Uhuru Street—only to discover that after their global peregrinations, the space is now too "small and dirty" for their comfort (Obradovic 1993, 328).

This form of traversing city space—unlike that practiced by Paulina in *Coming to Birth*—is not merely about claiming belonging in the (post)colonial city; it is also about asserting privilege to mobility beyond the space of the city and postcolonial nation-state. Urban cartography reflects linguistic hierarchies. The assumption of English supremacy emerges in how Dar es Salaam's roads are named. Uhuru means freedom or independence. In the passage above, the English word "independence" signifies an avenue, while Uhuru is relegated to a street. Avenues exude more prestige than streets. Independence Avenue is reserved for luxury stores and pavements that nurse coffee shops. Uhuru Street is set aside for the Indian diaspora, a second-class citizenry in a racialized space where the Africa autochthons occupy the lowest rank. *Uhuru Street* ends by depicting assertions of Indian claims to space in African cities as momentarily triumphant; however, we are left with no doubt that the struggle for supremacy between the two communities will continue. Vassanji's text depicts much unease over the spatial transgression of Indian or African characters in various parts of Dar es Salaam. Both *Coming to Birth* and *Uhuru Street* deploy the use of performance and verbal pictures to represent urban landscapes in terms of trespassing and mobility. Both writers privilege an understanding of urban environments that has much to do with belonging. One key difference between Macgoye's and Vassanji's texts, however, is the latter's interest in diaspora and the practice of transnational migration. In the next chapter, my examination of Ethiopian and Tanzanian literature demonstrates a long-standing rivalry between artists who wield literary allegories based on land and landscape and ruling regimes that ostensibly seek to monopolize such metaphorical aptitude. The battlegrounds for these political skirmishes, it turns out, are vernacular African languages and their embedded aesthetics and moral imaginings. I will demonstrate how such ontologies can be valuable given their ecological expertise.

African Languages, African Socialisms, and Representations of Lands and Landscapes

Ethiopia, the most loved of the Beloved, do you hear the drums above the clouds? Do you know that angels approach, and they come for you? . . . And after the storm, after the cleansing, we will open our arms again, and you will come, eager once more, and angels will guide our next steps, and we will move together
—Maaza Mengiste, *Beneath the Lion's Gaze: A Novel*

The furthest back I have traced my maternal and paternal family trees is to Waiyaki wa Hinga, Kinyanjui wa Gathirimũ, and Mariibe, all living in the 1890s. Two decades later, new kinds of names appear in my lineage: Gladys. Harrison. Hannah. Amos. Margaret. Salome. Sarah. Maria. Grace. Johnstone. These English and Christian monikers reflect Kenya's, and indeed Africa's, subordination as a stage for European imperialism. At the time, converting to Christianity and acquiring English literacy were acts of survival—and even low-key resistance—against white supremacy. Just as my grandparents' identities were morphing, so too did the spaces around them. They had previously lived in Gachie, Rirũta, and Manguo. Colonialists now imposed new place names to describe my kin's surroundings: Fort Smith, Fort Lugard, Scottish Mission (Thogoto), Karen, Fort Hall, Eastleigh, and Carrier Corps (Kariokor) barracks. Further afield, regional topography was *discovered* and renamed: the Aberdare Ranges, Lake Victoria, and even Lake Rudolf. In *Decolonising the Mind: The Politics of Language in African Literature*, Ngũgĩ wa Thiong'o describes how, in colonial Kenya, English became "*the* language, and all others had to bow before it in deference" (1986, 11; emphasis in original). The English tongue gained a prominence that was massively disproportionate to its use as a communication tool. English was a dialect, and much else besides. English symbolized Britain's imperial might, and the economic, political, and martial dominance of an occupying force. Truly, "English was the official vehicle and the magic formula to colonial elitedom" (12). One could not climb the colonial professional ladder without proficiency in English/ness. An English first name not only marked Kenyans as Christianized, and civilized, but also as worthy of such colonial tokens as employment in the civil service, administrative duties in the native reserves, or even finance to start a small business. It is for this reason that "vernacular African literatures more broadly have the potential to disrupt and resist the ongoing hegemony of colonial languages and institutions" (McGiffin 2019, 6). Or, as Ngũgĩ wa Thiong'o (1993, 39) has expressed in more poetic terms, "A world of many languages should be like a field of flowers of different colours." Ngũgĩ's equivalency between linguistic plurality and ecological diversity perfectly echoes my central argument: that conservation of African ecosystems necessarily involves preservation of its indigenous languages, knowledge systems, and ontologies.

The denigration of all things African, alongside the adoration of all things European, extends beyond naming to Africa's literary production. Mukoma wa Ngũgĩ's *The Rise of the African Novel: Politics of Language, Identity, and Ownership* (2018) argues that we should deliberately expand the African literary timeline to include texts in African languages published before the Sixties. Authors such as South Africa's Thomas Mofolo, R. R. R. Dhlomo, Samuel Mqhayi, A. C. Jordan, and Sol Plaatje had been publishing in isiXhosa, isiZulu, Sesotho, and even English between 1900 and 1930 (4). In Eastern Africa, there existed a sizeable Ethiopian canon in Geez and Amharic. Along the Indian Ocean, Kiswahili poets had established an extensive tradition of Utenzi. Some, but not all, of these writings were rendered in Ajami, Arabic script repurposed toward African languages—a reinvention that also occurred in the Sahel. Likewise, D. O. Fagunwa's Yoruba texts have been excluded from contemporary readings of African writing. The paradoxical expulsion of African languages from Africa's literary canon is best exemplified by the exclusion of Shaaban Robert and Fagunwa—and many others publishing in African languages—from the 1962 Makerere "Conference of African Writers of English Expression" (5). This is a truly strange omission. As Mukoma poses, why is it that "early African writing has not yet become part of the African literary and critical imagination" (7)? There exists an infrastructure of publishers, writers, readers, librarians, and critics who have, deliberately or otherwise, sidelined writing in African languages.

Literature in African languages, however, has not petered out. It may be shunned, but it still thrives in small pockets across the African continent. In

chapters 2 and 3, I argued that colonial and postindependence cities in Eastern and Southern Africa have repeatedly birthed vernacular art—literary,
musical, or performative—that resists hegemony. In this chapter, I pursue
Mukoma's plea by examining a writer who has a large Kiswahili corpus dating
as far back as 1969. Ebrahim Hussein's work has not garnered much critical
attention; in fact, the last book-length study on his work was by Alain Ricard
in 2000. I believe it is time to recover Hussein's work and reintroduce it to an
upcoming generation of decolonized Africanists, on the African continent,
and across the African diaspora. The two authors I discuss in this chapter offer
unique readership contexts. Ebrahim Hussein's Kiswahili drama was written
while Tanzania deployed Kiswahili as both an official language and a lingua
franca. Even those Tanzanians who may not have been literate could enjoy
the play when it was read out loud or performed in public.[1] These circumstances assured *Arusi* (Hussein 1980) a wide national audience. Berhane M.
Sahle Sellassie's work, on the other hand, was written in English in a country
where Amharic was the official language, and a lingua franca. The English-
speaking audience in Ethiopia during the Sixties was minimal. This upends
a common phenomenon where texts by postcolonial African writers such
as Chinua Achebe, Nadine Gordimer, Buchi Emecheta, and others attracted
sizeable national audiences. Sahle Sellassie's work could only be read internationally. Postcolonial African regimes monopolize the production of discourse and dissemination of tropes that deploy land as the central metaphor.
In this chapter, I argue that Sahle Sellassie's and Hussein's writings wrestle
allegories of land and landscape away from central governments. Doing so
recenters African indigenous languages as sources of ecological expertise that
contribute to contemporary conversations about the climate crisis. The two
texts examined in this chapter also shed light on how the language politics of
African literatures influence literary representations of lands and landscapes.[2]

DRAMATIC RENDERING OF TANZANIAN POLITICAL HISTORY

Literary representation of African lands and landscapes serves an important
historiographic purpose. Tanzanian history demonstrates the importance of
land as a unifying platform for anticolonial politics. Since 1885, the region
resisted European alienation of indigenous communities from their cultures and natural resources. The 1905 Maji Maji rebellion led by Kinjeketile
Ngwale, a traditional healer cum seer, was a good example of these initia-

tives. *Kinjeketile* (1969), Ebrahim Hussein's dramatic rendering of the Maji Maji uprising, is an apt illustration of African literature historicizing political events that revolve around land, space, and territory. Hussein's play highlights the theft of native lands as a key source of contention between German settlers and their colonized subjects. Consider, for example, this lamentation by Bibi (Mrs.) Kitunda.

> Bibi Kitunda: Isiwe njaa namna gani, wanaume wenyewe wote wanalima shambani kwa Bwana Kinoo? Njaa itakosa wapi? (Hussein 1)

> Bibi Kitunda: . . . famine is inevitable. All the men are working in Bwana Kinoo's plantation and not on their own. So, of course, there must be famine. (Hussein 1–2)

German colonialism entrenched highly oppressive labor practices. The redirection of indigenous labor away from food production to cash crop farming and the harvesting of raw materials for Berlin industries seriously undermined Tanganyikan food security. Depiction of alien terrains arises from cash crop farming superseding subsistence agriculture. Strange-looking farms bearing strange-looking crops symbolize foreign occupation. Jane Plastow (1996, 138) argues that Hussein's rewriting of the Maji Maji struggle is one of the subtlest historical-liberation plays written in Tanzania. Hussein's *Kinjeketile* links Tanzanian literature, anticolonial resistance, and the local environment. His drama memorializes past events and preserves them for future generations.

In chapter 1, I evidenced that supernatural elements are key in folkloric representations of African lands and landscapes. However, the relationship between African literature and representations of land can also be visionary—both drama and fiction acting as catalysts for socioeconomic equity. The 1970s was the era of pro-Ujamaa plays and two playwrights emerged supreme: Hussein and Penina Mlama. Immediately after 1967, *Ngojera* emerged to spread the message of Julius Nyerere's *Arusha Declaration*. Ngojera was essentially a "state art-form serving the party and explaining the party-line on topical issues, with minimal critical analysis of government positions" (Plastow 1996, 133). University students who graduated fired up with zeal for Nyerere also joined in this endeavor, espousing positions that ideologically matched up with the government narrative.[3] Some of the playwrights dramatized betrayal—of the poor, by an urban dweller. This (often sexual) treachery inspires its victims to establish new roots in an Ujamaa village; other dramatists addressed the challenge of "corrupt, at times, reactionary local leaders" who derail African socialism and must either be banished or revolutionized (135–36). In addition to praising the ruling regime, pro-Ujamaa theatre was united in its displeasure at such *bourgeois* ideas as love—despite numerous dramatic plots of sexual betrayal.

If the Seventies saw the rise of pro-Ujamaa plays, in the 1980s dramatists exercised their critical muscle and began to push against official narratives.[4] Once again, Hussein led the pack. And perhaps because of his trailblazing efforts, he more than other writers has been sanctioned by the Tanzanian state. For one year, as a university student, Hussein had moved into an Ujamaa village; his misgivings about African socialism have thus to be read as the firsthand experiences of a patriot. His sojourn, however, left him bitter at both the incompetency of state bureaucracy and the inability for genuine grassroots socioeconomic change. Such open criticism of Ujamaa irked political elites. This is more so because criticism emanating from Hussein is difficult to dismiss given his firsthand Ujamaa experiences. Hussein's dramaturgy includes *Kinjeketile* (1969; English translation, 1970), *Mashetani* (1971), *Wakati Ukuta* (1971), *Jogoo Kijijini* (1976), *Ngao ya Jadi* (1976), *Arusi* (1980), and *Kwenye Ukingo wa Thim* (1988).[5] Hussein has consistently viewed the purpose of his work as examining "the conflicts inherent in capitalism, imperialism, and gender relations" (Mwaifuge 2001, 11). *Mashetani* focuses on sociopolitical inequity in postindependence Tanzania, even as the country loudly proclaims its adherence to the edicts of socialism (Mwaifuge 2001, 7). More precisely, *Mashetani* criticizes the "neocolonial mentality" (Philipson 1989, 268) mythologized in Chinua Achebe's *A Man of the People* (1966). Both *Mashetani* and *Kinjeketile* share Hussein's frequent deployment of Tanzanian history. Furthermore, these two texts demonstrate the author's use of traditional symbols and his attempts to establish their continued relevance to present socioeconomic realities (Mwaifuge 2001, 11). Hussein repeatedly mines Tanzanian history for metaphors that can be recycled in the service of contemporary social justice concerns.

ARUSI: A DRAMA OF SHIFTING SIGNS

Arusi, a Kiswahili play by Hussein, is a play-within-a-play centered on a wedding ceremony (*arusi* in Kiswahili). The drama opens with the meeting of two lovers: Bukini and Mwanaheri. Bukini is about to embark on a long journey; we never learn the actual destination, but we get the sense that he is leaving Mombasa and going abroad for further studies. Mwanaheri is apprehensive. To solemnize the occasion, Bukini asks Mwanaheri to stretch out her hand and close her eyes; when she does, he slips a ring on her finger. Mwanaheri, too, takes a ring offered by her fiancé and slips it onto his middle digit. In the next scene, taking place in the play-within-a-play, a group of women dance and celebrate at Bukini and Mwanaheri's wedding. By the end of act 2, Kahinja—Bukini's brother—decides to escape from Mombasa, leaving behind his family and friends. Soon after, we learn that Mwanaheri is pregnant. Her husband has been away for more than a year, so the child is clearly not his. When Kahinja returns to Mombasa from his sojourn at a Tanzanian Ujamaa village, he is updated on village news—including Mwanaheri's scandalous pregnancy. Kahinja learns that his friend Ali impregnated Mwanaheri. We then learn that Kahinja has been arrested for embezzling funds. A government official reads from a letter Kahinja addressed to his fellow villagers defending himself and contending that the money he allegedly misappropriated was past dues for working at the Ujamaa village. His compatriots, understandably, disagree and lament that Kahinja turned out to be a thief. *Arusi* ends with Bukini and Mwanaheri back on stage. Mwanaheri appears shaken; she takes off her ring and returns it to Bukini.

Arusi documents representations of land and landscape as commentary on the rise of individualism at the expense of communalist norms (Mazrui 2007, 39). In addition to frequent use of Kiswahili words in vernacular circulation, Hussein deploys a form that requires several encounters before it can unfold itself to the reader. Despite disdain for Hussein's writing in the Eighties, no one disavowed the mastery with which he "manipulated language, plot and character" (Philipson 1989, 274). For instance, some of his work was labeled "morally questionable"—*Alikiona*—or "too abstruse"— *Jogoo Kijijini*—thus repelling highbrow readers (268). However, while critics have responded to this intricacy with derision, its richness and openness to multiple interpretations make *Arusi* a lasting gem of Tanzanian national culture. In *Arusi*, use of complex metaphors and figurative language has been viewed separately as either Hussein deliberately making his work difficult to comprehend or the effect of government control and official sidelining of his work, resulting in self-censorship. I argue, however, that Hussein demonstrates the use of African languages—Kiswahili in this case—and allegory in composing a Pan-Africanist literary canon. The key to breaking the code of metaphoric poetry with which Hussein shrouds his work lies in multiple interactions between this text and the audience. Hussein, through the voice of a traditional wedding counselor, advises Mwanaheri on how best to maintain romance between her and her groom. Somo, who acts as Mwanaheri's bridesmaid, urges her:

> *Mapenzi, somo yangu, hayataki*
> *Bayana; yanataka siri. Maisha usifanye*
> *Kuyadhihirisha*
> *. . . pendo*
> *Halitoki katika ridhaa, linatoka katika*
> *Sanaa ya kujitamanisha (Hussein, 11)*

> *You're jeopardizing your love by making it so obvious. . . .*
> *Romance, my friend, desires secrecy; not scrutiny.*
> *Don't publicize your romance;*
> *Like the shadow, leave when your lover comes.*
> *. . . Love thrives from desire. (my translation)*

Speaking through Somo, Hussein's instructions for a successful marriage can be read as coded instructions for a successful interpretation of his work. He, too, like the bride, is playing a game of hide-and-seek with the reader. While Hussein's writing style should also be understood within the realm of self-censorship, he elsewhere contends that, as a writer, his "goal is artistic expression, not political truth" (Plastow 1996, 193). Hussein occludes a facile understanding of his work, arguing that there might be more pleasure to be had from a text that playfully eludes obvious meaning—didactically political plays, for example, being notoriously boring.

Writing in African languages—Kiswahili, Gĩkũyũ, isiZulu, Igbo, Amharic, and so forth—does result in smaller book circulation. However, this is more than compensated for by the resulting audience engagement. On the African continent, there is an impatient readership yearning to see a literature that reflects its own ethnic diversity. While the subordination of political expediency for aesthetic goals is surely the writer's prerogative, the shift to complex language in Hussein's oeuvre demonstrates a major transformation in his work. Hussein's turn to complexity might have been precisely because it was frowned upon—a way of resisting the Tanzanian government's interference in aesthetic production. One consequence of this action, however, was the declining popularity of some of Hussein's texts. In 1988 *Wakati Ukuta* and the Kiswahili version of *Kinjeketile* were used as textbooks in Teacher Training Colleges (Philipson 1989, 268). This mass popularity of Hussein's work is a big contrast to the critical silence that *Arusi* met.[6] Hussein's Kiswahili representation of land and landscape in *Arusi* demonstrates that reading Africanist decolonial texts approximates to *reading* African ecologies. Close reading as an aesthetic exercise mirrors a caretaker/custodial praxis on African ecosystems. Ngũgĩ wa Thiong'o (1993, 39) argues for a linguistic plurality where "our different languages can, should, and must express our common being . . . our languages sing of the unity of the people of the earth, of our common humanity, and above all of the people's love for peace, equality, independence, and social justice." African languages serve as repositories of indigenous ontologies, knowledge systems, and ecological expertise. These modes of thought incorporate both the ancestors and the nonhuman world into a continuum of life. Similarly, Hussein describes capacious landscapes that accommodate the fullness of being. Kahinja's friend, Ali, reminds him of his philosophical pronouncement; Kahinja had apparently stated:

> *Naipenda fikra*
> *Iliyojaa*
> *Pana kama bahari;*
> *Nikiogelea*
> *Au nikipaa/*
> *Mwishowe si Dhahiri (Hussein, 9)*

> *I like ideas*
> *That are expansive*
> *Like the sea;*
> *When I swim*
> *Or if I fly,*
> *The end is not immediately obvious. (my translation)*

This vastness is contrasted to shallow thinking—which both deceives and jeopardizes our humanity. The sustainability of indigenous languages is linked to the resilience of communities and their ecosystems. For this to happen, there needs to be an ongoing level of innovation; African indigenous languages are capacious enough to accommodate reinvention.

THE AFERSATA AND LANGUAGE POLITICS IN ETHIOPIA

Berhane M. Sahle Sellassie has been at the center of Ethiopian language politics. Just a few years after the Makerere Writers' Conference, Sahle Sellassie wrote his first short novel, *Shinyega's Village* (1964), in Gurage, a vernacular from southern Ethiopia. Although the text's readership was minimal, the writer thought it important for Gurage to have its first written literature. Sahle Sellassie's other books have been written in both Amharic and English. *The Afersata* (1968), for example, was written in English. To better appreciate Ethiopian literature and its cultural meanings, it is necessary to unravel the country's language politics. Geez and Amharic hold supreme positions in Ethiopia; the former as a language deployed in religious texts—and court documents until the twelfth century—while the latter took over the role of royal chronicling in the thirteenth century (Demoz 1995, 17). The prominence of these two languages is set against a suppression of several hundred languages in Ethiopia as a whole. None of these tongues enjoy official status, and Amharic elites considered several of them downright barbaric. The *Fetha Negast*, Ethiopia's supreme law until the advent of a national constitution in the early 1930s, is an extensive legal document. This classic text represented landscapes as "unoccupied" unless cleared, tilled, and used for human settlement (Pankhurst 1966, 30). Through the *Fetha Negast*, the Ethiopian monarchy endorsed depictions of empty lands. Human economic activity, including crop and animal husbandry, determined varied forms of land ownership: *Gult*, land formally granted by the emperor or provincial administrators; *Semon*, land owned by the church in perpetuity; and *Mengist/Madeira*, large-scale state-owned farms (Wubneh and Abate 1988, 84). Although Ethiopian peasants often remarked that "land belongs to the king," this should not be taken literally; the autonomy of local communities demanded that land in and of itself was inalienable (Pankhurst 1966, 30).[7] This tension between state-level versus grassroots representations of land and landscape morphed into political opposition to Emperor Haile Selassie's reign—championed especially by university students, labor unions, and the military.[8]

Ethiopian landscapes have previously been depicted as the stage for martial prowess, territorial conquest, and political supremacy. Berhane M. Sahle Sellassie's *The Warrior King* (1974) is a retelling of the political career of Emperor Tewodros II. The text chronicles the rise of a young bandit from oblivion to the apex of Ethiopian power. Sahle Sellassie's rendition disguises social critique as historical fiction (Molvaer 1997, 3). For Ethiopia's writers, Tewodros II represented vision, reform, and modernization; authors discuss him in heroic terms as they attempt to influence government policy (Molvaer 1997, 166). This is like Ebrahim Hussein's work chronicling Tanzanian political history. Hussein and Sahle Sellassie demonstrate that African literatures often mine the past to adapt novel local and regional narratives. Such stories self-consciously reject not only neo-postcolonial dystopias (at the national level) but also antiblack racism (on a global scale). Emperor Haile Selassie's government had a paradoxical approach to the symbolic function of language. On the one hand, all public discussions of linguistic issues were banned. And, yet, each time a region rebelled or threatened to break away from the Crown, it was appeased with permission to establish a media outlet broadcasting in its ethnic language (Demoz 1995, 18). This encouraged continuous insurrections in search of cultural recognition. The yearning for cultural autonomy protested imperial overreach and attendant Amharic bigotry. For instance, there were numerous insults directed toward the "inarticulateness or the heavy accent" of the non-native Amharic speaker (Demoz 1995, 27). Consequently, Amharic speakers from other nationalities would rarely disclose their ethnic heritage.

B. M. Sahle Sellassie's *The Afersata* has secured its pivotal place in Ethiopian writing. Its significance, however, is complicated by the fact that the novel is written in English. In 1968—six years before Mengistu Haile Mariam's socialist revolution—this made Sahle Sellassie's text linguistically inaccessible to many Ethiopian readers. *The Afersata* is essentially a crime thriller. Its plot begins with Namaga's hut burning down in the middle of the night and follows with what happens in the months after as villagers investigate *who dunnit*. In addition to destroying Namaga's house, the culprit dug underneath the clay floor to retrieve a retirement fund worth $200 that Namaga and his wife had put away. To discover the arsonist, the community convenes a meeting—the eponymous Afersata. The first Afersata meets under an oak tree in the village meadow. First on the agenda is the election and swearing in of seven respectable elders who will conduct the meeting. The second Afersata would have been the last but rain clouds gathered and once it began to pour the meeting had to be adjourned. The third time round, the proceedings unfold uninterrupted. Unfortunately, the detectives are none the wiser as to whom the criminal was. Not finding the culprit, the village policy of collective responsibility mandates that community members contribute personally to compensate Namaga for his loss. As the cheka shum, a local bureaucrat, tells his fellow villagers, "we are all responsible for the burning of Namaga's hut" (Sahle Sellassie 1968, 89).

Sahle Sellassie demonstrates how Ethiopia, too, was debating the issue of African languages and literatures. The stakes of using European languages in Ethiopian literature are not like those in other African nations. In *Black Lions: The Creative Lives of Modern Ethiopia's Literary Giants and Pioneers*, Reidulf Molvaer (1997) outlines the events that led Sahle Sellassie to publish the text in English:

> When *The Afersata* was completed in its original form in 1968, he first considered publishing it in Ethiopia and went to see the chief censor about it, but he [the chief censor] was displeased it was not written in Amharic; however, he said that a decision about publication would be made in a month's time. But then [Sahle Sellassie] gave it to a friend in the censorship department to read, and he said that it would be a waste of time trying to get it published in Ethiopia—the censors would not permit it. So [Sahle Sellassie] sent it to the African Writers Series with Heinemann, and in about a month they wrote an encouraging letter. (371)

The need to evade censorship was a significant reason why the novel came out in English. But so too were Sahle Sellassie's positive experiences reading other African authors. Because some of this work was accessible in English, readers across the continent could participate in a Pan-African literary conversation (371). Through Amharic, Ethiopian writers have access to a nationwide language that sidesteps colonial ideologies. There is more Ethiopian literature published in Amharic than in English, French, Portuguese, or Italian. This is the reverse of most other African countries where literary production in European languages far surpasses that in indigenous ones (Kurtz 2007, 189). European languages are less consequential in Ethiopia than in other African nations.[9]

Ethiopian language politics are further complicated by Amharic chauvinism. It has been noted that "the rich development of Amharic literature is concurrent with the underdevelopment of the literatures of Ethiopia's other languages" (Kurtz 2007, 202). What is pertinent here is that non-native-Amharic speakers were metaphorically shut out from writing in Amharic, even if they spoke it. Other modes of defining national literatures have turned to the reader as the determining factor. The ideal situation, perhaps, is for writers to first create in their own language, and later pursue translations into national or regional lingua franca, or both, e.g., in Amharic or Kiswahili before finally publishing the works in non-African languages for other readers across the continent (Kurtz 2007, 201). Use of English enabled Sahle Sellassie to publish his book internationally. At the time, censors were increasingly stringent regarding what could be marketed to Ethiopia's reading public (Azeze 1985, 39). Given the contested nature of the Ethiopian linguistic terrain, English may also have appealed to Sahle Sellassie as a more neutral language. Not having been fully colonized, despite several years of Italian occupation, English occupies a very different position in Ethiopia as opposed to neighboring former British colonies: Kenya, Sudan, South Sudan, and Uganda. In Ethiopia, English is a language upon which none of the country's ethnic nationalities could lay claim. In former members of the British Empire, however, English is a neocolonial reminder of current (and long-standing) cultural, economic, and political ties to distant centers of hegemony.

Sahle Sellassie's choice of language seems to have been well received. Two of his English novels—*The Afersata* and *Firebrands* (1979)—sold well. *Firebrands* received positive reviews. It was compared to Ayi Kwei Armah's *The Beautyful Ones Are Not Yet Born* (1968) in the sense that both books have protagonists who "stand up for their principles" (Adera 1996, 128). *Firebrands'* success occurred even though the book was banned in Ethiopia and only distributed abroad (Molvaer 1997, 375). *The Afersata* has gone through two printings, sold 15,000 copies, and garnered much criticism—though most of it was negative because reviewers did not agree with the author's decision to include issues of land reform in a novel (Molvaer 1997, 372). Readers disapproved of the writer's attempt to discuss development policy in fictional form. *The Afersata* has been criticized for imposing Sahle Sellassie's authorial voice on the reader, often in a manner much closer to social or political commentary than fiction (Beer 1977, 108). *The Afersata* emerged from Sahle Sellassie's desire to chronicle knowledge about Ethiopia, especially for non-Amharic readers. Such aspirations reflect the mid-twentieth century wave of Pan-Africanism. Another important aspect about the text is that *The Afersata* portrays Ethiopia's rural poor in a positive light. While dominant narratives about destitute farmers cast them as "unenlightened, impoverished, callous, and sullen," Sahle Sellassie provides an alternative view of peasant life as "highly communal and self-sufficient" (Beer 1977, 107, 110). In addition, *The Afersata* deploys the hut as an image through which to comprehend Ethiopian society. This happens in three ways: Sahle Sellassie's deployment of the hut imagery as a synecdoche for land; his use of *demolition* as a symbol for political revolution; and, finally, his representation of the tension between peasant communities and the state.

"LAND TO THE TILLER": TRANSFORMING
ETHIOPIAN LANDSCAPES

There are numerous reports of Ethiopian peasants opposing despotic tax policies. In northern Ethiopia, for instance, Emperor Haile Selassie had to reverse his 1942 land tax schedule to placate a farmers' uprising in Gonder, Tigray, and Gojam (Wubneh and Abate 1988, 29). In 1960, villagers in Guidao attacked landowners in protest of unfair tax directives (Ministry of Information 1977, 9). Simultaneously, universities became increasingly militant between 1950 and 1965. This politicization culminated in demonstrations supporting land reform legislation; protestors chanted "land to the tiller" (Wubneh and Abate 1988, 37). Despite Haile Selassie's surveillance of cultural and political activity in Ethiopia, or perhaps precisely because of it, university students were among the crowds marching in Addis Ababa's streets in early 1974. The demonstrators demanded a radical change in government. As in previous 1965–66 protests, land was often the march-goers' rallying cry and call-to-arms. Historians cite several events as key contributors to, if not actual causes of, the February 1974 ousting of the Ethiopian monarchy. A 1977 May Day pamphlet notes that the Wollo (northern Ethiopia) famine that claimed more than 200,000 lives in the mid-Sixties was a big contributor to the fervor of revolt (Ministry of Information 1977, 18). This propaganda tract represents the Ethiopian landscape as a national breadbasket to be made available to all: irrespective of class, ethnicity, or proximity to urban areas.

By June 1974, a coalition composed of the armed forces and the police—popularly known as the Derg (Amharic for committee)—emerged as Ethiopia's power brokers. Within a year, the Derg nationalized land—supposedly to reverse the parasitic "exploitation of man-to-man" (Likke 1977, 8). This land reform produced a mixed bag of results. Peasants in southern Ethiopia, who had suffered land alienation in the late nineteenth century, benefited economically. Those from the north, however, reacted angrily (Wubneh and Abate 1988, 98). In Sidamo, Gonder, and Gojam peasants, once again, rose in protest. They opposed the Derg's directive to form cooperative farms (97). As in the past, such economic policies were seen to be overly autocratic. The Derg failed to attract any grassroots loyalty. Instead, the incoming military government resorted to censorship and efforts to muzzle free public discourse. After less than a year, the regime was already engaged in running battles with opposition groups in the capital. Eventually, the Derg sought to eliminate political engagement by sending university students into the countryside, under the pretext of setting up peasant associations and educating illiterate farmers. This state policy was not simply about reforming rural Ethiopia, but also ridding urbanized areas of militant students. A long tradition of rebellion against injustice, previously invoked against Italian Fascism and Haile Selassie's reign, was now directed toward the ruling junta. A significant part of this political heritage can be traced back to Ethiopia's literary canon.

A major thematic concern in *The Afersata* is transforming landscapes and land tenure as extremely vital for raising Ethiopian living standards. This ideological bend influences Sahle Sellassie's representation of land and landscape. Through the voice of two minor characters, Melesse and Tekle, the writer voices his misgivings about contemporary land practices and the unfair distribution of arable land. Using language that would later be echoed by Mengistu's military government, Sahle Sellassie identifies peasant exploitation as the main cause of poverty. "If the Ethiopian peasants could not improve their material life over the centuries it was probably because they could not enjoy fully the fruits of their labor," writes Sahle Sellassie (1968, 15). Despite his deep awareness of the problems that plagued his people, Melesse was "not important enough in the government to exert pressure to change the landholding system of the country" (33). The author sketches a character who, though well-versed in political economy and capable of identifying the evils of landlord-tenant relations, is impotent in the face of a centuries-old system. Melesse is acutely aware that "peasants are getting poorer while the absentee landlords are getting richer" and his conclusion is that "if the government does not distribute land to the peasants they will never be better off in the future" (52). Who then can execute this all-important change in Ethiopian society, the writer implicitly asks? If, indeed, as Sahle Sellassie states, Ethiopia "will never become rich without a proper land reform," whose mandate is it to accomplish such social transformation (53)? The author urges that land reform occur from the bottom-up.[10] Sahle Sellassie's call for rejuvenating landscapes echoes the student voices that marched in Addis Ababa in 1965–66 demanding that land be given to the tiller (Adera 1996, 132). This slogan seemingly inspired Sahle Sellassie to claim that "land reform must start with the redistribution of land to those who need it" (1968, 55). Writing three years after Ethiopian student demonstrations and only six years before the 1974 revolution, the author uses Melesse and his civil servant colleague, Tekle, to make an eloquent case for land equity in Ethiopia. It is also clear that Sahle Sellassie is heavily invested in determining whom among the various stakeholders with ties to land—Haile Selassie's monarchy, landlords, or tenants—should be mandated to implement this much-needed policy modification. Implicitly, there are also underlying questions about national wealth and inequity: Who gets to define Ethiopia's riches? Who has access to this bounty? Given that Mengistu and the Derg aligned themselves with global socialism, these enigmas go to the heart of national reckoning.

THE HUT AS A METAPHOR FOR THE ETHIOPIAN LANDSCAPE

In *The Afersata*, Sahle Sellassie depicts Namaga's hut as a symbol for the Ethiopian landscape. A popular argument among student activists, and disseminated via several political publications, concluded that "the only viable solution to Ethiopia's problems was the ultimate and complete destruction of the feudal regime" (Adera 1996, 131). This language of demolition is very similar to Sahle Sellassie's image regarding the devastation of Namaga's hut:

> The thatched roof of Namaga's hut smoked, sagged and crumbled down. The leaves that made up the circular wall emitted red and blue flames, glowed and broke down to the ground. Every piece that was part of Namaga's hut except the central pillar turned into ashes. (1968, 3)

First, much like Namaga's hut was destroyed by fire, the Ethiopian feudal regime was also, supposedly, burnt to the ground by revolutionary students, farmers, and urban workers. Although this deviates slightly from the actual events of February 1974, it is the version that the head of the Derg, Mengistu Haile Mariam, preferred. In his four-year anniversary address, Mengistu (Mariam 1978, 8) reminded his audience that "the feudo-bourgeois system was defused and burnt by a revolutionary fire." In both cases, fire serves not only as a tool for destruction, but as the impetus for change and the advent of a new order. Second, the imagery of *dismantling* was very popular in socialist Ethiopia as a way of interpreting the ousting of Haile Selassie. In his 1980 speech to a committee mandated with forming the Party of the Working People of Ethiopia, Mengistu described the 1974 events as the masses "dismantling the government" (Mariam 1980, 30). This idea of revolution as pulling the former regime to pieces was also reiterated in public presentations in 1979—as part of a policy document on economic development—and in 1986—to the constitutional drafting commission. In addition to detailing the "dismantling [of] the archaic system" (Mariam 1979, 11) Mengistu also described his own regime as involved in "the construction of a new order" and needing to "lay the necessary foundation for a [future Ethiopian] socialist society" (Mariam 1986, 6). The parallel between the initial destruction of an existing structure, by fire, and then its subsequent rebuilding is quite strong between Sahle Sellassie's text and the political rhetoric in Mengistu's Ethiopia.

Having demonstrated to the reader how Namaga's hut was destroyed, and after explaining the loss of his property, the author discusses the construction of a new hut for Namaga and his family. Based on how Namaga receives compensation for his damaged property, we can glean information about Sahle Sellassie's choice of stakeholders to undertake Ethiopian land reform:

> A few days later a group of villagers were busy constructing a new hut for Namaga. The cylindrical wall was already finished, and they were now busy with the conical roof. The unthatched structure resembled something like a giant, half-open umbrella. The central pillar and the poles that fanned out from the central pillar to sustain the cob-webbed roof were like the handle, the ribs, and the screen of an umbrella. (1968, 25)

The open framework that is described in this passage is a sign of things to come; it signals much bigger, and better, shelter for Namaga's family. Not only does the community undertake to help with building a new house but members also take it upon themselves to investigate the arson and accompanying theft. Use of the umbrella image signals the kind of overarching communal spirit that Sahle Sellassie hopes will inspire Ethiopian land reform. This manifestation of political power is embedded in an indigenous decision-making body that also upholds law and order. The Afersata tradition is founded on the philosophies of "collective responsibility" (Sahle Sellassie, 51). In other words, in the same way individuals share food during local festivals, they also share misfortune—a kind of communal insurance scheme. While frequent redistribution makes it difficult for any one person to accumulate much wealth, it also means that no one is ever entirely destitute. Whatever wealth is available is shared by all. As the local government administrator—the cheka shum— tells the village, they "are all responsible for the burning of Namaga's hut, and [they] are all condemned collectively to compensate him for his loss, because [they] have failed to find out the criminal" (Sahle Sellassie, 89). Sahle Sellassie depicts local communities as best suited for the business of redistributing wealth. He signals that at such grassroots levels, individuals know each other and relate in ways that privilege sharing over amassing. The Afersata pursues the image of communal responsibility and posits it as a viable alternative to the top-down bureaucratic nation-state.[11] Local self-governance emerges as an effective mode of political praxis—one that is more attuned to the people's needs and resists the allegory of revolutionary upheaval. Sahle Sellassie sketches Ethiopian lands and landscapes as intimately tied to local cultures, languages, and histories. This illustration grants ecological rights and responsibilities to grassroots activism. In the same way Namaga's neighbors practice community-level restorative justice, so too may they undertake environmental custodianship.

The Afersata foregrounds peasant communities as key stakeholders in socioeconomic reforms; this approach is starkly opposed to what the Mengistu government did. Not only did the Derg view peasants as former victims of the monarchy—and thus weak and powerless—it also mistook their illiteracy to mean they could make no meaningful contributions vis-à-vis national policies. These disparaging views eventually led to friction between poor farmers and the military government. Such conflict was related to the dilemma Sahle Sellassie had posed in his work: Who should be responsible for implementing land reform? Land reform marked a new phase in the interaction between Ethiopian masses and their government. The reforms

> created popular demands as to how taxes should be utilized—demands and attitudes unheard of during the imperial regime. The peasants . . . started to raise questions such as "where does the money we pay as tax end up?," "what do we get for our taxes?" (Stahl 1977, 79)

If the later years of Emperor Haile Selassie's reign were marked by increased repression of the opposition, this was only to mask what was a long tradition of peasants defying authority. This resistance varied from outward resignation to violent rebellion. As *Ethiopia: Power and Protest—Peasant Revolts in the Twentieth Century* (Tareke 1996, 14) makes clear, "although peasants may appear quiescent or deferential outwardly, they defy obligations imposed on them by using tactics [such as] . . . work or output withdrawal, pilfering, sabotage, deceit, banditry, flight or migration, and shift in patron allegiance."[12] Farmers in the countryside, away from Addis Ababa and other urban areas, also resented the manner in which urbanites dominated power. The antagonism between peasants and the state is exactly what Sahle Sellassie hoped to avoid by allocating the mandate for land reform and other attendant policy modifications to local communities. The author clearly favors a bottom-up approach; he asks that local infrastructure be left to deal with indigenous problems. The numerous problems experienced between Mengistu's regime and his subjects vindicate Sahle Sellassie. The overbearing nature of the central government demonstrates that Mengistu and his administration were too far removed from the lives of those previously oppressed by Haile Selassie's monarchy.

THE PEASANTRY POPULATING ETHIOPIAN LANDSCAPES

Despite much rhetoric to the contrary, Mengistu's regime maintained a notion of the Ethiopian peasant as backward and deserving nothing but contempt from Derg officials—this is a sentiment that had already been entrenched in Haile Selassie's reign. Mengistu and his ministers were quick to paint Ethiopians in general as helpless victims and in this way depict the military junta as the people's savior. The Derg was convinced that the peasantry it ruled over was "by nature a backward group incapable of understanding their own best interests" (Henze 1989, 5). With such an attitude in mind, the regime generally overlooked the people's demands. Lack of proper sanitation and appropriate farming technology were both cited as reasons why the peasantry was *indeed* backward. A 1964 government pamphlet titled *Awassa Community Development Training and Development Center* noted that villagers needed to learn "the dangers of insanitary water, flies, mosquitoes . . . villagers have to be taught also how to guard against epidemics and how to prevent the spread of infectious and contagious diseases" (Ministry of National Community Development 20). Although this document was produced during Haile Selassie's reign, the same image of peasants as dirty and disease-ridden can be found in government documents prepared under Mengistu. In *L'Éthiopie Rurale: Hier et Aujourd'hui* (*Rural Ethiopia: Past and Present;* 1978), the authors portray the Ethiopian nomad to be just as susceptible to disease as her flock. While the nomad suffers from malaria, her livestock are ravaged by epidemics of Rinderpest (*L'Éthiopie* 1978, 40). In 1978, the Ministry of Information and Propaganda noted that Ethiopian agriculture prior to 1974 was characterized by peasants' use of "very primitive" tools (*L'Éthiopie* 1978, 11). With such descriptions and images about the Ethiopian peasantry circulating, it is no surprise that Mengistu and his associates disregarded the poor and ignored their input vis-à-vis development—despite peasants being important stakeholders in Ethiopian development.

The Derg was quite eager to rewrite Ethiopian history and reinterpret it in ways that depicted the junta in a positive light. Mengistu's regime was invested in portraying the monarchy that it had helped overthrow as wholly corrupt. It became fashionable in socialist Ethiopia to denounce the failure of Haile Selassie's reign. For example, Mengistu's government would equate the amount of infrastructural improvement it had undertaken in one year to that delivered by ten years of the former emperor's administration (*L'Éthiopie* 1978, 5). This comparison was carried out in multiple ways including the production of tables to accompany propaganda material celebrating the ten-year anniversary of the Revolution.

There was an oft-repeated myth—that Mengistu and the Derg had liberated Ethiopians from Haile Selassie's chains of servitude. Documents from the Ministry of Information and Propaganda, the Ministry of Agriculture, as well as a 1979 speech by Mengistu—"Towards Economic Development in Ethiopia"—all perpetuated the idea that before the rise of the military government, Ethiopians had been enslaved by Haile Selassie. All three texts deploy an image of the 1974 revolution as having, finally, made Ethiopian peasants "masters of their lands" (*L'Éthiopie* 1978, 11). The ubiquity of this representation of political liberation not only points to a regime that maintained close scrutiny on its missives and sought to coordinate them, it also indicates the ways in which *production* of these texts was often interconnected. In addition to writing texts for mass education, the Ministry of Information also had the task of creating an archive and memorializing the revolution. The ministry's employees produced pamphlets to celebrate the one-year, four-year, five-year, and ten-year anniversary of the February 1974 revolution In addition, it was tasked with printing numerous Mengistu public addresses such as his May Day speeches in 1975, 1978, and 1984. In all these documents, the message was identical: Ethiopians should be grateful to the military government for freeing them from the chains of imperial bondage. In this book's conclusion, I argue that an alternative path toward national cohesion and regional partnership awaits to be unlocked in the ontologies nurtured by African languages.

A complement to the argument that peasants were backward, unsanitary, and primitive was an image of the country as a vast pool of resources waiting to be exploited. Whether this meant human resources—for instance, a fighting army with which Mengistu could meet insurrections in northern Ethiopia or stem a Somali invasion—or natural resources, Ethiopia was a bountiful chest of wealth waiting to be consumed. In classic nationalist fashion, Mengistu referred to the nation as a gendered subject—the Motherland—

that, much like Ethiopia's women, awaited a strong hand to unveil its "real self . . . [formerly] masked during the feudo-bourgeois era" (Mariam 1979, 17). This image of *unveiling* or *disrobing* the feminized nation to reach the vast "mineral resources in the bosom of our Motherland" was also mentioned while invoking foreign expansionist efforts into Ethiopia as attempts to "violate the integrity of our Motherland" (16). In this missive the military regime not only underlined its role as liberator but also invoked its right as sole progenitor endowed with the sacred duty of making Ethiopia's fertile, but unyielding, lands (*and mothers*) productive. Mengistu's political outlook, like that held by Haile Selassie's regime, had seemingly accepted the myth that there existed *empty land* in certain parts of Ethiopia that could be offered to encourage loyalty. This cynical representation of Ethiopian landscapes ignores multigenerational custodial relationships between communities and their ecosystems. It is an erroneous view of land as experienced by poor farmers and nomads who have unique relationships to the territories and environments on which they subsist. Attempting to unilaterally nullify those multigenerational interactions—and judging them less valid than, for example, state ownership of cooperative farmland—placed the state in conflict with its people. This view has been rather hard to shake off. In 1991, the incoming government of Meles Zenawi declared that private investors would acquire "open and fertile lands . . . after ascertaining first that this will not result in evictions or affect the interests of peasants and nomads as well as those who practice shifting cultivation" ("Ethiopia's Economic Policy" 1991, 25). As inclusive as these practices sound on paper, the reality has been vastly different. Ethiopia is now one of several African nations that has leased large tracts of land to foreign conglomerates in controversial deals. In addition to possibly alienating communities, these land leases do not always contribute to the country's food security. Similarly fraught relationships between the state and its citizenry can be deduced from Ebrahim Hussein's work.

UJAMAA AND THE DEPRIVATION OF URBAN LANDSCAPES

Ujamaa unintentionally impoverished laborers. These destitute citizens were then unable to engage in their local urban economies. The connection between rapidly deteriorating landscapes and novel economic relations under Ujamaa is exemplified by Kahinja's return. Hussein employs Kahinja's tragic end to depict tension between individualism and communalism, as well as the "quest for a truly interior liberty" (Ricard 2000, 127). Ironically, the sense of duty to one's family that Kahinja acts upon is deemed individualistic and much opposed to the communal beliefs that are central to Ujamaa. More importantly, this irreconcilable difference results in further alienation for Tanzania's peasants:

> Diwani: (Anasoma barua)
> Siku ile nilipotoka
> Hapo kijijini . . . kwenda
> Mombasa kuwaona jamaa . . . niliikuta
> Hali ya nyumbani mbaya sana
> Kwanza walikuwa wagonjwa, tena
> Walikuwa wamo katika deni. Na
> Kama isingelipwa deni hiyo
> Nyumba yao, ambayo ni nyumba
> Wanayokaa na kupangisha ingeuzwa. (Hussein 1980, 44)

> Diwani: (Reading Kahinja's letter)
> When I left the village,
> I traveled to Mombasa to visit my folks.
> I found them desperate.
> Somebody was ill, and they were also in debt.
> If this bill had not been cleared
> Their house, where they live and sublet, would have
> Been auctioned. (my translation)

Kahinja's arrival at home is met by worries about ill health, debt, and fear of homelessness. Possibly losing the family domicile threatens to render two women rootless, belonging nowhere in both social and spatial routes of mobility. Hence, financial resources are required to recalibrate the balance upset by the risks of vagrancy. Kahinja steals an Ujamaa village's funds to pay off outstanding bills. Theft is a low-level act of resistance for a character who is torn between family obligations and loyalty to the political ideals of African socialism. Hussein depicts the threat of rootlessness as a social phenomenon that communal efforts cannot resolve: a sense of alienation that produces *reactionary* individualism. Moreover, Hussein's text highlights the plight of numerous Tanzanian villagers who were forcefully turned out of their homes and moved to ill-equipped government villages. Although this Kenyan urban plot is not simply allegorical of villagization, Hussein *is* suggesting that Kenya and Tanzania are perhaps not so different by inserting the Ujamaa plot into this scene of Kenyan strife.

As it turns out, it is the Tanzanian political bureaucracy that delayed achievement of socioeconomic equality. In *Tanzania: A Political Economy* (1982), Andrew Coulson comments on an incident much reminiscent of the theft with which Hussein ends *Arusi*. Coulson relates a news report in which a man is accused of stealing an Ujamaa village's money (235, 244). This newspaper entry is significant in how closely it mirrors the tale at the end of Hussein's play. In Coulson's narrative, the Ujamaa village disintegrates after the local official runs off with the funds. In Hussein's text, however, he leaves the conclusion open-ended as though forcefully willing for a different history to be written about this socialist endeavor to which he, too, had seemingly offered so much of himself. Ultimately, both *Arusi* and *The Afersata* shed light on how postcolonial African regimes seek to dominate the production of discourse and the dissemination of tropes that deploy land as the central metaphor. Writers, on the other hand, attempt to wrestle the use of such allegories from central governments. Often enough, this contest is resolved by the state's capacity to censor and muzzle critical voices. This chapter has been concerned with the post-Sixties transformation of landscapes in two independent African nations: Tanzania and Ethiopia. The raising of national flags—to herald the end of colonial projects—was met with jubilation and high hopes for the future. As African masses soon discovered, however, postindependence regimes dashed many of those aspirations and drove their citizens to bitterness. Both *Arusi* and *The Afersata* critique African states. In the next and final chapter, Kenya's Yvonne Owuor and Uganda's Monica Arac de Nyeko not only pursue an indictment of African nation-states but they also seek to reverse conflict over land—often projected as sexual violence against women and the marginalization of minorities.

CHAPTER 5

Representations of Lands and Landscapes at the Humanity-Ecology Interface

They thought
the leaving

would be like the banyan tree
rising to spread wide
branches turned down become
root again, grow new life.
  —Hope Wabuke, *The Leaving*

Over the past century, my kin practiced subsistence agriculture across various spaces in Eastern Africa. Maize, beans, peas, potatoes, pumpkins, sweet potatoes, arrowroots, sugarcane groves, and fruit orchards. My folks practiced agroforestry—planting trees for timber, fuel, soil conservation, or beauty. Food crops and trees existed alongside livestock: cattle, goats, sheep, donkeys, rabbits, and various kinds of poultry. The primary incentive for plant and animal husbandry was, and still is, securing enough food for the family. Building wealth, and disposable income, is consistently out of reach for these small-scale agriculturalists. Family lore credits women for supplying most of the labor to keep farms productive. My father remembers gardening with his mother, often walking an hour to a variety of fields owned, rented, or managed by my paternal grandmother. My mother and her cousins recall going to Kīrīti with their grandmother, my great-grandmother. In the literature I consider in this chapter, we find similar socioeconomic patterns: mothers, grandmothers, and older women engaged in the daily business of sustenance and creating. The spaces that my family settled modified their identity. Forests. Grazing pastures. Well-drained arable lands. Riverine estuaries. Dry savannahs. Each ecosystem demanded unique husbandry and navigational skills. In a June 2017 conversation, Yvonne Adhiambo Owuor argues that humanity's "odd, broken, impulse to destroy life" has wreaked havoc on the planet (Mũchiri 2020). Owuor connects this destructive urge to the racial and gender violence enacted under the auspices of reason, Enlightenment, imperialism, and European colonialism. Owuor's larger point, however, is that the ecosystem does not merely exist as a victim of this Anthropocene present. Rather, ecology and humanity influence one another. This relationship goes both ways. Our economic and social policies have environmental effects; similarly, our surrounding ecologies affect not just our physical well-being but also our actions as well as our mental and psychological health.

Yvonne Adhiambo Owuor's novel *Dust* (2014) and Monica Arac de Nyeko's short stories "Strange Fruit" (2004), "The Banana Eater" (2008), and "In the Stars" (2003) contend that environmental destruction stems from the same hegemonic framework as gender-based violence. In my previous chapter, I read Ethiopian and Tanzanian literature and demonstrated a long-standing rivalry between artists who wield literary allegories based on land and landscape and ruling regimes that ostensibly seek to monopolize such metaphors. Here, I argue that Owuor's and Nyeko's writing demonstrates how trauma on lands and landscapes often accompanies gender-based violence against women and the state's marginalization of minorities. I indicate how both writers generate metaphors of food as evocative imagery that links representations of ruin on the land to food insecurity.[1] In Yvonne Owuor's *Dust*, her description of trauma against the body is, first, achieved through depiction of the land as tactile and animate. M. Arac de Nyeko's short stories expose erasure of female subjects from representations of lands and landscapes, while also inviting an exploration of why claims of territoriality are often laced with ethnic prejudice. Nyeko's fiction displays varied representations of land in rural versus urban spaces. Hence, her writing is a powerful cultural artifact and analytical tool for discussions regarding narrative and its potential for resistance, the pastoral as a literary genre, and violence—especially as it is manifested on female bodies. Finally, Nyeko's "Banana Eater" exposes gender and ethnic marginalization as experienced across urban landscapes. Owuor's novel represents a new kind of engagement with land and landscape. *Dust* depicts the land as "tangible and sentient" (Mũchiri 2019). Christina Kenny (2016, 4) identifies the "insatiable desire for home" that landscapes inspire, no matter that, in *Dust*, this quest often fails. As Amy Rushton (2017, 53) contends, home is paradoxically "desired yet feared." *Dust* portrays lands and landscapes not merely as objects influenced by human actions but also as subjects.[2] "Landscape in Africa: Process and Vision" (Luig and von Oppen 1997) argues that landscape is a continuous aesthetic, historical, and political praxis. Owuor's characters traverse large distances, and while such voyages engender cross-cultural encounters, peregrinations across space produce a "mobility-induced anxiety" (Knudsen and Rahbek 2017, 118). I agree with Russell West-Pavlov (2017) who reads topographical features in *Dust* as manifesting nonhuman instrumentality. Elsewhere, Annie Gagiano (2021) demonstrates Owuor's ability to depict local memories that intersect with regional social movements; history, in Owuor's skillful hands, haunts and lingers.

In this chapter, I find the idea of a "subsistence perspective" to be especially productive (Mies and Shiva 1993, 20). This is an ecological outlook that respects both the "diversity and the limits of nature . . . [and is] rooted in the everyday subsistence production" (19). Emphasis on the vernacular links subsistence production to two key goals pursued by the womanist perspective: "societal healing [and] reconciliation of the relationship between people and nature" (Phillips 2006, xxix). At a sociocultural level, this presents itself as "living in a particular way in a particular place" (Styles 2019, 34). That aesthetic stands in stark opposition against imperialist, capitalist, patriarchal objectification of women.[3] *Different Shades of Green: African Literature, Environmental Justice, and Political Ecology* argues that "women's objectification is legitimized through their association with nature, while nature, being feminized, is positioned as in need of male mastery" (Caminero-Santangelo 2014, 58). What emerges from this prejudice is the kind of violence we witness in both Nyeko's and Owuor's work. This is a "dysfunctional relationship" often manifested as abuse and trauma not only toward women, children, and marginalized persons but also directed at animals, plant life, and the ecosystem at large (Fike 2017, 150). It is this violence, under a colonial and imperial guise, that many of the authors previously discussed in this book contend with in their narratives. Though previously part of the colonial demarcation titled the Northern Frontier District, Owuor's Turkana setting houses multiethnic characters who successfully argue for a reinterpretation of identity and belonging. *Dust* examines "older forms of cosmopolitanism, diaspora, and nomadic life [and explores how these] came to coexist and compete with the modern territorial state" (Weitzberg 2017, 3). This renegotiation and recalibration of identity is at the core of what many of the authors I've examined achieve.

NYEKO'S REPRESENTATIONS OF SPACE

Prior to my discussion of Owuor's writing, I'd like to survey short fiction by Monica Arac de Nyeko for its representations of space. Given Nyeko's use of natural imagery—alternating between urban and rural spaces—her work, especially "Strange Fruit," is a powerful cultural artifact and analytical tool for illustrating landscapes and belonging. Her fiction explores narrative and its potential for resistance, the pastoral as a literary genre, and violence—especially as it is manifested on female bodies. "Strange Fruit" begins with a dream.[4] The female narrator, Lakidi Sofia, conjures up her husband, Mwaka, as she sleeps, in apparent attempts to relive the happy days before he was abducted by Joseph Kony's Lord's Resistance Army (LRA). She remembers her mother's desperate attempts to stop her and Mwaka from getting married, as well as her mother's eventual, and reluctant, acknowledgment that Mwaka was a worthy husband for her daughter. Months later, after Mwaka has risen through the LRA ranks and can make a short visit home, the narrator smells how different a man her husband has become. She is shocked to discover that her husband had "tasted human blood, licked at it and smeared it upon his body" (2004, 9). Mwaka eventually flees from the LRA and returns home one night; Sofia insists he take a bath and change into fresh clothing. The next day, members of Kony's militia find their way to Sofia's compound in search of Mwaka. They soon discover him hiding in an outdoor shed dressed in his wife's gown. They drag him outside and beat him. Mwaka does not divulge the information his former comrades demand and he is consequently punished: hanged on his favorite mango tree. Sofia watches her husband dangle "like strange fruit, waiting to be plucked," as LRA soldiers rape her (16). Songs, from traditional dance music to childhood jingles, pop music, and sing-alongs found in oral literature, litter the narrative. Nyeko deploys music to further highlight the connection between the story's title, "Strange Fruit," and the similarly titled famous Billie Holiday track.

Nyeko's "Strange Fruit," keenly attuned to the fallacy of a rural-urban divide, performs rhetorical labor against the myth of a pastoral idyll. Nyeko exposes urban snobbery from Kampala that paradoxically imagines Kitgum (northern Uganda) as both remotely idyllic and savagely violent. Her fiction critiques the pastoral convention. While Nyeko's work is pastoral in how it "describes the country with an implicit or explicit contrast to the urban," additional nuances of this genre deserve elaboration; for one, her work is keen on challenging "an idealization of the reality of life" in

Uganda's northern countryside (Gifford 1999, 2). Unlike earlier examples of this tradition, Nyeko's rural communities are characterized by a "bleak battle for survival" as determined by political and socioeconomic actualities (Gifford 1999, 3, 120, 128). Ultimately, Nyeko's writing moves beyond the pastoral—lodging squarely in the postpastoral. The postpastoral recognizes an endless cycle of creation and dying, juxtaposes natural features as allegories for inner human psyches, and demonstrates that environmental exploitation stems from the same sentiment as marginalization of women and minorities (Gifford 1999, 153, 156, 165). Nyeko not only writes back against the pastoral's arcadian view of the countryside—contending that the rural is wholesome in its own right—but also transcends and exposes the genre's shortcomings.

"Strange Fruit" reveals the ethnic and gender chauvinism underlying nationalist imaginations of the pastoral.[5] Nationalist theorizing of the rural overlooked not only ethnic competition but also the gendered labor that was required to maintain rural productivity. Nyeko's short story foregrounds love and its enabling capacity for subjects to transcend conflict and victimhood; that is, the business of loving in rural Uganda is political. Sofia Ahlberg (2009) argues that the choices Nyeko's protagonist makes to love, to trust, and to create a family are as political as Joseph Kony's antigovernment war. Furthermore, activism is not limited to the character's actions; Nyeko's act of creation—as an artist—is also an example of resistance. What authors do is simultaneously "an act of love" and "a struggle for peace" (409). Amplifying women's romance is vital because Nyeko's deployment of the postpastoral motif enables her to expose the misogyny upon which nationalist narratives are often founded. The postpastoral is an effective tool for Nyeko to deconstruct several concepts: one, the "separation of the urban and the rural"; two, the idea of the "rural as a privileged and mythologized location"; and three, the depiction of the rural as a space devoid of "terror and political violence" (Ramlagan 2011, 99, 100, 103). By refuting "a politics of space" that splits the urban from the rural, Nyeko exposes the pastoral fallacy that the countryside is "apolitical" (99). Hegemonic discourse viewed rural Africa as a wild space lacking Western domestication.

Nyeko rewrites the Ugandan countryside in more inclusive terms. Her work seeks to rise above the histories of violence that have been inscribed onto the region's landscapes—both geographic and psychic.[6] There is a desire for a renewed and empowered existence in Nyeko's work. In "Strange Fruit," the protagonist reconjures her abducted husband as she attempts to survive trauma by recalling and narrating. "Strange Fruit" has been performing the labor of memory across varied temporalities and cultural contexts. Abel Meeropol's poetic version and Billie Holiday's musical rendition both mythologize African American suffering at the hands of white supremacists. These two artists focus on the black male body and its parallel hypersexualization and liability to physical assault. The poem and the song refuse to let go of the nightmarish scene of numerous "black bod[ies] swinging . . . hanging from the poplar trees" ("Strange Fruit," Meeropol). In the way violence against black communities in the United States was, simultaneously, about capitalism, race, citizenship, and disenfranchisement, it was also about land. Specifically, it was about what kinds of spaces were conducive to black communal life. The image of "poplar trees" in the song is, after all, not accidental; reference to southern flora invokes the pastoral idyll. Land, space, and a scrutiny of ethnic-based claims to territory form the backbone on which Nyeko's short fiction is based.[7] While this is much more apparent in "Strange Fruit," we find similar themes in Nyeko's "The Banana Eater" and "In the Stars." Across her oeuvre, Nyeko is interested in land for its productive potential. What the land yields, especially food crops such as bananas and fruits, is of extreme importance.

In two of her short pieces of fiction, Nyeko provides her audience with a clear link between prejudice and interpersonal friction. Both "Strange Fruit" and "The Banana Eater" expose ethnic chauvinism and connect it to respective moments of misunderstanding, or even worse, interethnic war. Nyeko is interested in how food—the fruits of the land—props up thinly veiled ethnic discrimination.[8] In addition, urban snobbery about the countryside is one instance on a spectrum of bigotry whose logical end point is the destruction of lives and property visible in northern Uganda. The narrator's mother in "Strange Fruit" attempts to superimpose false partitions between rural and city folk. As Sofia narrates, her mother was "always going on and on about the city and how different people from the city should be when they come to the village" (Nyeko 2004, 2). When faced with the violence that takes place in Kitgum, the othering of rural populations serves as one way for the narrator's mother to psychologically shield herself from the suffering. By then, of course—with her daughter deeply involved as the wife of an abducted husband/soldier—Mother's attempts are largely frustrated. And yet there exists an alternative to this manufactured ethnic rivalry. In the concluding section of this book, I demonstrate how production of knowledge in African languages is a key step along the path toward decolonial praxis.

CUISINES AND ETHNIC PREJUDICE

"Banana Eater" starts with Amito, the narrator, explaining the beauty of her mother's flower garden in Kampala and the guests it attracted. Many came to appreciate the garden's splendor, but some, notably local market vendors, left it much worse. The first person to comment on the market sellers' rudeness is Brother Aculu; he has been romancing Amito's mother for several weeks when he finally acquires the courage to broach the subject. Red Devil, as the narrator nicknames Brother Aculu, suggests that the narrator's mother confront the market vendors who visit every afternoon, sit on the lawn, and leave scraps of paper, "packets of milk and cardboard boxes, banana peels and maize husks" strewn all over (Nyeko 2008, 2). When Ma attempts to eject the market folks from her flower garden—doing so by claiming ownership—she is quickly rebuked and reminded that she lives on government space. "No one came into the estates with any piece of land," she is told (2). The flower garden, it seems, is public property—despite the private labor put into beautifying it. Government housing estates are contrasted to "Kampala's hills, where the houses were large and double-storied and there were dogs and long walled fences to keep people away" (2). The text also explores prejudice, religious—such as that against Kampala's Jehovah's Witnesses—and ethnic—such as that held by Amito's mother against the Baganda community, the eponymous banana eaters (4). Nyeko's third short story, "In the Stars," reads like a letter to the editor. It is a fictional first-person narrative that humanizes the suffering in northern Uganda. It provides faces for the rebel perpetrators—the narrator's uncles—as well as for the victims—the narrator's schoolmates, fellow villagers, and extended family members. What is clear is that the civilians of northern Uganda have no one to turn to: neither government forces nor LRA militia. Both armies use their assumed civilian mandate to exert more agony on the very people they claim to protect.

Given the importance of food in this narrative—the title "Banana Eater" highlights this—it is no surprise that meals become a synecdoche for entire cultures. Amito's mother is highly skeptical of anything from outside her local space. Ma, we are told, "saw no point in learning cuisines whose ingredient names were so foreign they could have been strange illnesses" (2008, 1). The peculiarity of imported dishes conjures images of sickness; that which is foreign inspires imaginings of infection and disease. As it turns out, the alien includes Ugandan cultures other than one's own. Amito has a playmate, Naalu, whose father her mother abhors. Ma disliked Naalu's father for three simple reasons: "he was Catholic, like the unforgiving nuns of her school-days; he supported the Democratic Party; and he was a Muganda. . . . Ma said it often that Baganda treasured money over loyalty. They would steal your hand if you turned away. The Baganda were banana eaters" (4). Once again, food—a banana dish—becomes a focal point for hatred. It is with much disdain that the narrator's mother adds the last statement to her appraisal of this community, "the Baganda were banana eaters." The meal in of itself has nothing to do with religion, politics, or betraying one's country, the three reasons given for disliking the Baganda people. However, closing this statement of ethnic chauvinism with the community's staple food indicates that bananas have come to symbolize everything Ma hates.

As it were, the mother abhors the Baganda for eating bananas, and she hates bananas because they are eaten by the Baganda. For the mother, bananas are a peculiar fruit; they serve as an icon onto which she can project her ethnically based chauvinism. Ma projects her anger against the Baganda, and the power struggles that ensue between them and the northerners, onto the banana. The nutrients a community consumes take on a much larger significance; hence, the mother is elated when she sees Naalu try, and appreciate, a meal made from millet. Viewing this as a triumphant moment over Naalu's father—and the Baganda community in general—she commands the girl thus: "tell that to your father . . . tell him you eat millet these days, not bananas!" (4). As often happens, Naalu's father reciprocates the prejudice. In his case, he "thought northerners were to blame for every single thing that had ever gone wrong in the country—the coups d'états, the bad roads, the hospitals without medicine, the high price of sugar, his addiction to nicotine, and the fact that the country was landlocked" (4). Clearly, Nyeko is intent on satirizing ethnic biases; that Naalu's father blames northerners for Uganda's geographic disadvantage at not having access to the sea is absurd. At most, Naalu's father could blame the haphazard imperial desires of nineteenth-century European nations. In any case, both Naalu's father and the narrator's mother rely upon the oversimplification of distant cultures to nourish their prejudice.

NATURAL MOTIFS AS SITES OF MEMORY

As a self-reflective writer, Monica Arac de Nyeko has contributed to some of the critical conversation concerning her short fiction.[9] A member of FEM-RITE, the Ugandan Women Writers' Association, Nyeko envisions a social role for herself and other authors; hence, for example, she has commented on gender-based violence. In a 2005 piece titled "Ugandan Monologues," she decried the government's ban on the staging of the renowned feminist play *Vagina Monologues*. Citing possible moral corruption, the Ugandan state minister of information James Nsaba-Buturo refused to issue performance licenses for the production (Nyeko 2005, 101). Nyeko described the injunction as "tantamount to silencing women's voices" even as she underlined the drama's potential to shift public discourse about rape and sexual assault (101). The writer points out the way survivors are twice victimized: "first by the perpetrator of the violence and then by the common view that they have become 'defiled' and unacceptable for marriage" (101). The advocacy with which Nyeko approaches issues concerning the female body in these journalistic pieces also serves as an undercurrent in her fiction. Female bodies appear repeatedly in Nyeko's stories; women's torsos are a motif the author uses while portraying Uganda's landscapes.

Apart from feminist activism, Nyeko sees literature as a vehicle for transmitting (hi)stories—especially collective memory. Nyeko writes to better comprehend herself and "the things that have come and passed, and those that are yet to come" (Wood 2007, 1). Here Nyeko outlines a trajectory that excavates the past while also making major intrusions into the future. For Nyeko, however, such narratives need not be linear or singular; she catalogues her own subjectivity in multiplicity rather than singularity—simultaneously manifested as "Arac, a woman, Acoli, Ugandan, a daughter, an aunt, [and] a sister" (1). The symbolism associated with geological features in Nyeko's work denotes a violent countryside that is much unlike the paradise depicted by nationalist pastorals. After her husband's abduction by the LRA, Sofia mourns her spouse as though he were confirmed dead. Having embarked on the grieving process, she is eager to fulfill burial requirements—no matter that she does not actually have her husband's body. Instead, Sofia turns to her immediate environment; by finding objects she may use to substitute for Mwaka's missing corpse, she makes rocks and human corpses analogous. She decides "to lay four large stones in the cemetery to evoke Mwaka's spirit back home to rest with his ancestors under the big *kituba* tree" (Nyeko 2004, 8). This stone-body motif is also repeated in Nyeko's "In the Stars." Having lost her son, the narrator's grandmother "laid four large stones to show where we should have laid [my uncle's] body" (2003, 1). It is unclear why the number four recurs in both cases; I speculate it suitably represents all four cardinal points on a compass, and hence can help reorient a relative's spirit from wherever it may be presently lost.

Nyeko's fiction deploys natural motifs—rocks, water, and trees—as sites of memory, strongly connecting her work to cultural production in the African Diaspora.[10] Billie Holiday's image of black bodies strung from branches not only became the rallying cry for civil rights politics, but also served to sustain an African American culture of resistance. In both contexts, natural vegetation serves to critique pastoral rural-scapes that exploited women—and additionally, in the American South, African Americans. Nyeko seemingly borrows even more from this tradition of black struggle. Like Toni Morrison and George Lamming who—in the aftermath of the Middle Passage—have depicted the sea in their attempts to discuss grieving and loss, Nyeko's work deploys rivers and similar water bodies as depositories of family history and communal memory. This is the case, for instance, in her description of the Aringa River in "Strange Fruit." Indigenous myths about the waterway note that "during those days before the war . . . [the Aringa River] did not house so many troubled souls under it. The river was not filled with too many leeches like it is now. Lost souls did not cry out in the night begging for rescue" (Nyeko 2004, 8). Armed conflict between the LRA and the Ugandan state has turned the river into a repository of death, loss, and unvoiced mourning. The Aringa's continuous movement from source to mouth is an apt allegory of the constant untethering of bodies in northern Uganda. Bodies float in and out of Nyeko's fiction and appear in many unexpected ways. For instance, child-like male bodies appear in place of soldiers, with some so young they seem "weighed down by the size of their guns" (6). Also, body parts are applied onto other bodies; hence, Sofia can tell from her husband's breath that "he'd tasted human blood, licked at it, and smeared it upon his body" (9). The local community has focused its sorrow and bereavement on flowing water. In the absence of the victims' bodies, relatives project their sense of loss onto the river.[11] The water becomes at once a reminder that the cycle of life includes birth and death—however painful the latter may be—even as it houses organisms, leeches, that are appropriate metaphors for military activity in Kitgum. Nyeko's text reduces both LRA militias and the Ugandan armed forces into blood-sucking vermin that have drained the life out of northern Uganda. This has occurred either through the abduction of older male relatives—and the subsequent breaking up of families—or through the abduction of young boys and girls—hence jeopardizing the community's continuity.

Nyeko's work depicts landscapes by exposing the emptiness of nationalist and militarist pastorals and their disregard for women's and minority agency. Unlike the pastoral, where trees and streams are doorways into innocent childhoods, Nyeko's postpastoral fiction emphasizes the violence enclosed within rural spaces. Consequently, death is perpetually less than an arm's length away, haunting the land and filling it with ghostly apparitions. In two of Nyeko's pieces, "Strange Fruit" and "In the Stars," kituba trees are known to serve as resting places for souls. After the death of the narrator's uncle, a second uncle also joined the war and "combed Kituba trees where they say spirits live . . . to fight the demons of his brother's death that haunted him" (2003, 1).[12] Unfortunately, such efforts end in failure; there are neither spirits located in local flora nor is there peace in the very act of searching. Consequently, kituba trees remain in the local imaginary as sites of memory where unnamed, *and* unseen, victims may be mythologized. Additionally, the production of memory invades the individual psyche, especially the realm of dreams, seeking to fulfill the quest that was earlier frustrated. Noting that "memories of nights in rain and gripping fear creep to our dreams," the narrator demonstrates how the trauma of trying to survive, and the guilt of surviving, continuously assault any attempt at nocturnal repose (2003, 1). That "sleep should be the one place where there is no worry. It should be dreamland, hopeland" immediately alerts the reader that sleep in Kitgum *is not* any of these (2003, 1). Readers anticipate the narrator's desire that in addition to finding one's "dreamland" and "hopeland," the residents of Kitgum should also be able to inhabit their "home/land," yet they do not. Therefore, it is quite appropriate that "Strange Fruit" begins with Sofia's dream—a reverie in which she sees Mwaka although he was abducted by the LRA months before. Locating her husband in her mind's eye enables Sofia to re-create the family that was broken by Kony's militia, thus completing Sofia and Mwaka's home for their daughter.

FINDING HOME

The desire to find a home—any space that enables the full articulation of one's subjectivity—is also a key quest in Nyeko's "The Banana Eater." More specifically, competition between public and private concerns causes friction between urban communities. Unlike in the two previous tales, Nyeko explores how characters' desire for home is achieved in the urban environment. The pluri-cultural nature of Uganda's capital city makes an already complex pursuit even more mystifying. In "The Banana Eater," we witness a renegotiation of the terms *public* and *private* as they apply to Kampala's real estate. The narrator describes how her mother's garden served as a haven for market women. "Our backyard was a place to forget about the market and its unsold sacks of potatoes and bananas, a place to gossip, a place to laugh out loud at anyone, including our distinguished house guests" (2008, 1). Market sellers choose this garden because of its attractive flowers and easy access. Once they invite themselves there, they are impossible to dislodge. The narrator's mother experiences this difficulty as she attempts to evict the men and women of the market who visit her garden, trample on flowers, litter, and generally destroy the private labor that has been invested in beautifying the plot. Retailers told off Ma, saying

> no one came into the estates with any piece of land on their heads. They called my mother a whore. They said she was a husbandless slut, a fanatic Christian, a sex-starved bitch who should migrate back to the north of the country where people were uncivilized and lacked manners. (2008, 2)

As the sellers correctly point out, the narrator and her mother live on city council of Kampala property; their home has been *rented* from the government and hence can only be classified as *quasi private*. However, as the vendors contend, quasi private really means public, regardless of private efforts and resources invested. Since nobody brought land with them to the housing projects, the traders assert, all land in that part of the city is up for grabs, for public consumption. These merchants reconceptualize public space as a hybrid public good (Brown, Msoka, and Dankoco 2014). The market men and women caricature the narrator's mother as an "uncivilized Northerner"; she has misunderstood what should be private and what should not. While land should be public, female sexuality should not. They admonish the woman as someone who freely offers her body in the public sphere—hence she is a loose woman. Of particular concern, it seems, is the fact that the narrator's mother has no man in her life; this fact unnerves the vendors who see her attempts at creating romance with a fellow churchgoer as clear indication of her immorality. Traders weaponize patriarchy to discipline this single mother.

Demarcating spaces and deploying borders, it turns out, are also effective ways of differentiating public from private. Mama Benja, one of the narrator's neighbors at the estate, demonstrates the use of fences against public invasion of quasi-private gardens. Mama Benja's "plant fence was high, thick, and threatening enough to keep the vendors away. It was said that her backyard was host to a family of cobras which she kept tamed and nourished. If anyone ever tampered with her, she sent the cobras after them" (Nyeko 2008,

3). Nyeko's tale does not provide clear evidence that Mama Benja truly had domesticated reptiles that she used to settle vendettas. What is clear about the rumors—for whom we have no absolute originator—is that they associated Mama Benja's fence with malevolence. The crowd dislikes Mama Benja but cannot explicitly accuse her of the social crime that truly irks them: thwarting attempts to invade her backyard. The vendors' trespassing is reminiscent of Paulina's transgression in chapter 3. In Macgoye's work, of course, this spatial disobedience is deployed against a colonial hegemony. Here, instead, vendors fabricate accounts about Mama Benja taming snakes and use that to discredit her. There is the same impetus at work that derided the narrator's mother as a "savage from the North." Urban social mores recruit neighborhood gossip to chastise women who have contravened rules of cataloguing the public versus the private. Demonstrably, ethnicity and gender are crucial identity markers amid negotiations for land—a scarce yet essential source of livelihood in both the rural and urban spheres.

Nyeko turns to legal language to resolve this urban conflict. Her discussion, however, raises concerns regarding the positioning of center versus periphery—within a state and internationally—and the political repercussions. Thus, while city council ordinances successfully adjudicate over urban space, the Ugandan constitution is contravened in Kitgum by the LRA. Nyeko (2008) deploys city council by-laws to help discipline unruly market sellers and frustrate the proliferation of the public at the expense of the private. Through this motif, Ma achieves some respite from the onslaught of people daily trampling her garden. Salvation comes from her sworn enemy: Naalu's father, the Baganda man. Naalu's father explained to the market operators

that the market and the estates were two different entities. It was irrelevant that they were both owned by Kampala city council. If the men wanted to use such flimsy arguments, he said, we should as well go and camp at the state house and tell the president it was our right as citizens. (Nyeko 2008, 4)

He then enacted a new law, in his capacity as estate manager; the following day a novel edict "was erected right next to Ma's newly planted red euphorbia fence: Anyone caught crossing over to the estates would be fined twenty thousand shillings" (2008, 5). This is a positive application of the law that has immediate benefits for those aggrieved; the same, however, cannot be said of the foundational document ratified in Kampala's National Assembly to govern the country in its entirety—including the smallest hamlet in the north.

Kitgum's residents have no legal recourse to turn to; unlike Ma, who lives at the center of Uganda's power structure, Kitgumians reside at the periphery. Nyeko's description of their plight—especially their inability to safeguard their rights to a home—demonstrates that communities in northern Uganda are considered *inferior* citizens in comparison to others much closer to Kampala and the seat of government.

Nyeko further complicates the effectiveness of using the legal arm to resolve conflict by demonstrating the successes and failures of different levels of law: local versus international. The local council ordinance regarding private plots in Kampala's housing estates seems quite appropriate in mediating between Ma's interests versus those of the market traders. It is an example of *functional* law. However, international human rights law does not have much success in creating solutions to the northern Uganda war. Such statutes are merely fictive. The victims of this conflict continue to suffer amid "treaties signed by important men"; furthermore, they remain ignorant of terms such as the "*universal declaration of human rights*" (Nyeko 2003, 2; emphasis in original). Once again, Kitgum is depicted as a region impenetrable not only to the constitutional gaze emanating from Kampala's House of Representatives but also from The Hague's International Criminal Court. The lofty ideals set by such institutions fall short of the terror that affected communities endure.[13] Nyeko's fiction is skeptical about international legal agreements and the extent to which they can empower marginalized communities. Ultimately, neither national constitutions nor human rights charters buttress socioeconomic reform—that task is best performed by postpastoral fiction, or the kinds of grassroots decision-making organs previously examined in my fourth chapter.

As the narrator describes, a war that began back in 1986 mostly as "a joke" has gone on to destroy the Acholi tribe, accompanied by media reports that "the war will end real soon" (Nyeko 2003, 1–2). In the almost three decades since the beginning of the conflict, the region has learnt not to place its hope in the government, or in international humanitarian organizations. Each stakeholder has their own sinister motives for getting involved, and for posing as though *they* hold the key to its resolution. For example, "low-ranked government soldiers, who are sent to protect us, run and hide in their brick-walled barracks to protect themselves when the rebels come . . . [then] return when it's calm to rape our grandmothers [and] light our huts for pleasure" (2003, 2). High-level government officials, on the other hand, embezzle foreign funding allocated to those affected and use it for personal gain: to "buy banks, government property and own the entire nation" (2). With all realistic options seemingly exhausted, victims have resigned their dreams and hope for a miraculous end to the conflict in "the immortal stars" (2). The utopian vision that aid will come from celestial powers, coupled with Nyeko's use of environmental features— rocks, trees, and rivers—as repositories of communal memory, complements the narrator's allusion to the "night sky" as the only source of salvation victims can rely on (2). Two years after winning the 2007 Caine Prize for African Writing, Monica Arac de Nyeko characterized her vocation as one where fiction "unpacks the bigger and more complex [sociopolitical] issues by giving these collective memories a human and much more intimate face and story" (Patel 2009). Nyeko foregrounds literary production as an ontology through which to comprehend the human, physical, and natural environments around us. In the rest of this chapter, I will examine how Yvonne Owuor manifests literature's capacity to connect humans to their ecologies.

THE LANDS AND LANDSCAPES OF ANAM KA'ALAKOL

When *Dust* begins, Odidi Oganda is fleeing a hail of bullets in Nairobi's back alleys. Odidi is murdered by the Kenyan police. Nyipir Oganda, Odidi's father, and Ajany Oganda, Odidi's sister, prepare his body for burial on the same day Kenya ignites in the 2007–8 postelection mayhem. Simultaneously, Isaiah Bolton journeys from England to Wuoth Ogik, the Oganda home, in search of his father, Hugh, a colonial settler who mysteriously disappeared. Isaiah, summoned by Odidi before his death, travels despite his mother's pleas. *Dust* ends with love, hinting that Ajany and Isaiah might get married. Akai Ma, Odidi's mother, heads into the Turkana scrubland with a longtime admirer. Nyipir, accompanied by a former jailor and torturer, goes to Myanmar, hoping to find where his elder brother and father died during World War II.

Ajany and Odidi grew up in the desert lands around Anam Ka'alakol (Lake Turkana)—the same region where archaeologists uncovered early human remains. This territory is the cradle of mankind, and *Dust* portrays the siblings' childhood as embedded in the surrounding ecosystem. Ajany and Odidi experience an inner life that is as varied as the physical landscapes they call home. Odidi and his younger sister

> were chance offspring of northern-Kenyan drylands. Growing up, Odidi and
> Ajany had been hemmed in by arid land geographies and essences . . . they had

marveled at Anam Ka'alakol, the desert lake that swallows three rivers—the Omo, Turkwel, and Kerio. They learned the memories of another river—the Ewaso Nyiro—four moody winds, the secret things of parents' fears, throbbing shades of pasts, met assorted transient souls, and painted their existence on a massive canvas of glowing, rocky, heated earth upon which anything could and did happen. They mapped their earth with portions of wind, fire, sky, water, and nothingness, with light, piecing tales from stones, counting footsteps etched into rocks, peering into crevices to spy on the house of red rain. (Owuor 2014, 6–7)

Dust depicts Anam Ka'alakol, the desert lake, as a mythical place. Rivers, winds, rocky promontories, and the scrubland all loom larger than life. The natural elements that have formed this landscape not only act as guardian spirits but also as playmates. Owuor's description suggests an intimacy between Ajany, Odidi, and the ecosystem. This form of oneness is far from the bifurcated approach to the natural world previously instituted by European imperialism.

We see a similar sense of awe and wonder at the end of the novel. Owuor closes the plotline with a vivid description of how the desert lands rejuvenate in the aftermath of a flash flood. In the teeming abundance of young life—both flora and fauna—Owuor's prose conjures a sense of renewal. We witness the planet replenish itself as the cycle of life marches forth.

A congregation of birds chirp, a raucous choir in need of a sane conductor. Transient storm-rivers disappear as the Ewaso Nyiro starts its reluctant crawl back to old boundaries. Oryx gambol; giraffes browse on the extended banks of stream, among pockets of flowering shrubs of all hues, mostly peach, a desert supernova of frozen flame, fragile blossoms, frantic in bloom, as if they were angels relishing a temporary reprieve from celestial certainty. (364)

Birdlife, oryx, giraffes, flowers, and shrubs emerge from the desolation of a watery inundation. Owuor goes as far as to invoke the beginning of the universe; this "desert supernova" echoes the spark that ignited the formation of stars, planets, chemical elements, monocellular organisms, and eventually *Homo sapiens sapiens*. How is it that the text fleets across fourteen billion years of the universe's existence?

Dust often shifts its timeline. That happens through allusions to the cosmic Big Bang, or through a plot structure that moves back and forth between the 1950s, 2008, and the early part of the twentieth century (Mũchiri 2019). The novel is invested in a space-time continuum, rather than adopting discrete moments in chronology and place. *Here-now* is often linked to *there-then*. The past and the present are repeatedly and closely intertwined with the future. Hence, for instance, as Ajany and her father fly back home with Odidi's body, they observe:

> This is their territory. Teleki's volcano, a brown bowl, windy landforms. They pass over Loiyangalani, toward Mount Kulal. Shift northeast toward Kalacha Goda. They level over the salt flats fringing the Chalbi. Hurri Hills in the dusk light, and then, below, a wide unkempt stripe carved into the land. The plane flies through the layers of time, reveals the hollowed brown rock below from which Ajany and Odidi would survey the rustling march of desert locusts, dry golden-brown pastures where livestock browsed, and they would run after homemade kites, eat cactus berries, and curse one of the land's visiting winds, which had ripped the kites to shreds. (26)

Ajany and her family interact with the landscape by immersing themselves in it. This traversing of the land is embedded in the action words from the passage above: pass, shift, survey, and run. I argue that the Oganda clan, like the nomadic communities they live among, imitates the restlessness of the natural world. They roam like the winds roam; they flow like the waters flow; and they drift like the desert sands drift.

It is indicative that Owuor characterizes this funeral procession as flying through time. Such language hints at the ways in which human perception is affected not only by emotional trauma—for instance, the grief of losing a son or brother—but also by environmental conditions. Elsewhere in the novel, we learn that Nyipir views the open horizons of Wuoth Ogik with some trepidation. To Nyipir, the surrounding vistas register as "an eternal landscape that seems to foreshadow the end of life" (36). The beauty that the Oganda family lives among simultaneously inspires reverence and fear at nature's potential. "A convoluted silence warps the landscape"; the districts around Anam Ka'alakol may seem vacuous, but these spaces are also miraculous (46). There is much that lies beneath the surface, partially hidden from human life cycles. The text indirectly summons the sublime, describing the setting as "spare pastures [and] ephemeral watering holes" (32). Grasslands and waterways are the lifelines of nomadic pastoralists.[14] These communities have adapted to Turkana's harsh conditions—learning how to become one with the terrain to survive. Mortality is never far. The beauty of the bare landscapes masks the reality that drought, famine, wildfires, floods, or any number of adverse weather conditions may devastate the people's livelihoods. In this precarity, Anam Ka'alakol and its surroundings are a "cosmos of grief" (85).

Dust succeeds as a novel not only for how meaningfully the text mines Kenya's political history but also for the stunning representations of space. The world of the novel is one where the winds have "texture" (63). Overall, the "landscape unfurls into eternity, shimmering past origins" (336), and, as Isaiah Bolton comes to realize, "everything breathes here, even the damn stones" (78). One cannot easily pin down what is living and what is not. That is precisely how it should be. The callous disregard of Anthropocene luxury and its environmental consequences comes undone. *Dust* challenges the artificial boundaries between man and nature, masculine and feminine, or even center and periphery. Literary aesthetics that privilege the supernatural—as seen in writing by Ogot, Ogola, Vera, and Kanengoni—blur and disturb bifurcations of reality, especially as endorsed by racist, sexist capitalism. In the next chapter, my coda, I elaborate on how this book's overall argument regarding representations of land and landscape might be further enhanced through the use of African languages in Africanist scholarship.

Mũthia

Harĩa Tumĩte

Kĩrĩra gĩakwa ibuku-inĩ rĩrĩ nĩ atĩ mĩgũnda na ithaka nĩ çia bata harĩ waan-
dĩki wa ngerekano çia Abirika. Aandĩki arĩa marĩ haha maumĩte kũndũ
ngũrani: Kenya ya rũgũrũ, Uhabeshi ya gatagatĩ, Tanganyika ya mũkoroni,
Tanzania ĩna wĩyathi, Zimbabwe, Nairobi, Dar es Salaam, iria rĩa Turkana,
Kampala, na Kitgum kũrĩa rũgongo rwa Uganda. O ibuku o ibuku rĩronania
ũrĩa aandĩki a ngerekano içi matũmagĩra ĩthaka, mĩgũnda, na teri kũũmba,
kũgemia, gũthakaria, na kũagĩria ng'ano çiao. Itanya rĩa mbere rĩonanirie ũrĩa
ngerekano çia Grace Ogot na Margaret Ogola çĩena mĩtaratara ĩtaratwarana.
Ng'ano çiao çia tene itũmagĩra mimera, nyamũ, na marimũ naçio ngerekano
çia kĩĩrĩu ikamũrĩka andũ na çieko çiao. Ndindĩkire uhoro ũyũ wa marimũ
harĩ mabuku ma Yvonne Vera na Alex Kanengoni. Itanya rĩrĩ rĩa keri rĩrorire
ũtũmĩri wao wa ng'ano çia magegania makĩregana na birosobi ya ũtunyani na
ũkoroni. Harĩ itanya rĩa gatatũ, rĩrĩa rĩkũnainie na mĩçie ya Nairobi na Dar
es Salaam, ndungatire ũrĩa aikari a kũndũ gũkũ maunaga mawatho marĩa
mareganĩte namo. Uni wa mawatho nĩ wa bata harĩ aikari a mĩçie ĩratun-
gatwo nĩ mũkoroni—muno akĩgeria kũingata andũ airũ. Nĩnjarĩrĩirie ũhoro
wa kũandĩka na thiomi çia kĩ-Abirika harĩ itanya rĩa kana. Ndũmĩrĩte ithako
rĩa ngerekano rĩa kuma Tanzania na rũgano rwa kuma Ethiopia, nĩnjorotire
mũng'eng'ano wa aandĩki na thirikari harĩ ũtũmĩri wa ithaka na mĩgũnda
ta çiũnereria çia maũndũ ngũrani. Ngĩrĩkĩrĩria, ng'ano çiao Yvonne Owuor
na Monica Arac de Nyeko ironania atĩ gũthookia kwa marĩa matũrigiçei-
rie gũtwaranaga na harũ, kũnyita atumia na airĩtu kĩa hinya, na kũnyarira
ndũũrĩrĩ ngũrani. Owuor na Nyeko matumaga irĩma, mĩtitũ, na thĩ nyũmũ ta
çiũnereria çia çaikorojia ya andũ arĩa marĩ ngerekano-inĩ çiao.

CODA: THIS FUTURE LIES IN THE PAST

My overall argument in this book—that representations of land and landscape perform significant metaphorical labor in African literatures—evolves across several geographical spaces. Each chapter's analysis is grounded in a particular locale: western Kenya, central and southern Ethiopia, colonial Tanganyika, postindependence Tanzania, Zimbabwe, Nairobi, Dar es Salaam, Anam Ka'alakol (Lake Turkana), Kampala, and Kitgum in northern Uganda. Moreover, each section contributes to a deeper understanding of the aesthetic choices that authors make when deploying tropes revolving around land, landscape, and the environment. In my first chapter, I argued for mystical realism as a narrative technique that decolonizes our reading and highlights the nonhuman and the supernatural in both the fictional and the natural worlds. I demonstrated the contradictions in fiction by Grace Ogot and Margaret Ogola—straddling both folklore and social realism. I further pursued the aesthetic use of nonhuman life in Yvonne Vera's and Alex Kanengoni's nonlinear narratives. My second chapter examined the incorporation of mysticism and realism into a womanist gaze on Zimbabwean land and landscape. In chapter 3, which focused on the urban landscapes of Nairobi and Dar es Salaam, I investigated how cit(y)zens strategically trespass and transgress. These self-conscious acts of disobedience are important substitutes for belonging—especially in colonial urban spaces that are singularly hostile toward their African residents. My discussion of publishing in African languages related to drama and fiction from Tanzania and Ethiopia, respectively. In that fourth chapter, I expounded on the fraught relationship between artists and ruling regimes, especially regarding use of literary tropes derived from landscapes. Finally, the chapter on Yvonne Owuor and Monica Arac de Nyeko explored how trauma on lands and landscapes often accompanies sexual violence against women and the marginalization of minorities. Owuor and Nyeko transform topographical features into allegories of their characters' psychological landscapes.[1]

This book has chronicled representations of African lands and landscapes from a variety of platforms, including but not limited to decolonial studies, ecofeminism, and African indigenous ontologies. I will use this coda to argue that we transform our reading of literatures from the African continent by engaging and flexing the region's indigenous languages. Doing so distinguishes colonial versus decolonial depictions of ecologies and languages. As

I was reflecting on the rich, yet largely unacknowledged, ecological expertise housed in Africa's indigenous languages, I also pondered on the production of academic knowledge regarding the continent's environment. My book self-consciously emerges from my family's history. In these circles, then and now, Gĩkũyũ and Kiswahili, not English, reign supreme. For many of my extended family who never graduated high school, English is intimidating. They are literate and fluent enough to navigate government or even banking bureaucracy, but they are much more confident, and eloquent, in Gĩkũyũ. Why would I create knowledge about their lives and then lock that content behind a linguistic wall?

I experimented with Gĩkũyũ and Kiswahili translations as one attempt to break down these barriers. I begin and end this coda with Gĩkũyũ and Kiswahili translations of my summation paragraph, respectively. The very oddity of this gesture points to the great need for more Africanist scholarship to embrace the continent's linguistic diversity. In examining representations of land and landscape in literature from Eastern Africa, my project uncovers indigenous ontologies and their use in challenging Enlightenment racism, European imperialism, and the utilitarian approach to global ecologies undergirded by a bifurcated view of nature/culture. I have also demonstrated that African languages serve as rich depositories of local and regional ecological expertise. Throughout this book, my investigation of literary texts emerges from juxtaposing texts and delving into close readings. My reading of Eastern and Southern African fiction exposes intertextual patterns in the aesthetic use of land, landscape, and a wide variety of ecological tropes. I take seriously the Eastern African literary world created over the last half century. I approach this fictional realm not only to uncover postindependence utopias but also to experience a recalibration of Western ontologies. The artistic production that I examine—while often couched in the form of a Western literary device, the novel—simultaneously seeks to undermine its own foundation.

These texts, I argue, strategically advance decolonial modes of resistance in response to global marches of empire and irreparable environmental destruction. My project teases out meaning through connections, configurations, and parallels across an Eastern and Southern African oeuvre rarely juxtaposed and read in conversation. The central argument chases apparitions whose presence in the texts chosen is not explicit. Rather, ideas are hinted at or alluded to. My thesis succeeds by stringing together literary experiences that, while tenuous, are discursively profitable when substantially reflected upon. The literary terrain over which this book exists has few signposts, and even less clarity. Instead, I rely on the smells, sounds, sights, and wind patterns that manifest as authorial word choice, stylistic devices, and intertextuality. These are the navigational instruments that support a critical exploration of allusions to land, depictions of landscapes, and the presence of nonhuman animals and topographical features in work by Eastern and Southern African writers. Across the canon considered herein, we encounter geographic features slightly altered. Lands and landscapes are not fully transparent; whether dimly lit or brightly featured, they are, however, always present. I demonstrate this by adopting the moon as an allegorical device for my own critical engagement. Under a clear night sky, with the moon reflecting rays from a sun hidden since dusk, human and nonhuman life appears otherworldly. So too, do the topographies on which these life forms exist. While imagining the critical intervention that land and landscape accomplishes, I was drawn to the imagery of reflection and illumination, especially as it pertains to moonlit experiences. I wish to conclude by briefly elaborating on the use of African languages in the critical scholarship of African literatures. There remains considerable scope for incorporating hundreds, perhaps even thousands, of Africa's languages into the production of knowledge about the continent, for an audience based on the continent, and beyond.[2] The rest of this concluding section suggests how the use of indigenous languages might be enhanced and elaborated upon in future scholarship. To demonstrate this point, I discuss Peter Hewitt's *Kenya Cowboy: A Police Officer's Account of the Mau Mau Emergency* (1999), Ngũgĩ wa Thiong'o's *Petals of Blood* (1977), as well as Ronjaunee Chatterjee, Alicia M. Christoff, and Amy R. Wong's "Undisciplining Victorian Studies" (2020).

AN APOLOGIA FOR WHITE SUPREMACY

Peter Hewitt's *Kenya Cowboy* is based on the author's professional experience as a colonial cop. The Kenya police, joined by the British military—and civilian vigilante groups known as the Kenya Police Reserve—were tasked with decimating an armed uprising coordinated under the Ithaka na Wĩyathi (Kenya Land and Freedom) Army. Forty-five years after his residency in the White Highlands, Hewitt's autobiography is a virulently racist defense of his police work. It is a one-sided discussion of settler life. A more comprehensive account is hampered not only by Hewitt's inability to seek out any legitimacy to armed struggle against the British Crown but also by his lack of fluency in either Gĩkũyũ or Kiswahili—the two most common languages at his Kipipiri office. The text opens with Hewitt's arrival in Kenya and follows with his police training. The rest of the memoir compiles his interactions with white settler farmers. Hewitt also chronicles his operations seeking and hunting down Itungati—the Ithaka na Wĩyathi soldiers he choicely refers to as "barbaric," "inveterate oath-takers," "primitive," "bloody repugnant," or simply "inhuman and so beastly" (Hewitt 1999, 168. 170. 171. 173). That Hewitt's text was first published just twenty years ago destroys commonly held, though unstated, hopes that such open antiblackness is neatly confined to the nineteenth century, or at most not beyond the 1950s. That there have been two additional printings of this book, in 2001 and 2008, demonstrates that what would otherwise be viewed as fringe beliefs still have portent currency. David Maughan-Brown's *Land, Freedom, and Fiction: History and Ideology in Kenya* (1985) deftly lays out the overt bigotry associated with colonial narratives in support of empire. Caroline Elkins's *Imperial Reckoning: The Untold Story of Britain's Gulag in Kenya* (2005) and David Anderson's *Histories of the Hanged: The Dirty War in Kenya and the End of Empire* (2005) have both exposed Britain's human rights abuses as it fought Kenya's campaigns for political autonomy. Why, then, does Hewitt's text still peddle a revisionist approach to the violent story of Britain's Kenya colony? Having styled himself a Kenya *cowboy*, Hewitt must needs have his *Indian*—no matter that he is several thousand miles too far from the American West. To do so, the author describes repeated "whooping" and "warbling" whenever Ithaka na Wĩyathi troops attacked colonial settlements, police stations, and farmhouses (Hewitt 1999, 136, 183). This is incredibly odd because not only would the dictates of stealth and surprise attacks on a much better armed British militia encourage silence, but no other historian records these "shouts and whoops" (Hewitt 1999, 135). Neither the previously mentioned historiographies by Elkins and Anderson nor Paul Maina's *Six Mau Mau Generals* (1977) relate the bloodcurdling screams that supposedly so enamored Hewitt.

Despite this, Hewitt unwittingly makes a strong case for wider use of African languages, not just in the academy but also in the twenty-first-century knowledge economy. For one, Africanist scholarship that wholly eschews Africa's linguistic diversity problematically mirrors Hewitt's own research and writing process. It is incredulous to take *Kenya Cowboy* as an authoritative text given that Hewitt's self-confessed "pathetic command" of Gĩkũyũ and Kiswahili limits his interactions with indigenous communities to simple salutations and rambunctious orders (Hewitt 1999, 77). Hewitt demonstrates great understanding of the settlers' point of view, with good reason: this is the only side whose case he listens to and asks questions of. Certainly, there were Kenyan leaders and agitators with whom Hewitt could have conversed in English. But not only is Hewitt quite suspicious of such learned uppity, most of his daily experiences were with subsistence farmers: fluent in Gĩkũyũ, but illiterate in English.

In addition, Hewitt resorts to a common trope in colonial narratives: the destructive nature of indigenous agriculture as opposed to the productivity of the settler farmstead. While describing the biography of one guerrilla soldier he hunted and captured, *Kenya Cowboy* reports that

> his mother, Wanjiru, like all Kikuyu women, was contentment itself clearing and planting the virgin forest land. She would, inevitably, reap rich harvests twice a year for several years and then, when the earth was exhausted, she would leave the plot for nature to rejuvenate in the course of time, and move on to another virgin plot. . . . It was subsistence farming with no care for the future or of land husbandry. Her abiding preoccupation was to provide enough food for today. All her fellow tribeswomen applied themselves in similar fashion so why shouldn't she perpetuate the tribal practice? (Hewitt 1999, 209)

The writer's accusation of destructive indigenous farming is premised on a complete misunderstanding of Gĩkũyũ agroforestry and the practices of shift cultivation. As I noted in my introductory discussion of Kissidougou, colonial readings of African environments often, and erroneously, reversed the forest-farmland transition. What they perceived as local deforestation in pursuit of farmland was communal reforestation. Gĩkũyũ farmers mixed trees with food crops, and when the forest cover was no longer conducive to subsistence production, they would move on to treeless spaces and begin the same cycle. Wanjiru, despite Hewitt's assertion, was not cutting down trees for farmland. She was in fact tilling grassland, planting indigenous trees, and expanding forest cover. Indeed, Nobel laureate Wangari Maathai's Green Belt Movement—and its countrywide reforestation efforts—is premised upon this local knowledge.

Hewitt's caricature of Gĩkũyũ agriculture is not, of course, meant to be representative. Instead, this depiction serves as a rhetorical foil to the abundantly productive settler farmer. Of one such settler homestead, *Kenya Cow-*

boy describes how "the fields were neatly tilled and planted, cattle grazed peacefully in slowly moving herds, the water of a dam shone enticingly by the side of a solid thicket of cedar" (Hewitt 1999, 212). Of another pioneer, we learn that he possessed "three thousand acres of wheat and oats, and a hundred and fifty of pyrethrum plus a hundred head of cattle. Then there were his pigs, wattle plantations and maize shambas" (165). The author paints white farmers as especially gifted and fruitful. He deploys the pastoral idyll as an aesthetic, painting rural pictures of agricultural paradise threatened by "woolly-haired [Gĩkũyũ] boys" who form a "blindly ecstatic blood-lusting mob" (135, 136). Hewitt never describes indigenous crop and animal husbandry using figures to demonstrate their high yields. Evidently, the white man "was entitled to his claim as one of the colony's top farmers. Just the sort of successful settler at whom the covetous wrath and discontent of land-hungry Kikuyu was directed" (166)! Rather than delve into the politics of land alienation, or the economics of farming subsidies and affordable capital, Hewitt recasts Gĩkũyũ grievances as naked envy. Jealousy, quite naturally, cannot be resolved through political self-rule, economic sovereignty, or cultural renaissance.

Paradoxically, Hewitt begrudgingly covets the ecological expertise of his Ithaka na Wĩyathi enemies. It is worth noting that the Kenya Land and Freedom Army never referred to itself as Mau Mau. The latter was an equivalent of the n-word in the United States: a derogatory epithet intended to put down those who opposed white supremacy. Ithaka na Wĩyathi soldiers lived off the land, and indeed deployed the Kenyan terrain against the British. Hewitt, during one of his police operations, encounters a rebel hideout; he is quite impressed, describing the space as a "classic of improvisation and of a coming to terms with nature" (274). Elsewhere, he confesses to "having paid tribute to [the guerrillas'] excellent bush-craft and elusiveness" (231). Blinded by his racialized lenses, however, the writer does not question how Ithaka na Wĩyathi soldiers gained this knowledge in the first place.

The ecological mastery that Hewitt describes here marks Africans as more animal than human. This proficiency, Hewitt suggests, has not been uncovered through multigenerational custodianship of the environment. Instead, this competence is irrefutable evidence that "there are varying levels of human evolution and many of these terrorists have barely reached the accepted stage of evolution as human beings" (176). With this statement, which the author ascribes to a rich settler called Mr. Harry Dawling, Hewitt connects his work to centuries' worth of quasi-scientific research about human diversity. It is no surprise, then, that Ithaka na Wĩyathi oath ceremonies supposedly included public orgies, animal bestiality, and the "foulest of sights—excrement, semen in gourds, menstrual discharge from the women, blood of the slaughtered beast, even such nauseating objects as a dismembered human penis" (176). Through the palpable hate in this description, Hewitt prepares his audience for a revelation that among the Gĩkũyũ cannibalism is an ancient practice, one that "many were indulging in when the white man arrived in Kenya" (177). Aside from accusing Gĩkũyũ fighters of evil, Hewitt describes them as harboring an "unriddable [*sic*], all-pervading and unforgettable Mau Mau terrorist's special odour" (201). The purpose of these characterizations in the text is to camouflage British atrocities. If the enemy whom Hewitt and his colleagues in the security apparatus face is less than human, then there can be no recourse to the Geneva Convention on conducting war nor any misgivings regarding human rights abuse. In fact, there can be no space to reflect on, and critique, the conduct of war in defense of colonial imperialism.

BRITISH ARMED FORCES AND ENVIRONMENTAL DESTRUCTION

Ultimately, despite Hewitt's finger-pointing at Gĩkũyũ farmers for environmentally unsound practices, his book describes remarkable colonial damage wrought on local fauna. Regardless of the despicable politics enshrined in *Kenya Cowboy*, the text aesthetically depends upon representations of land and landscape for its argumentative thrust. Hewitt's Afro-pessimism and naked racism set him apart from any of the Pan-African writers I've discussed in previous chapters. However, his use of literary tropes based on land, landscape, and the environment is a key point of similarity. One member of the Kenya Land and Freedom Army is quoted as saying that what they truly feared in the forests was

> wildlife injured during bombing sorties. Animals maddened by the pain of great wounds cavorted dangerously through the forest and would charge out on terrorists quite unprovoked. It was the bigger game, usually so inoffensive, that kept them petrified in their hideouts after a heavy bombing raid on the moorlands, valleys and bamboo thickets. (Hewitt 1999, 233)

This confession is noteworthy for its explicit link between animal wounding and British use of explosive ordnance. As previously noted in chapters 1 and 2, the presence of nonhuman life serves as a key rejoinder to European imperial projects. Animal casualties of colonial wars bring us back full circle to my discussion regarding folklore and the agency afforded flora, fauna, and the supernatural. Aside from wounded wild animals, we also witness "acres of ten-foot-high reed falling before an army of glinting, slashing, weaving [machetes], like an impossibly enormous human scythe" (Hewitt 1999, 282). In the aftermath of clearing this swamp, numerous hippopotami were "shot in mistake for terrorists by jittery soldiers . . . The morning patrols invariably came across a dead or dying cow or bull hippo" (285). Finally, approximately "2,800 bombs were flung into a square-mile target area" to flush out insurgents (284). Injured big game, dying hippos, and bomb-cratered landscapes are ecological collateral damage.

Hewitt demonstrates the pitfalls of a colonialist scholarship that ignores the cultural heritage of its subjects. Conversely, decolonial work acknowledges Africa's indigenous languages and, by extension, a community's sociohistorical tradition. I referenced Ngũgĩ's memoir in my introductory chapter; similar liberatory concerns are evident in his fiction. Novels such as *Petals of Blood* (1977) demonstrate that an important part of this activism involves highlighting the deep connections between global capitalism and its adverse effects on ecosystems all around the world.[3] Critics view Ngũgĩ's oeuvre as staging a "set of irresolvable questions pertaining to the legacy of colonialism, the possibility of postcolonial revolution, and the place of culture and the role of the intellectual in the postcolony" (Amoko 2010, 2). Ngũgĩ's literary career, embarked on at the twilight of Britain's East African colonies, has queried the land issue from multiple perspectives—especially Marxist criticism from the late Seventies onward.[4] Ngũgĩ's discussions of the (post)colonial nation-state are filled with communities alienated from their land—which had previously inspired a feeling of home and sense of belonging. Disenfranchised by colonial settlers and postcolonial rulers, Ngũgĩ's heroes and heroines repeatedly resort to fellow peasants and factory workers for political agency and a chance to resist economic oppression.

It is in *Petals of Blood* that Ngũgĩ crystalizes his critique of the African postcolony. The text begins with an exploration of land alienation as it was perpetrated by colonial authorities. Ngũgĩ's characters lament that "the white man first took the land, then the goats and cows, saying these were hut taxes or fines after every armed clash"; it was only after this that colonial forces captured young Africans to provide farm labor (1977, 18). Moreover, the rural folk depicted in *Petals of Blood* are deeply suspicious of mercantile activities; they still remember how the European settler "took their land, their sweat, and their wealth and told them that the coins he had brought, which could not be eaten, were the true wealth" (18). Ngũgĩ further demonstrates his misgivings toward global capitalism and the rhetoric of development, especially as it is applied to the Global South. By mimicking newspaper language, he produces an obituary for three politicians murdered in Ilmorog—where most of the novel's action takes place—that compares local political elites with former colonial explorers. Ngũgĩ notes that the "the three will be an irreplaceable loss to Ilmorog. They built Ilmorog from a tiny nineteenth-century village reminiscent of the days of Krapf and Rebman into a modern industrial town" (5). The author is complicating the story of postcolonial progress and development by making more vivid the link between violent alienation of land in colonial epochs and the continued disenfranchisement of the poor at the hands of black political elites. Just as colonial rhetoric celebrated Johannes Ludwig Krapf's and Johannes Rebman's civilizing touch, Ngũgĩ parodies the politicians' modernizing hand; in both cases, progress is determined by outsiders—colonial or otherwise—whose paternalism overrules Ilmorog's future aspirations.[5] Later in the text, Ngũgĩ provides another example not only of the destructive nature of colonial technologies but also of the toll these took on African landscapes. In the olden days,

> the land was not for buying. It was for use. It was also plenty, you need not have beaten one yard over and over again. The land was also covered with forests. The trees called rain. They also cast a shadow on the land. But the forest was eaten by the railway. (82)

Petals of Blood is deeply antagonistic toward capitalist colonial forms of economic production and their inherently rapacious and unsustainable use of natural resources. Unfortunately, postindependence regimes continued in much the same vein, betraying the people's hopes of socioeconomic reform that was in line with local beliefs. By depicting "the Bible, the Coin, [and] the Gun" as the "Holy Trinity," Ngũgĩ also aims his censure at colonial religion (88).

Colonial alienation of land was traumatic for indigenous communities due to the resultant loss of sovereignty and material well-being. Ngũgĩ's characters in *Petals of Blood* lament that "there was a time . . . we had power over the movement of our limbs. We made up our own words and sang them and we danced to them. But there came a time when this power was taken from us" (115). Ngũgĩ employs the metaphor of dance, choreography, and movement—key elements of precolonial African performativity—to think through indigenous political institutions before the advent of European rule. By doing so, the writer further underlines the homegrown nature of precontact African forms of life—whatever their limitations. In the aftermath of colonial incursions, African populations moved, "but somebody else called out the words and the song" (115). This is starkly contrasted to epochs when "Ilmorog, or all Africa, controlled its own earth"; Ngũgĩ's interest in precolonial self-determination demonstrates that political and economic systems in precontact times were inherently more organic (125).[6] The postindependence modernization of the Kenyan state has been painful for Ilmorog's community, with many of them dispossessed while the rest provide unskilled labor for agribusiness and manufacturing concerns. Despite their efforts, Ilmorogians can at best only hope to dwell in informal settlements; they are shut out from upper class neighborhoods and the bungalows formerly owned by European settlers (302). This crisis in wealth accumulation—by the few at the expense of the many—causes deep soul-searching.[7] As Ngũgĩ asks, "Why, anyway, should soil, any soil, which after all was what was Kenya, be owned by an individual? Kenya, the soil, was the people's common shamba" (302). At the core of this dilemma is the tension between individual ambitions versus communal needs.[8] While Ilmorogians, and Kenyan peasants and laborers at large, view the country's natural resources as available for public needs, a faction within the state has usurped power to amass personal fortunes.[9] I take it for granted that African communities have robust ideas about economic, legislative, and political reform.[10] In my next, and final section, I sketch out how best to harness Africa's *tradition of innovation*: through explicit use of African indigenous languages in knowledge production.

(UN)DISCIPLINING AFRICAN(A) STUDIES

The missing piece in Eastern and Southern African decolonization has been land reparations and genuine efforts at restorative justice. These can be achieved through dignity restoration—an initiative founded on "principles of restorative justice [that] seeks to rehabilitate the dispossessed and reintegrate them into the fabric of society through an emphasis on process" (Atuahene 2014, 4). One immediate and effective way for African nation-states to incorporate their citizens into the governing process is through the production of knowledge in indigenous languages.[11] A conducive ecosystem for the successful implementation of this aspiration includes not only policy directives but also financial and infrastructural investments.[12] While the translations that bookend this coda are no more than a few hundred words, they threaten to upend standardized North American processes of publishing, peer reviewing, and disseminating critical scholarship. For one, my own facility with Gĩkũyũ is minimal. Though I speak the language fluently, none of the Kenyan private schools I attended taught it. And while I did take twelve years of Kiswahili grammar and literature, I need collaborative expertise to polish up the language. These challenges, however, I see as opportunities for a more expansive kind of African literary criticism. Indigenous languages are unique ontologies with specific ways of seeing the world, interacting with nature, and understanding the human condition. Aside from being good scholarly practice, deliberate use of indigenous languages ignites fresh ways of problem solving. This process could help us think outside the academy.[13] Moreover, the scope for collaborating with nonacademic cultural practitioners to augment institutional expertise is sizeable.[14] The academy often speaks about public-facing humanities, and I think indigenous languages are one concrete way to begin that shift. Finally, representation matters. Wangui wa Goro's (2007) argument in an essay titled "Translating Africa and Leadership: What Is Africa to Me?" is instructive. Goro muses that "translation produces ways for societies to understand the workings of communities other than their own" (158). For millions of people around the globe, chances of seeing academic research or even state-produced knowledge in their own languages are few and far between. Inevitably, this either causes a feeling of alienation or perpetuates a disconnect between local concerns and top-down directives.

The very recent debates about "Undisciplining Victorian Studies" are a case in point. Ronjaunee Chatterjee, Alicia M. Christoff, and Amy R. Wong (2020) incite a rejection, radical rethinking, and fundamental unmaking of the academic "partitioning and co-opting of knowledge." Superficially, we have previously done this. Some of the most enticing and readable scholarly work borrows strands of thought from across diverse knowledge areas. What Chatterjee, Christoff, and Wong urge, however, is far more groundbreaking. They solicit for a revision of the very processes of creating and curating knowledge. What they envision

is not quick or easy, nor is it work that is necessarily ever completed. Ours is an ongoing, careful, and deliberate effort. We want to develop a truly relational thinking that does not stop at engaging scholarship across fields and disciplines for a richer cross-fertilization of ideas, but that might extend into coalition-based politics and activism and a refashioning of academic structures to better serve the purposes of equity and justice. (Chatterjee, Christoff, and Wong 2020)

I think the "refashioning of academic structures" described above necessarily includes a strategic repositioning of African languages in the critical scholarship of African literatures. To date, first-tier academic journals have yet to devise scalable, sustainable models for production of Africanist scholarship in African languages. The *African Studies Review* deliberately aims for regional balance by consolidating book reviews into broadly conceived categories: East, West, Central, and Southern Africa. The *Journal of the African Literature Association* regularly publishes peer-reviewed articles in French, though most of the pieces are in English. Cleary, these publications are attempting to address the cultural, linguistic, and sociopolitical diversity on the African continent. However, neither of these venues, nor even *Research in African Literatures* and *African Literature Today*, feature critical work in Igbo, Zulu, Twi, Amharic, Somali, or any other African language. Ngũgĩ 's "Rũrĩmĩ na Karamu: Ithoga Harĩ Athamaki a Abirika" (2013), published by the *Journal of African Cultural Studies*, is an exception to the rule. This Gĩkũyũ essay was simultaneously published in translation as "Tongue and Pen: A Challenge to Philosophers from Africa." *Mũtiiri*, a journal Ngũgĩ established as a platform for Gĩkũyũ culture and writing, is no longer in circulation.

It is not necessarily that journals would have to wholly overturn their publications. Perhaps special editions on the novels, poetry, drama, or short fiction in an African language would spawn a collection of critical work in Kiswahili, isiXhosa, Hausa, and so forth. Fruitful collaborations with academic departments on the continent and beyond could help. The strategic use of translations would also provide a growing body of work. In the way Chatterjee, Christoff, and Wong outline "the need for all scholars, and not just scholars of color, to integrate considerations of race and racial capitalism— the most urgent questions of our time—into their work. And to do so rigorously: after deep reading and learning and listening," I perceive similar opportunities in the use of African languages. Questions regarding the use of African languages "are not ornaments or accessories. They should radically shape—that is to say, at its very roots—how we construct and conduct [Africanist] intellectual inquiry and imagine its stakes" (Chatterjee, Christoff, and Wong 2020). Garrett Hardin (1968) described a class of solutions that were quite unlike the technical kind. The ontological revisions suggested here entail a "change in human values or ideas of morality" (1243).

My own attempts, which bracket this conclusion, are belated and, relatively, miniscule. That they've been a long time coming, despite graduate training and mentorship by senior colleagues, suggests this is an area of need that has yet to be recognized as such. While exemplary avenues such as the Mabati-Cornell Kiswahili Prize for African Literature encourage a new generation of authors and poets, they risk perpetuating the divide: African languages produce primary sources, which is then *processed* using European languages. This paradigm is replicated elsewhere: a spring 2020 special edition of the *Yoruba Studies Review* contains several English-language essays based on a Yoruba historical novel by Chief Isaac Oluwole Delano. Delano's *Aiye D'Aiye Oyinbo* (1955) is available in an English translation as *Welcome to the White Man's World,* and yet none of the literary scholarship on the text is availed in the novel's original Yoruba. Why is there such a disconnect? And more importantly, how can the academy support fieldwork and language study so that future scholars get comprehensive training? I get the sense that many fields in the humanities and social sciences—history, political economy, geography, and so on—foreground field trips and language preparation in a way that literary criticism does not. Archival visits are a key exception to this, though if the historical records are in English, French, and other European languages there may not be a similar need for translators and language study. My proposal is not that readers should seek advanced fluency in Gĩkũyũ before encountering the world of Ngũgĩ's *Wizard of the Crow* (2006)—originally published as *Mũrogi wa Kagogo* (2004)—but that they creatively imagine how familiarity, intermediate fluency even, with the author's first language opens fruitful realms of interpretation. In the same vein, how would an understanding of Igbo cosmology, and the language within which this ontology is housed, enrich our encounters with Chinua Achebe's *Things Fall Apart* (1958)? The technologies of digital humanities will enhance the permutations in which these experiments with African languages might occur. And our ongoing efforts to craft public-facing humanities will benefit.

KIISHIO: PALE TULIPOTOKA

Mada yangu katika kitabu hiki—kwamba ardhi na mazingira ni za umuhimu katika fasihi za bara la Afrika—ninaiendeleza katika jiografia mbali mbali.

Sura zangu zinao msingi katika mahali haswa: magharibi mwa Kenya, kusini
na katikati mwa nchi ya Uhabeshi, Tanganyika ya mkoloni, Tanzania huru,
Zimbabwe, Nairobi, Dar es Salaam, Ziwa Turkana, Kampala, na Kitgum huko
Uganda kaskazini. Kila sehemu inaonyesha jinsi waandishi huumba hadithi
zao wanapotumia mifano na vielelezo vinavyoambatana na udongo, ardhi, na
mazingira. Katika sura ya kwanza, nilionyesha jinsi vitabu vya Grace Ogot na
Margaret Ogola vinao usanii wenye utata—ilhali hadithi za kale zinasisitiza
mimea, wanyama, na mazingaombwe, riwaya inawapendelea binadamu na
matendo yao. Nililifuatilia wazo hili la wasanii kutumia uhai usio wa kib-
inadamu katika ngano za Yvonne Vera na Alex Kanengoni. Hadithi zao,
badala ya kuufuata mpangilio wa moja kwa moja, zinao mfumo wa mviringo.
Sehemu hii ya pili ilichunguza matumizi ya falsafa ya "womanism" katika
mtazamo wa kimazingira. Kwenya sura ya tatu, inayolenga miji ya Nairobi na
Dar es Salaam, nilizichambua tabia haramu za wakaazi ambao hukiuka she-
ria ili kusisitiza utu wao. Uhalifu huu ni mbadala ya haki miliki, hasa katika
miji ya ukoloni ambayo inawatimua wakaazi wao wa Kiafrika. Nilizungum-
zia uchapishaji katika lugha za Kiafrika nikitumia tamthilia ya kiTanzania
na riwaya ya Kihabeshi. Katika sura hii ya nne, nilifafanua mgogoro mkali
kati ya wasanii na serikali, haswa kwenye matumizi ya vielelezo vinavyo-
husu ardhi au mazingira. Mwishowe, sehemu ya tano inafanya utafiti kuhusu
maandishi ya Yvonne Owuor na Monica Arac de Nyeko. Owuor na Nyeko
wanaonyesha jinsi uharibifu wa mazingira hujitokeza kama dhulma ya kijin-
sia na unyanyasaji wa jamii mbalimbali. Waandishi hawa wawili wanavitu-
mia vipengele vya kijiografia kama vielelezo vya kisaikolojia katika maisha
ya wahusika wao.

NOTES

INTRODUCTION

1. *Swahili beyond the Boundaries: Literature, Language, and Identity* by Alamin Mazrui (2007) describes the evolution and consolidation of a Kiswahili literature and identity.

2. See, for example, Bessie Head's *Maru* (1971) and Rebeka Njau's *Ripples in the Pool* (1978) and *The Sacred Seed* (2003). All three texts depict land and landscape in ways that chronicle deep connections between communities and topographies.

3. Jaji's previous *Beating the Graves* (2017) similarly evokes the Zimbabwean landscape in interrogations of contemporary politics and the experience of diaspora.

4. Jorge Gertel, Richard Rottenberg, and Sandra Calkins (2014, 1) demonstrate that land is vital in forming identities; they aptly summarize the importance that land holds in contemporary Kenya.

5. The *OED Online* (2021) traces "landscape" as a technical term in painting first appearing in 1598. The colloquial "landskip," originally a Dutch import into the British Isles, presumably precedes the standardized form. In ca. 825 "land" had acquired meaning as soil designated for specific use; a century earlier, by ca. 725 "land" already referred to "territory [demarcated] by natural or political boundaries." All these nuances are layered onto each other in contemporary uses of the word.

6. Jennifer Wenzel (2020, 8) describes this immense diversity encountered across the African continent as a "*multiscalar reading practice* [that] shuttles between the microscopically specific and the world-historical" (emphasis in original).

7. At a transhemispheric level, Paul Gilroy's *The Black Atlantic* (1993) argues for the rise of a Black identity that was/is unstable, mutable, and "always unfinished, always being remade" (xi).

8. Lazarus (2011, 11) suggests that, even as recently as ten years ago, there existed room for a renewed focus on representations of land and landscape against a colonial history of commodity production and the "forced integration of hitherto uncapitalised societies, or societies in which the capitalist mode of production was not hegemonic, into a capitalist world system."

9. A decade before Lazarus's polemic, Ato Quayson's *Postcolonialism: Theory, Practice or Process* (2000) envisioned a postcolonial analysis that linked disparate phenomena to changes in colonized societies, cultures, and politics (19). Unlike Lazarus, Quayson does not place explicit focus on the capitalist underpinning from which colonialism emerged.

10. This dissonance is best theorized by Homi Bhabha's (1990, 1) work on the "particular ambivalence that haunts the idea of the nation, the language of those who write of it and the lives of those who live it."

11. As Graham Huggan and Helen Tiffin (2010, 6) point out, colonized peoples were administratively lumped together with local flora and fauna, animalized, and "forced or co-opted over time into western views of the environment." *The Green Breast of the New World: Landscape, Gender, and American Fiction* (Westling 1998) reads Willa Cather, Ernest Hemingway, William Faulkner, and Eudora Welty to argue that gendering the landscape as female is a common trope in twentieth-century American writing.

12. To the extent that there is truth in my interpretation, it also unduly posits African communities as wholesale imbibers and replicators of colonial hegemony. Although colonized communities recognized themselves in the caricatures offered by European depictions of the African continent, they also complicated such top-down views. I think an alternative explanation as to why land was/is gendered female in these transactions has to do with the import accorded marital negotiations. Historically, the in-law relationship is a sacred one, binding what were previously two strangers into familial networks that were all but irrevocable. Gendering land as female encourages two parties unfamiliar with each other into honest dealings given the permanency of building a home, starting a farm, or investing in a business. Like the in-law connections that are the aftermath of all successful nuptials, land transactions add a new member to the community. Concerns about that newcomer's character are channeled through tenuous claims to kinship. The imagined family will discipline the new arrival, if need for such censure ever arose. My anecdotal evidence raises further questions: How does the buyer's identity influence the rhetoric of land transactions? Would a woman buying land be a recipient of the msichana formula? How about a male-female couple? Nuances of the buyer's age, gender, class, and perhaps even sexual orientation (as "read" by the seller) would presumably elicit a variety of responses. This line of inquiry deserves more work.

13. Inevitably, a study of colonial cultures is an examination of "the struggle between the colonizers and the colonized" (Desai 2001, 4). What is particularly pertinent to my project is the continuation of exploitative global capitalism. In other words, "the 'post' in postcolonial marks not an end of colonialism, but an end of a particular mode of colonialism which then shifts its gears and evolves to another stage (obviously triggering a concomitant shift in the global struggles against it)" (Mukherjee 2010, 5–6). Upamanyu Mukherjee's "global struggles" manifest in Eastern and Southern African literature and especially its aesthetic representations of space and place. That is, this ideational contest is played out on the land.

14. Writing by Kenya's Wangari Muta Maathai, Nobel Peace Prize laureate, and Nige-

ria's Ken Saro-Wiwa, author and community organizer, is a good example. For example, *The World We Once Lived In* (Maathai 2010, 11) indicts the misperception of planetary ecology that "there are always more trees to be cut, more land to be utilized, more fish to be caught, more water to dam or tap, and more minerals to be mined or prospected for . . . [it is this instrumentalist approach] that has created so many of the deep ecological wounds visible across the world." See also *The Talking of Trees* (Nderitu 2021), a play based on Wangari Maathai's environmental stewardship.

15. To better appreciate literature's power, we need only revisit Europe's invention of an Oriental Other: "a place of romance, exotic beings, haunting memories and landscapes, [and] remarkable experiences" (Said 1979, 1). What began as phantasm on the canvases and manuscripts of European artists soon morphed into territorial desires and government policies. What was previously conceived finally manifested in the choices of realpolitik.

16. Other important studies of forests and the transition from countryside to urban area include *Forests: The Shadow of Civilization* (Harrison 1993) and *The Country and the City* (Williams 1973).

17. As James Fairhead and Melissa Leach (1996, 15) conclude, reversing the way Kissidougou's landscape has been read necessarily means overturning the entrenchment of power.

18. The *Routledge Companion to the Environmental Humanities* advances the recognition of ecological disasters as a "fundamentally cultural process" (Heise, Christensen, and Niemann 2017, 9).

19. We must approach the challenge of rising sea levels, melting polar icecaps, and extreme weather patterns not only with an "environmental and scientific literacy" but also with a "critical and historical" expertise (Clark 2012, 4).

20. However, what Henri Lefebvre's (1991, 39) *The Production of Space* posits as representational space "dominated—and hence passively experienced space—which the imagination seeks to change and appropriate" is more closely aligned to the exact colonial and imperial landscapes that African ecocriticism is eager to reframe.

21. "Political Mobilization and Conflict on Kenya's Coast: Land, Indigeneity and Elections" (Harris 2014) makes a similar argument about the manipulation of ethnic identities and election-related violence in Mombasa.

22. Yi-Fu Tuan (1977) notes that "space is a common symbol of freedom" (54).

23. This connection is aptly made in the title of Simon Schama's *Landscape and Memory* (1996). Schama persuasively argues that the mingling of culture and "human perception" necessarily means that "landscape is the work of the mind" (7).

24. Besi Brillian Muhonja's *Radical Utu: Critical Ideas and Ideals of Wangari Muta Maathai* (2020) connects the struggle for personhood, women's empowerment, and environmental rights in the work of Kenyan Nobel Peace Prize laureate Prof. Wangari Muta Maathai.

25. In Australia, Peta Mitchell and Jane Stadler (2011, 47) examine the ways in which colonial literature is "profoundly tied up with national myths of land, landscape, and

identity." Elsewhere, Rebecca Weaver-Hightower (2011, 124) argues that underneath the bluster, colonial writers often betrayed "suspicion of the colonial mission and even guilt over the dispossession of indigenous people."

26. Elsewhere, in *For Space*, Massey (2005, 9) argues that space is necessarily a "product of interrelations."

27. Alongside numerous other brilliant examinations of Ngũgĩ 's writing, see, for example, David Cook and Michael Okenimkpe, *Ngugi wa Thiong'o: An Exploration of His Writing* (1983); James Ogude, *Ngugi's Novels and African History: Narrating the Nation* (1989); Simon Gikandi, *Ngugi wa Thiong'o* (2000); and Brendon Nicholls, *Ngugi wa Thiong'o, Gender, and the Ethics of Postcolonial Reading* (2010).

28. Trinh T. Minh-ha (1989) poignantly captures the competing concerns that female writer-activists face, more so when they also happen to be women of color. In *Woman, Native, Other*, Minh-ha disentangles a series of questions that women writers of color encounter: "Writer of color? Woman writer? Or woman of color? Which comes first? Where does she place her loyalties" (6)?

29. Lisa Brooks (2018) argues that "land itself is an archive that demands interpretation" (13). Brooks examines indigenous languages as a "vastly underutilized archive of place names and concepts" (7).

30. Discussing representations of land and landscape in the current Anthropocene moment demands that we conceptualize "human life at much broader scales of space and time"; this radically alters how we view much of what has been previously familiar to us (Clark 2015, 13).

31. Juxtapose, for instance, Marzec's (2007, 11) analysis about the enclosure of the commons in colonial centers and the cultivation of colonized spaces with Mike Davis's (2001, 9) assertion that in the same fifty years during which "peacetime famine permanently disappeared in Western Europe, it increased so devastatingly throughout much of the colonial world." Food insecurity was not only exported to the Global South but also simultaneously produced the rationale for colonial land acquisitions.

32. Lorenzo Cotula's *The Great African Land Grab? Agricultural Investment and the Global Food System* (2013) places this rupture within the legal-political sphere. Both colonial and postcolonial governments have commoditized land and monetized social relations. There has been a significant erosion of the "social and political embeddedness that characterizes land relations in the real world of local contexts, and the role of land as a basis of social identity and spiritual value" (176). Tobias Haller (2019) makes a similar point about preservation of the commons as a key ingredient in supporting sustainable livelihoods.

33. See also "Lost in Translation: Pro-Poor Development in the Green Revolution for Africa" (Bassett and Munro 2022); "Land of Plenty, Land of Misery: Synergetic Resource Grabbing in Mozambique" (Bruna 2019); "Large-Scale Land Acquisitions as Commons Grabbing: A Comparative Analysis of Six African Case Studies" (Haller et al. 2019); Samrawit Getaneh Damtew, "Land-Grabbing and the Right to Adequate Food in Ethiopia," *African Human Rights Law Journal* 19, 1; a 2019 *Land Use Policy* article by

Ellis Adams et al., "Land Dispossessions and Water Appropriations: Political Ecology and Water Grabs in Ghana"; a June 7, 2016 European Parliament resolution, "New Alliance for Food Security and Nutrition"; a May 2015 Act!onAid report, "New Alliance, New Risk of Land Grabs: Evidence from Malawi, Nigeria, Senegal, and Tanzania"; *Losing Your Land: Dispossession in the Great Lakes* (2014), edited by An Ansoms and Thea Hilhorst; Ruth Hall, "Stop Selling Off African Land—Invest in Farmers Instead," *Guardian*, January 23, 2014; and An Ansoms, "Large-Scale Land Deals and Local Livelihoods in Rwanda: The Bitter Fruit of a New Agrarian Model," *African Studies Review* 56 (3) (2013).

34. The Banjul Charter's unique distinction between human rights and people's rights—as well as its elaboration of duties—are both reminiscent of intergenerational custodial ties associated with communal land stewardship. These caretaking obligations were in deference to both the ancestors and the unborn. This custodial relationship is also embedded in the 1992 United Nations Framework Convention on Climate Change, which explicitly sought to "protect the climate system for present and future generations" (3).

CHAPTER 1

1. Indigenous relationships to land were comprehensive and dynamic. "Land as Indigenous Epistemology" (Dei, Karanja, and Erger 2022) chronicles the multifaceted connections between communities and their landscapes: cultural, economic, epistemological, pedagogical, philosophical, spiritual, and supernatural.

2. In Ogot's *Land without Thunder and Other Stories* (1968), we see a similar deployment of the supernatural. In the eponymous short story, interventions by the non-human in the daily lives of a community include the sacrifice of a young female virgin to Lake Nam Lolwe to bring rain and end a harsh spell of drought (116).

3. Ogola's protagonist, Akoko Obanda, is reminiscent of the strong female characters that Alina Rinkanya (2014) chronicles in several texts by Kenyan women writers. These female characters exude hope and a democratic vision for Kenya; they rely on the natural world, mythology, and spirituality to build coalitions that help manifest their goals. For a more comprehensive review of fiction by African women writers, see Anthonia Kalu's "Women's Literature in African History" (2020).

4. Elsewhere, we witness the ever-present danger that local elites hijack processes of land tenure reform for their own private gain (Achiba and Lengoiboni 2020).

5. Mahmood Mamdani's *Neither Settler nor Native: The Making and Unmaking of Permanent Minorities* (2020) argues that a key objective in the decolonial process is a fundamental recalibration of "who belongs" in the political community (34). African independence in the Sixties was a missed opportunity to overthrow homogenizing notions of the European nation-state; a more decidedly decolonial approach would have pursued the epistemological starting point that "political identities . . . are not natural and are not forever" (35). Instead, postcolonial nations wholly adopted "territorial indirect rule," a system of colonial modernity that privileges the fantasy of pure "tribal

homelands" (13). The ensuing violence erupting from political schemes of ethnic cleansing and national homogeneity was largely predictable.

6. Perhaps in an attempt to reverse some of these harms the African Union's *Declaration on Land Issues and Challenges in Africa* (2009) explicitly foregrounds "the centrality of land to sustainable socio-economic growth" across the continent.

CHAPTER 2

1. *Apartheid and Beyond: South African Writers and the Politics of Place* (Barnard 2006) argues that similar policies of spatial control were underway in apartheid South Africa. See also "Sense of Frustration: The Debate on Land Reform in South Africa" (Müller and Kotzur 2019) for analysis on efforts to reverse land alienation.

2. *On Decoloniality: Concepts, Analytics, Praxis* (Mignolo and Walsh 2018) conjoins theory and practice. Sidestepping binary thinking, Walter Mignolo and Catherine Walsh argue that "theory is doing and doing is thinking" (7). In other words, knowledge and praxis are intertwined. This is encapsulated as simultaneously engaging in "the thinking-doing and doing-thinking of decoloniality" (9).

3. Alice Walker's *In Search of Our Mothers' Gardens: Prose* (2011) and Layli Phillips' introduction to *The Womanist Reader* (2006) both provide foundational definitions of womanism. I am especially interested in womanism's efforts in "restoring the balance between people and the environment/nature" (Phillips 2006, xx).

4. I see strong parallels between this contemporary disruption of colonial histories and the assembly of imperial projects since the 1700s. European colonial projects were characterized by acts of "geographical violence through which virtually every space in the world [was] explored, charted, and finally brought under control" (Said 1995, 225). The exploration and mapping of distant territories were immensely important to colonial ventures. These twin activities constituted a production of knowledge about the native. Consequently, "stories are at the heart of what explorers and novelists say about strange regions of the world; they also become the method colonized people use to assert their own identity and the existence of their own history" (xii).

5. The history of stories as curative is long and varied. "Some Principles of Ecocriticism" (Howarth 1995, 71) describes the "medicine rites of early people [during which] shamans sang, chanted, and danced stories to heal disease or prevent disaster."

6. *The Colonizer and The Colonized* describes this as a "discouraging geography" that surreptitiously condemns its victims to "eternal dependence" (Memmi 1965, 67).

7. Historiographies of anticolonial resistance repeatedly place struggles for cultural artifacts ahead of political campaigning. Likewise, Walter Mignolo and Catherine Walsh (2018, 1, 10) center a profound awareness of "the integral relation and interdependence amongst all living organisms" with planet Earth as a precursor to the successful decoupling from the fantasies of modernity: development, growth, progress, and Western civilization.

8. At the end of empire, as colonial administrators, clergy, educators, scientists, and

soldiers (somehow) packed up and (partially) returned to the colonial centers, they left behind a vastly altered society. Representation of land and landscape was an important political act not only in the run-up to political independence but more so afterward.

9. Land alienating policies are evident in spaces as disparate as present-day South Africa, Zimbabwe, Kenya, and Algeria. The dismantling of such legislation was a big incentive in the formation of anticolonial movements. And yet, as we've witnessed in the last six decades, issues of land reform, redistribution, and access have merely accelerated since the advent of flag independence.

10. "Magic Mountain: 'The Ancestors Cannot Be Relocated'" (Coplan and Moopelo 2021) chronicles the use of caves and mountains as conduits to the supernatural. These geologic features serve as points of contact with ancestral spirits.

11. See "The Imagination of Land and the Reality of Seizure: Zimbabwe's Complex Reinventions" (Chan and Primorac 2004); *Zimbabwe's Land Reform: Myths and Realities* (Scoones et al. 2010); "Divergent Perspectives on the Land Reform in Zimbabwe" (Tarisanyi 2019); "The Politics of Youth Struggles for Land in Post-Land Reform Zimbabwe" (Chipato, Wang, and Zuo 2020); and "Revisiting Zimbabwe's Land Rights, Human Rights and Social Justice: The Post-Mugabe Era" (Chipuriro and Mkodzongi 2022) for a more comprehensive analysis of how the land reform debate has unfolded in Zimbabwe over the last two decades.

12. Southern African communities have responded to the phenomenon of land alienation in a variety of ways: in Lesotho there is use of chiefs, local councils, and other grassroots power brokers to secure land tenure (Leduka, Ntaote, and Takalimane 2018); in Namibia, individuals unite to practice community-based conservation (Welch 2018); finally, in Maputaland, the tri-border region at the nexus of Mozambique, South Africa, and eSwatini, women's vernacular walk songs map and narrativize a sense of place (Impey 2018). White citizens in the Okavango Delta use storytelling as "an important means of asserting and performing senses of belonging" (Gressler 2015, 3).

13. The "Frameworks and Guidelines on Land Policy in Africa" (United Nations Economic Commission for Africa 2010, 8) notes that to the "vast majority of societies in Africa land is regarded not simply as an economic or environmental asset, but as a social, cultural, and ontological resource. Land remains an important factor in the construction of social identity, the organization of religious life and the production and reproduction of culture. . . . land is fully embodied in the very spirituality of society."

CHAPTER 3

1. See "A Prequel to Nollywood: South African Photo Novels and Their Pan African Consumption in the Late 1960s" (Krings 2010) for more information.

2. *Nairobi's Matatu Men: Portrait of a Subculture* (wa Mūngai 2014) provides an in-depth study of Matatu-ism and its cultural aspects.

3. Although the African (Banjul) Charter on Human and People's Rights (1986, Article 14) enumerates citizens' right to housing, this is far from a universal condition.

In *The Challenge of Slums: Global Report on Human Settlements 2003*, United Nations secretary-general Kofi Annan lamented the urbanization of poverty," with informal settlements representing "the worst of urban poverty and inequality" (UN-Habitat 2003, foreword).

4. Macgoye's early writing is often read alongside both Ngũgĩ wa Thiong'o and Grace Ogot. For example, Macgoye's *Song of Nyarloka and Other Poems* (1977) attends to the same themes of rapid social change in Kenya during the Sixties and Seventies as do Ogot's and Ngũgĩ's work. See "Nyarloka's Gift: The Writing of Marjorie Oludhe Macgoye" (Kurtz 2005) and *Urban Obsessions, Urban Fears: The Postcolonial Kenyan Novel* (Kurtz 1998).

5. Sociocultural shifts accompanying the economic dominations inherent in the colonial and neocolonial moments have provided much inspiration for African writers; consequently, "novelists exploit self-reflexive techniques to signal changing circumstances in society" (Mwangi 2009, ix). Mwangi's *Africa Writes Back to Self: Metafiction, Gender, Sexuality* further argues that due to "growing suspicions of the grand narratives of national unity" propagated from the Fifties through the Seventies, African authors sought other means to express themselves; metafiction emerges as one such narrative technique (8).

6. Remnants of this controlling impulse are also visible in the postindependence era. In northern Kenya, for example, the use of fences to restrict access to conservation areas and private ranches has sparked conflict. Local communities advocate for or against porous boundaries and fences as the demands for grazing lands dictate (Løvschal and Gravesen 2021).

7. There is historical evidence that Nairobi's urban planning in the Fifties looked to South Africa as the model to emulate in creating spaces for white minorities living among a black majority. To the extent they could, Nairobi's European settlers instituted their own form of racial segregation, complete with a "color bar" that dictated where black/brown/white could (or could not) go.

8. Vassanji's commitment to multiple histories is especially evident in *Gunny Sack* where he deploys the gunny sack as a motif to free acts of "remembrance and hence of narrative itself, from the strictures of teleology and closure, something which allows the stories to originate from multiple sites and times without losing their connectedness" (Simatei 2000, 30).

9. Vassanji is also critical of the more conservative political tendencies in Asian East African communities. In his quest for "those dynamic, multidirectional, and revolutionary histories of the national people," Vassanji's work on the East African Indian diaspora invites comparison with other fiction that seeks to lay claims of "Africanness" on behalf of communities with Asian heritage (Simatei 2011, 57). The South African political landscape offers examples of how an Indian diaspora has attempted to integrate itself within the host community. *Afrindian Fictions: Diaspora, Race, and National Desire in South Africa* (Rastogi 2008), a text focused on "how different *nonwhite* constituencies interact *with each other in non-western* geographies," suggests "an Africanization of Indian selfhood and an Indianization" of African selfhood as a way to resolve cultur-

al hang-ups produced by the presence of an Indian diaspora in South Africa (Rastogi 2008, 2; emphasis in original). In addition to coining the term "Afrindian" to accommodate the heritage that each group brings to the union, Rastogi documents how Indian South African writers navigate their identity(ies).

10. As a British protectorate, following the demise of Germany's colonial empire with the defeat in World War I, the region was called Tanganyika. It was not till its unification with Zanzibar island that the United Republic of Tanzania was formed.

11. Vassanji's characterization of urban space is quite unlike what we encountered in my previous chapter through Yvonne Vera's description of Selbourne Avenue. Vera's Selbourne, steeped in white supremacy, is insular. Vassanji's Uhuru Street, despite colonial and imperial machinations, is pluralist.

CHAPTER 4

1. "African-Language Literature and Postcolonial Criticism" (Barber 1995, 12) argues that there exists a "network of allusions and cross-references [that] enables audiences in whatever state of literacy to access [literary/performative] texts in one way or another."

2. *The Power of Babel: Language and Governance in the African Experience* (Mazrui and Mazrui 1998) ridicules the artificiality of borders used to classify African indigenous cultures and languages.

3. Notable plays from this era include Penina Mlama's *Hatia* (Guilt), G. Z. Kaduma's *The Canker*, Ngalimecha Ngahyoma's *Huka* (Huka) and *Kijiji Mfanobora* (A Model Village), Emmanuel Mbogo's *Giza Limeingia* (The Dawn of Darkness), K. K. Kahigi and A. A. Ngemero's *Lengo Letu* (Our Objective), and Gervas Moshiro's *Chama Chetu* (Our Party).

4. Across the border in Kenya, Kiswahili novels published since the 1990s have consistently explored allegorical dystopia as sociopolitical intervention (Gromov 2014).

5. Hussein also has a play titled *Alikiona* (no date); a collection of his Kiswahili poetry was published as *Diwani ya Tunzo ya Ushairi ya Ebrahim Hussein* (2016).

6. There has been a similar aversion to his work—with a few exceptions—both in Tanzania and abroad. This phenomenon suggests that critics of African literature, globally, tend to mirror the hierarchies of literary value fashioned within African national public spheres—often characterized by political machinations.

7. As we saw in chapter 1, similar sentiments can be found in Ancient Egypt and over the last millennia of Southern African political entities.

8. Since 2015, there has been tension between the Ethiopian federal government and Oromia communities around Addis Ababa. The main cause for contention has been the government's desire to expand the capital city at the expense of local communities— or so the perception has been (Ademo 2015). What is remarkable is that once again, Ethiopian university students have been at the forefront of antigovernment campaigns to halt all land acquisitions.

9. What makes a piece of literature *Ethiopian*, and by extension *African*? Sahle

Sellasie argues that in Africa's multilingual societies, national literatures should not be classified through language (Kurtz 2007, 193). Therefore, *The Afersata*, even though not written in an Ethiopian language, is part and parcel of Ethiopian culture because of its interest in the country's peasantry, its representation of Ethiopian landscapes, and its participation in a national conversation regarding socioeconomic reform.

10. "Land Tenure, Gender, and Productivity in Ethiopia and Tanzania" (Melesse and Awel 2020) is one of numerous studies that demonstrate positive gains in agricultural productivity when women's land tenure is secured.

11. The extensive terraced landscapes of Konso, southwest Ethiopia, demonstrate another instance of organizational initiative where individual contributions are aligned with communal well-being (Waton 2009).

12. Although extreme, banditry was an option that subjects deployed if all other means of seeking redress failed. Banditry was a sign of open rebellion; "to be a *shifta* meant to rebel against someone in authority or against an institution that had failed to render justice" (Abbink, De Bruijn, and Van Walraven 2003, 95).

CHAPTER 5

1. Africans' rights to "self-determination" and the ability to "free themselves from the bonds of domination" can—in the twenty-first century—be interpreted to include freedom from extreme poverty, food insecurity, and the ravages of climate change (African Union 1986). There's a liberatory bend to the Banjul Charter that autocracies repeatedly overlook, but which Pan-African forces of resistance can channel into decolonial movements.

2. Here, Owuor's aesthetic echoes W. J. T. Mitchell's argument in *Landscape and Power* (1994).

3. "Ecological Postcolonialism in African Women's Literature" (Nfah-Abbenyi 1998) and *Africa's Narrative Geographies: Charting the Intersections of Ecocriticism and Postcolonial Studies* (Crowley 2015) both provide far-ranging surveys of ecocriticism as envisioned by African writers.

4. Monica Arac de Nyeko was shortlisted for the 2004 Caine Prize in African Writing for "Strange Fruit." She won the award in 2007 for another short story, "Jambula Tree."

5. Article 15 of the *Protocol to the African Charter on Human and Peoples' Rights on the Rights of Women in Africa* establishes that women be provided with safe drinking water as well as resources to ensure food security (African Union 2003). The *Framework and Guidelines on Land Policy in Africa: A Framework to Strengthen Land Rights, Enhance Productivity and Secure Livelihoods* (African Union, African Development Bank, and United Nations Economic Commission for Africa 2010) states that "to redress gender imbalances in land holding and use, it is necessary to deconstruct, reconstruct and reconceptualize existing rules of property in land under both customary and statutory

law in ways that strengthen women's access and control of land." The challenge, as always, is that action plans and regional policy initiatives do not wholly translate into improved access to land for African women (Sandilands 1999; Madhavan and Narayan 2020; Ashukem 2020; Ananda, Moseti, and Mugehera 2020; and Laloyo and Tabitha 2022). Nyeko's work exposes this gap between legislative aspirations and lived experiences.

6. Multiple studies tie inequity in land tenure to political violence. This pattern is apparent in northern Uganda (Kobusingye, van Leeuwen, and van Dijk 2017) as well as in eastern Uganda (Kandel 2017). Regionally, we see similar circumstances in the South Sudanese Nuba Mountains (Komey 2010) and in Kenya (Manji 2020; Gravesen 2021).

7. Nyeko's thematic interests closely mirror scholarship that demonstrates links between secure land tenure, not only to the right to food (De Schutter 2010; Chitonge and Mine 2019) but also to environmental rights (Pepper and Hobbs 2020).

8. The strong link between nutritional security and national security has been well established. High agricultural productivity and food security reinforce communal wellbeing (Bonabana, Kirinya, and Muganola 2020; Mwesigye, Barungi, and Guloba 2020; Koech 2020; Adema et al. 2022). The second United Nations Sustainable Development Goal (2021) aims to "end hunger, achieve food security and improved nutrition and promote sustainable agriculture." Similarly, the Paris Agreement (2015, 1) recognizes "the fundamental priority of safeguarding food security and ending hunger." What neither aspirational document acknowledges is that resolving challenges of food insecurity is not merely a policy or governance issue but an ontological task as well. Solutions demands rethinking citizenship and civic participation in one's ecological community.

9. Nyeko's view of writing is that it is both a "vocation" and "a calling" (Ava-Mathew 2009, 1).

10. For instance, the silk cotton tree in the Caribbean is sometimes viewed as the final resting place for ancestors' souls.

11. This is reminiscent of narratives that circulated in Uganda during Idi Amin's reign of terror (1971 to 1979) and the dumping of victims' bodies into the Nile River.

12. The Digital Library of Language Resources lists Kituba as a Creole with approximately 5.5 million speakers and derived from the Kongo language. Here, however, I am more interested in Kituba references to trees as deployed by both Nyeko and Okot p'Bitek in his groundbreaking *Song of Lawino* (1966).

13. There are several studies on effective ways to provide Eastern African women with secure land tenure: *Women's Land Rights and Privatization in Eastern Africa* (Englert and Daley 2008); *Women, Land Justice in Tanzania* (Dancer 2015); and "A History without Women: The Emergence and Development of Subaltern Ideology and the 'Land Question' in Kenya" (Meroka-Mutua 2022).

14. Farther south of Turkana, in the Mara/Serengeti ecosystem, there is renewed appreciation of pastoralism and nomadism as important systems of environmental management and conservation (Kurajian 2022)

CODA

1. The paragraph that opens this coda is a Gĩkũyũ translation of this summative paragraph. Likewise, the very last paragraph in this coda is a Kiswahili translation of the same text.

2. Indigenous knowledge systems, for instance, have much to contribute to conversations about climate change (Siwila 2022; Kilonzo 2022).

3. Although *Petals of Blood* was originally published in English, Ngũgĩ was already thinking deeply about his Gĩkũyũ oeuvre. Less than a year after the novel was published, Ngũgĩ directed *Ngaahika Ndenda (I Will Marry When I Want)* a Gĩkũyũ drama performed by community members at Kamirithu, Kenya.

4. For example, Ngũgĩ's short story, "Mugumo" (1975), in a collection titled *Secret Lives and Other Stories*, is named for the Gĩkũyũ word for fig tree.

5. Johann Ludwig Krapf (1810–1881) and Johannes Rebmann (1820–1876) were German missionaries in East Africa. They spread the Christian gospel in the middle of the nineteenth century.

6. Ngũgĩ describes the African postcolony as a "New Kenya. No free things. Without money you cannot buy land: and without land and property you cannot get a bank loan to start a business or buy land" (254). Even after independence, land has remained a vital source of economic empowerment; unfortunately, access to land rights is still as restricted as during colonial rule.

7. For instance, in 1969, elite members of the Gikuyu community met at President Jomo Kenyatta's home and took an oath that, while mimicking Mau Mau practices, was utterly opposed to nationalist ideals. Instead, these ceremonies swore members into ethnic solidarity that would willingly sabotage Kenya's future for Gikuyu advancement (Odhiambo 2003, 39). This level of ethnic chauvinism is opposed to the forms of cultural nationalism that formerly helped establish anticolonial politics in Kenya; the sabotaging of indigenous cultural institutions by elites bent on amassing riches serves as an additional form of disenfranchising the poor—they are not only robbed of national resources but also of their cultural heritage—causing deep ambivalence toward the postcolonial state.

8. Hence, for instance, "large plots of 100 acres, in addition to former European residences, were given to each African social and political elite"; many members of this group *also* acquired land through national settlements designed for small-scale farmers (Gaston 1979, 44).

9. In "Matunda ya Uhuru, Fruits of Independence: Seven Theses on Nationalism in Kenya," E. S. A. Odhiambo points out that it was the "petty bourgeoisie" who scrambled after Kenya's independence in the hopes of concretizing their way into a national bourgeoisie (Odhiambo 2003, 40). Furthermore, this group had no commitment to the ideals that rallied anticolonial politics: "freedom, unity and equality"; indeed, these concepts were uttered with falsehood (Odhiambo 2003, 40).

10. For example, "Mapping Black Ecologies" (Roane and Hosbey 2019) argues for channeling the ecological know-how of the African diaspora in the Americas in addressing the ongoing climate crisis.

11. There have been several experiments in the use of indigenous languages across the continent. South Africa, for example, has eleven official languages. Aside from English and Afrikaans, the list includes Sepedi, Sesotho, Setswana, siSwati, Tshivenda, Xitsonga, isiNdebele, isiXhosa and isiZulu (Constitution, Chapter 1). Tanzania has had a long history teaching the curriculum in Kiswahili (elementary education) and English (secondary and postsecondary education) (Marwa 2014). Kiswahili has recently been adopted as an official working language of both the East African Community and the African Union (Independent 2022). In an unrelated move, the United Nations Educational, Scientific and Cultural Organization (UNESCO) designated July 7 as World Kiswahili Language Day (CGTN Africa 2022).

12. Aside from decoupling concepts of development from Western neocolonialism, use of indigenous languages would be beneficial in increasing women's literacy rates. There is a wide chasm between countries that boast women's literacy rates in the ninetieth percentile (Equatorial Guinea, Namibia, Seychelles, and South Africa) versus those with women's literacy rates at less than 30 percent (Benin, Burkina Faso, Central African Republic, Chad, Guinea, Guinea-Bissau, Liberia, Mali, Niger, Sierra Leone, and South Sudan) (World Bank 2020). Subsistence farmers like Wanjiru, the Gĩkũyũ woman whose farming activities Hewitt castigates, profit from administrative and financial systems that are available in their first language.

13. Research (Blot, Zarate, and Paulus 2003; Kharkurin and Wei 2015) on English-Spanish bilingual speakers establishes a positive correlation between code switching between languages and creativity. Work such as *Necroclimatism in a Spectral World (Dis) order? Rain Petitioning, Climate and Weather Engineering in 21st Century Africa* (Artwell and Munyaradzi 2019) exemplifies the innovative rethinking that African ontologies and indigenous languages could offer to contemporary global crises.

14. Potential areas of collaboration include dispute resolution for land-related conflicts; see Kariuki Muigua's "Effective Application of Traditional Dispute Resolution Mechanisms in the Management of Land Conflicts in Kenya: Challenges and Prospects" (2022).

WORKS CITED

Acam-Oturu, Assumpta. 1995. "Arise to the Day's Toil." In *African Women's Poetry*, edited by Stella Chipasula and Frank Chipasula, 142. Portsmouth, NH: Heinemann.

Achebe, Chinua. 1958. *Things Fall Apart*. New York: Anchor Books.

Achebe, Chinua. 1966. *A Man of the People*. New York: John Day.

Achiba, Gargule A., and Monica N. Lengoiboni. 2020. "Devolution and the Politics of Communal Tenure Reform in Kenya." *African Affairs* 119 (476): 338–69. https://doi .org/10.1093/afraf/adaa010

Adem, Andrew, Rashidah Namatovu, and Michael Farrelly. N.d. "Women's Land Rights as a Pathway to Food Security in Uganda." *African Journal on Land Policy and Geospatial Sciences* 5 (1). https://doi.org/10.48346/IMIST.PRSM/ajlp-gs.v5i1.30465

Ademo, Mohammed. 2015. "Students Protesting Development Plan Met with Violence in Ethiopia." *Al Jazeera America*, December 8. http://america.aljazeera.com/articles /2015/12/8/students-protesting-land-grab-met-with-violence-in-ethiopia.html

Adera, Taddesse. 1996. "Ideology in Sahle Sellassie's Firebrands." *Northeast African Studies* 3 (3): 127–37.

African (Banjul) Charter on Human and Peoples' Rights. 1986.

African Union. 2009. *Declaration on Land Issues and Challenges in Africa*.

African Union, African Development Bank, and United Nations Economic Commission for Africa. 2010. "Framework and Guidelines on Land Policy in Africa: A Framework to Strengthen Land Rights, Enhance Productivity and Secure Livelihoods."

Ahlberg, Sofia. 2009. "Women and War in Contemporary Love Stories from Uganda and Nigeria." *Comparative Literature Studies* 46 (2): 407–24.

Ali, Suki, Kelly Coate, and Wangui wa Goro, eds. 2000. *Global Feminist Politics: Identities in a Changing World*. New York: Routledge.

Amadiume, Ifi. 1987. *Male Daughters, Female Husbands: Gender and Sexuality in an African Society*. London: Zed Books.

Amoko, Apollo. 2010. *Postcolonialism in the Wake of the Nairobi Revolution: Ngũgĩ wa Thiong'o and the Idea of African Literature*. New York: Palgrave Macmillan.

Ananda, Grace A., Bernard Moseti, and Leah Mugehera. 2020. "Women's Land Rights Scorecard: The Failure of Land Policy and Legal Reforms in Securing Women's Land

Rights in Africa." Oxfam International Pan Africa Programme. https://oxfamilibra ry.openrepository.com/bitstream/handle/10546/621108/rr-womens-land-rights-sc orecard-241120-en%20(2).pdf?sequence=1

Anderson, David. 2005. *Histories of the Hanged: The Dirty War in Kenya and the End of Empire*. New York: W. W. Norton.

Appiah, Kwame Anthony. 1991. "Is the Post- in Postmodernism the Post- in Postcolonial?" *Critical Inquiry* 17 (Winter): 336–57.

Armbruster, Karla, and Kathleen Wallace. 2001. "Introduction: Why Go beyond Nature Writing and Where To?" In *Beyond Nature Writing: Expanding the Boundaries of Ecocriticism*, edited by Karla Armbruster and Kathleen Wallace, 1–27. Charlottesville: University of Virginia Press.

Arnfred, Signe, and Akosua Adomako Ampofo. 2009. "Introduction: Feminist Politics of Knowledge." In *African Feminist Politics of Knowledge: Tensions, Challenges, Possibilities*, edited by Signe Arnfred and Akosua Adomako Ampofo, 5–27. Norway: Nordiska Afrikainstitutet.

Artwell, Nhemachena, and Mawere Munyaradzi. 2019. *Necroclimatism in a Spectral World (Dis)Order? Rain Petitioning, Climate and Weather Engineering in 21st Century Africa*. Bamenda and Buea, Cameroon: Langaa RPCIG.

Ashcroft, Bill, Gareth Griffiths, and Helen Tiffin. 1989. *The Empire Writes Back: Theory and Practice in Post-Colonial Literatures*. New York: Routledge.

Ashcroft, Bill, Gareth Griffiths, and Helen Tiffin. 2006. *The Post-Colonial Studies Reader*. 2nd ed. New York: Routledge.

Ashukem, Jean-Claude N. 2020. "Land Grabbing and Customary Land Rights in Uganda: A Critical Reflection of the Constitutional and Legislative Right to Land." *International Journal on Minority and Group Rights* 27 (1): 121–47. https://doi.org/10.11 63/15718115-02701003

Attree, Lizzy. 2002. "Language, Kwela Music and Modernity in Butterfly Burning." In *Sign and Taboo: Perspectives on the Poetic Fiction of Yvonne Vera*, edited by Robert Muponde and Mandi Taruvinga, 63–80. Harare: Weaver Press.

Atuahene, Bernadette. 2014. *We Want What's Ours: Learning from South Africa's Land Restitution Program*. Oxford: Oxford University Press.

Ava-Mathew, Lois. 2009. "FEMRITE and Ugandan Women Writers." *Belletrista*, no. 2. http://www.belletrista.com/2009/issue2/features_2.php

Azeze, Fekade. 1985. "Ethiopian Creative Writing and Criticism in English: A Review and Bibliography." *Journal of Ethiopian Studies* 18: 34–50.

Barasa, Violet. 2009. "Reconstructing Kenyan Women's Image in Marjorie Oludhe Macgoye's Coming to Birth." PhD diss., University of the Witwatersrand, Johannesburg.

Barber, Karin. 1995. "African-Language Literature and Postcolonial Criticism." *Research in African Literatures* 26 (4): 3–30.

Barmard, Rita. 2006. *Apartheid and Beyond: South African Writers and the Politics of Place*. Oxford: Oxford University Press.

Bartolovich, Crystal. 2002. "Introduction: Marxism, Modernity, and Postcolonial Studies." In *Marxism, Modernity, and Postcolonial Studies*, edited by Crystal Bartolovich and Neil Lazurus, 1–17. Cambridge: Cambridge University Press.

Bassett, Thomas J., and William Munro. 2022. "Lost in Translation: Pro-Poor Development in the Green Revolution for Africa." *African Studies Review* 65 (1): 8–15. https://doi.org/10.1017/asr.2021.99

Beer, David. 1977. "The Sources and Content of Ethiopian Creative Writing in English." *Research in African Literatures* 8 (1): 99–124.

Berman, Nina. 2017. *Germans on the Kenyan Coast: Land, Charity, and Romance*. Bloomington: Indiana University Press.

Bertz, Ned. 2015. *Diaspora and Nation in the Indian Ocean: Transnational Histories of Race and Urban Space in Tanzania*. Hawaii: University of Hawaii Press.

Bhabha, Homi. 1990a. "DissemiNation: Time, Narrative, and the Margins of the Modern Nation." In *Nation and Narration*, edited by Homi Bhabha, 291–322. New York: Routledge.

Bhabha, Homi. 1990b. "Introduction: Narrating the Nation." In *Nation and Narration*, edited by Homi Bhabha, 1–7. New York: Routledge.

Boehmer, Elleke. 2005. *Colonial and Postcolonial Literature: Migrant Metaphors*. 2nd ed. Oxford: Oxford University Press.

Bonabana, J., J. Kirinya, and B. Mugonola. 2020. "Land Tenure and Food Security in Uganda: A Review." *Makerere University Journal of Agricultural and Environmental Sciences* 9 (1): 58–72.

Boone, Catherine. 2012. "Land Conflict and Distributive Politics in Kenya." *African Studies Review* 55 (1): 75–103.

Bradley, Kenneth, and Kenneth Ingham. 2020. "Zimbabwe." *Encyclopædia Britannica*. . https://www.britannica.com/place/Zimbabwe/Climate#ref480964

Brooks, Lisa. 2018. *Our Beloved Kin: A New History of King Philip's War*. New Haven: Yale University Press.

Brown, Alison, Colman Msoka, and Ibrahima Dankoco. 2014. "A Refugee in My Own Country: Evictions or Property Rights in the Urban Informal Economy?" *Urban Studies*, August, 1–16. https://doi.org/10.1177/0042098014544758

Brownell, Emily. 2020. *Gone to Ground: A History of Environment and Infrastructure in Dar es Salaam*. Pittsburgh: University of Pittsburgh Press.

Brownell, Emily, and Toyin Falola. 2013. "Introduction: Landscapes, Environments and Technology—Looking Out, Looking Back." In *Landscape, Environment and Technology in Colonial and Postcolonial Africa*, edited by Emily Brownell and Toyin Falola, 1–18. New York: Routledge.

Bruna, Natacha. 2019. "Land of Plenty, Land of Misery: Synergetic Resource Grabbing in Mozambique." *Land* 8 (113). https://doi.org/10.3390/land8080113

Burke, Timothy. 1996. *Lifebouy Men, Lux Women: Commodification, Consumption, and Cleanliness in Modern Zimbabwe*. Durham: Duke University Press.

Cabral, Amilcar. 1994. "National Culture and Liberation." In *Colonial Discourse and Postcolonial Theory: A Reader*, edited by Patrick Williams and Laura Chrisman, 53–65. New York: Columbia University Press.

Caminero-Santangelo, Byron. 2014. *Different Shades of Green: African Literature, Environmental Justice, and Political Ecology*. Charlottesville: University of Virginia Press.

Caminero-Santagelo, Byron, and Garth Myers, eds. 2011. "Introduction." In *Environment at the Margin: Literary and Environmental Studies in Africa*, 1–21. Athens: Ohio University Press.

Caulker, Tcho Mbaimba. 2009. *The African-British Long Eighteenth Century: An Analysis of African-British Treaties, Colonial Economics, and Anthropological Discourse*. Lanham: Lexington Books.

Césaire, Aimé. 2000. *Discourse on Colonialism*. New York: Monthly Review Press.

Cezula, Ntozakhe Simon, and Leepo Modise. 2020. "The 'Empty Land' Myth: A Biblical and Sociohistorical Exploration." *Studia Historiae Ecclesiasticae* 46 (2): 2020. https://doi.org/10.25159/2412-4265/6827

CGTN Africa. 2022. "African Union Adopts Swahili as Official Working Language," February 10. https://africa.cgtn.com/2022/02/10/african-union-adopts-swahili-as-official-working-language/

Chan, Stephen. 2005. "The Memory of Violence: Trauma in the Writings of Alexander Kanengoni and Yvonne Vera and the Idea of Unreconciled Citizenship in Zimbabwe." *Third World Quarterly* 26 (2): 369–82.

Chan, Stephen, and Ranka Primorac. 2004. "The Imagination of Land and the Reality of Seizure: Zimbabwe's Complex Reinventions." *Journal of International Affairs* 57 (2): 63–80.

Chatterjee, Ronjaunee, Alicia M. Christoff, and Amy R. Wong. 2020. "Undisciplining Victorian Studies." *Los Angeles Review of Books*, July 10. https://lareviewofbooks.org/article/undisciplining-victorian-studies

Chemhuru, Munamato. 2019. "The Moral Status of Nature: An African Understanding." In *African Environmental Ethics: A Critical Reader*, edited by Munamato Chemhuru, 56–82. Cham, Switzerland: Springer.

Chigumadzi, Panashe. 2018. *These Bones Will Rise Again*. London: Indigo Press.

Chipato, Fadzai, Libin Wang, Ting Zuo, and George T. Mudimu. 2020. "The Politics of Youth Struggles for Land in Post-Land Reform Zimbabwe." *Review of African Political Economy* 47 (163): 59–77.

Chipuriro, Rejoice Mazvirevesa, and Grasian Mkodzongi. 2022. "Revisiting Zimbabwe's Land Rights, Human Rights and Social Justice: The Post-Mugabe Era." In *The Future of Zimbabwe's Agrarian Sector: Land Issues in a Time of Political Transition*, edited by Grasian Mkodzongi. London: Routledge.

Chitonge, Horman, and Yoichi Mine, eds. 2019. *Land, the State and the Unfinished Decolonisation Project in Africa: Essays in Honour of Professor Sam Moyo*. Bamenda and Buea, Cameroon: Langaa RPCIG.

Clark, Timothy. 2012. "Introduction: The Challenge." In *The Cambridge Introduction to Literature and the Environment*, edited by Timothy Clark, 1–12. Cambridge: Cambridge University Press.

Clark, Timothy. 2015. *Ecocriticism on the Edge: The Anthropocene as a Threshold Concept*. London: Bloomsbury Academic.

Collen, Lindsey. 1993. *The Rape of Sita*. New York: Feminist Press.

Collen, Lindsey, and Barbara Waldis. 2004. "'De l'art de la Rébellion': Entretien avec Lindsey Collen, écrivaine et militante à l'île Maurice." *Nouvelles Questions Féministes: Postcommunisme: Genre et États en Transition* 23 (2): 97–111.

Coly, Ayo. 2019. *Postcolonial Hauntologies: African Women's Discourses of the Female Body*. Lincoln: University of Nebraska Press.

Cook, David, and Michael Okenimkpe. 1983. *Ngũgĩ wa Thiong'o: An Exploration of His Writing*. Nairobi: Heinemann.

Coplan, David B., and Kearabetswe Moopelo. 2021. "Magic Mountain: 'The Ancestors Cannot Be Relocated.'" https://wiser.wits.ac.za/system/files/seminar/CoplanandMoopelo2021.pdf

Cotula, Lorenzo. 2013. *The Great African Land Grab? Agricultural Investments and the Global Food System*. New York: Zed Books.

Coulson, Andrew. 1982. *Tanzania: A Political Economy*. Oxford: Clarendon Press.

Coundouriotis, Eleni. 2014. *The People's Right to the Novel: War Fiction in the Postcolony*. New York: Fordham University Press.

Crowley, Dustin. 2013. "'A Universal Garden of Many-Coloured Flowers': Place and Scale in the Works of Ngũgĩ wa Thiong'o." *Research in African Literatures* 44 (3): 13–29.

Crowley, Dustin. 2015. *Africa's Narrative Geographies: Charting the Intersections of Ecocriticism and Postcolonial Studies*. New York: Palgrave Macmillan.

Damtew, Samrawit Getaneh. 2019. "Land-Grabbing and the Right to Adequate Food in Ethiopia." *African Human Rights Law Journal* 19 (1): 219–45. https://doi.org/10.17159/1996-2096/2019/v19n1a11

Dancer, Helen. 2015. *Women, Land and Justice in Tanzania*. London: James Currey.

Darian-Smith, Kate, Liz Gunner, and Sarah Nuttall. 1996. "Introduction." In *Text, Theory, Space: Land, Literature and History in South Africa and Australia*, edited by Kate Darian-Smith, Liz Gunner, and Sarah Nuttall, 1–20. London: Routledge.

Davis, Mike. 2001. *Late Victorian Holocausts: El Niño Famines and the Making of the Third World*. London: Verso.

Davis, Mike. 2004. "Planet of Slums." *New Left Review* 26 (April): 5–34.

Davis, Rocio G. 1999. "Negotiating Place: Identity and Community in M. G. Vassanji's 'Uhuru Street.'" *ARIEL: A Review of International English Literature* 30 (3): 7–25.

Deane, Seamus. 1990. "Introduction." In *Nationalism, Colonialism, and Literature*, 3–20. Minneapolis: University of Minnesota Press.

Declercq, Robrecht. 2020. "'From Cape to Katanga': South African Expansionism, White Settlers and the Congo (1910–1963)." *South African Historical Journal* 72 (4): 604–26. https://doi.org/10.1080/02582473.2020.1832142

Dei, George J. Sefa, Wambui Karanja, and Grace Erger. 2022. "Land as Indigenous Epistemology." In *Elders' Cultural Knowledges and the Question of Black/African Indige-*

neity in Education, edited by George J. Sefa Dei, Wambui Karanja, and Grace Erger, 113–26. Cham, Switzerland: Springer. https://doi.org/10.1007/978-3-030-84201-7_5

Delano, Isaac Oluwole. 1955. *Aiye d'Aiye Oyinbo*. London: Thomas Nelson & Sons.

Delano, Isaac Oluwole. 1953. *Welcome to the White Man's World*. London: Thomas Nelson.

DeLoughrey, Elizabeth, and George Handley. 2011. "Introduction: Toward an Asthetics of the Earth." In *Postcolonial Ecologies: Literatures of the Environment*, edited by Elizabeth DeLoughrey and George Handley, 3–39. Oxford: Oxford University Press.

Demoz, Abrham. 1995. "State Policy and the Medium of Expression." In *Silence Is Not Golden: A Critical Anthology of Ethiopian Literature*, 15–38. Lawrenceville, NJ: Red Sea Press.

Desai, Gaurav. 2001. *Subject to Colonialism: African Self-Fashioning and the Colonial Library*. Durham: Duke University Press.

Desai, Gaurav. 2011. "'Ambiguity Is the Driving Force or the Nuclear Reaction behind My Creativity': An E-Conversation with M. G. Vassanji." *Research in African Literatures* 42 (3): 187–97.

De Schutter, Olivier. 2010. "The Emerging Human Right to Land." *International Community Law Review* 12 (3): 303–34. https://doi.org/10.1163/187197310X513725

Diop, Cheikh Anta. 1974. *The African Origin of Civilization: Myth or Reality*. Chicago: Lawrence Hill.

Edoro, Ainehi. 2018. "Gods of Fiction." *Africa Is a Country* (blog). November 23. https://africasacountry.com/2018/11/gods-of-fiction-african-writers-and-the-fantasy-of-power/

Elkins, Caroline. 2005. *Imperial Reckoning: The Untold Story of Britain's Gulag in Kenya*. New York: Henry Holt.

Ethiopia's Economic Policy during the Transitional Period. 1991. Addis Ababa: Transitional Government of Ethiopia.

Éthiopie: Quatre années de processus révolutionnaire. 1978. Addis Ababa: Comite d'Information et de Propaganda.

Fairhead, James, and Melissa Leach. 1996. *Misreading the African Landscape: Society and Ecology in a Forest-Savanna Mosaic*. Cambridge: Cambridge University Press.

Fanon, Frantz. 1963. *The Wretched of the Earth*. New York: Grove Press.

Fike, Mathew. 2017. *Anima and Africa: Jungian Essays on Psyche, Land, and Literature*. London: Routledge.

Flanagan, Kathleen. 1996. "African Folk Tales as Disruptions of Narrative in the Works of Grace Ogot and Elspeth Huxley." *Women's Studies* 24 (4): 371–81.

Gaston, Jessi R. 1979. "Land Issue in Kenya Politics: Pre-and Post-Independence Development." *Ufahamu: A Journal of African Studies* 9 (2): 30–58.

Gathogo, Julius. 2020. "Settler-Missionary Alliance in Colonial Kenya and the Land Question." *Studia Historiae Ecclesiasticae* 46 (2): 20.

Gertel, Jorge, Richard Rottenberg, and Sandra Calkins. 2014. "Disrupting Territories: Commodification and Its Consequences." In *Disrupting Territories: Land, Commodification and Conflict in Sudan*, 1–30. Rochester, NY: Boydell and Brewer.

Gifford, James. 2010. "Vassanji's Toronto and Durrell's Alexandria: The View from across or the View from Beside?" In *Indian Writers: Transnationalisms and Diasporas*, edited by Jaspal Singh and Rajendra Chetty, 171–82. New York: Peter Lang.

Gifford, Terry. 1999. *Pastoral*. London: Routledge.

Gikandi, Simon. 2000. *Ngũgĩ wa Thiong'o*. Cambridge: Cambridge University Press.

Gikandi, Simon. 2005. "Globalization and the Claims of the Postcoloniality." In *Postcolonialisms: An Anthology of Cultural Theory and Criticism*, edited by Gaurav Desai and Supriya Nair, 608–34. New Brunswick, NJ: Rutgers University Press.

Gikandi, Simon, and Evan Mwangi. 2007. *The Columbia Guide to East African Literature in English since 1945*. New York: Columbia University Press.

Gilroy, Paul. 1993. *The Black Atlantic: Modernity and Double Consciousness*. Cambridge, MA: Harvard University Press.

Glissant, Edouard. 1999. *Caribbean Discourse: Selected Essays*. Charlottesville: University of Virginia Press.

Glotfelty, Cheryll. 1996. "Introduction: Literary Studies in an Age of Environmental Crisis." In *The Ecocriticism Reader: Landmarks in Literary Ecology*, edited by Cheryll Glotfelty and Harold Fromm, xv–xxxv. Athens: University of Georgia Press.

Goro, Wangui wa. 2007. "Translating Africa and Leadership: What Is Africa to Me?" In *Under the Tree of Talking: Leadership for Change in Africa*, edited by Onyekachi Wambu, 157–72. London: Counterpoint.

Graham, James. 2009. *Land and Nationalism in Fictions from Southern Africa*. New York: Routledge.

Gravesen, Marie Ladekjaer. 2021. *The Contested Lands of Laikipia—Histories of Claims and Conflict in a Kenyan Landscape*. Leiden, The Netherlands: Koninklijke Brill. https://brill.com/view/title/58014

Gressier, Catie. 2015. *At Home in the Okavango: White Batswana Narratives of Emplacement and Belonging*. New York: Berghahn.

Gromov, Mikhail. 2014. "Visions of the Future in the 'New' Swahili Novel: Hope in Desperation?" *Tydskrif Vir Letterkunde* 51 (2). http://dx.doi.org/10.4314/tvl.v51i2.4

Hall, Catherine. 2000. "Introduction: Thinking the Postcolinial, Thinking the Empire." In *Cultures of Empire: Colonizers in Britain and the Empire in the Nineteenth and Twentieth Centuries*, edited by Catherine Hall, 1–33. Manchester: Manchester University Press.

Hall, Stuart. 1996. "Cultural Identity and Diaspora." In *Contemporary Postcolonial Theory: A Reader*, edited by Padmini Mongia, 110–21. London: Arnold.

Haller, Tobias. 2019. "The Different Meanings of Land in the Age of Neoliberalism: Theoretical Reflections on Commons and Resilience Grabbing from a Social Anthropological Perspective." *Land* 8 (104). https://doi.org/10.3390/land8070104

Haller, Tobias, Timothy Adams, Desirée Gmür, Fabian Käser, Kristina Lanz, Franziska Marfurt, Sarah Ryser, Elisabeth Schubiger, Anna von Sury, and Jean-David Gerber. 2019. "Large-Scale Land Acquisitions as Commons Grabbing: A Comparative Analysis of Six African Case Studies." In *Global Perspectives on Long-Term Community*

Resource Management, edited by Ludomir R. Lozny and Thomas H. McGovern, 125–64. Cham, Switzerland: Springer. https://doi.org/10.1007/978-3-030-15800-2

Hardin, Garrett. 1968. "The Tragedy of the Commons." *Science* 162 (3859): 1243–48.

Harris, Danielle Marie. 2014. "Political Mobilization and Conflict on Kenya's Coast: Land, Indigeneity, and Elections." MA thesis, University of California, Los Angeles. http://search.proquest.com/docview/1552737584

Harrison, Robert Pogue. 1993. *Forests: The Shadow of Civilization*. Chicago: University of Chicago Press.

Heise, Ursula. 2008. *Sense of Place and Sense of Planet: The Environmental Imagination of the Global*. Oxford: Oxford University Press.

Heise, Ursula. 2017. "Introduction: Planet, Species, Justice—and the Stories We Tell About Them." In *The Routledge Companion to the Environmental Humanities*, edited by Ursula Heise, Jon Christensen, and Michelle Niemann, 1–10. New York: Routledge.

Henze, Paul. 1989. *Ethiopia: Crisis of a Marxist Economy*. Santa Monica, CA: Rand Corporation.

Hewitt, Peter. 1999. *Kenya Cowboy: A Police Officer's Account of the Mau Mau Emergency*. Johannesburg: 30 o South Publishers.

Highfield, Jonathan. 2012. *Imagined Topographies: From Colonial Resource to Postcolonial Homeland*. New York: Peter Lang.

Howarth, William. 1996. "Some Principles of Ecocriticism." In *The Ecocriticism Reader: Landmarks in Literary Ecology*, edited by Cheryll Glotfelty and Harold Fromm, 69–91. Athens: University of Georgia Press.

Huggan, Graham, and Helen Tiffin. 2010. *Postcolonial Ecocriticism: Literature, Animals, Environment*. New York: Routledge.

Hussein, Ibrahim. 1969. *Kinjeketile*. Oxford: Oxford University Press.

Hussein, Ibrahim. 1971. *Mashetani*. Nairobi: Oxford University Press.

Hussein, Ibrahim. 1980. *Arusi*. Nairobi: Oxford University Press.

Hussein, Ibrahim. 1988. *Kwenye Ukingo wa Thim*. Nairobi: Oxford University Press.

Huxley, Elspeth. 1959. *Flame Trees of Thika: Memoirs of an African Childhood*. Great Britain: Chatto and Windus.

Iheka, Cajetan. 2017. *Naturalizing Africa: Ecological Violence, Agency, and Postcolonial Resistance in African Literature*. Cambridge: Cambridge University Press.

Iheka, Cajetan. 2021. "The Media Turn in African Environmentalism: The Niger Delta and Oil's Network Forms." *Journal of Visual Culture* 20 (1): 60–84.

Iheka, Cajetan, and Stephanie Newell. 2020. "Introduction: Itineraries of African Ecocriticism and Environmental Transformations in African Literature." *African Literature Today* 38: 1–10.

Imperial Ethiopian Government, Ministry of National Community Development. *Awassa Community Development Training and Development Center*. 1964. Ethiopia

Impey, Angela. 2018. *Song Walking: Women, Music, and Environmental Justice in an African Borderland*. Chicago: University of Chicago Press.

Independent. 2022. "East African Community to Add Kiswahili, French as Official Languages." April 28. https://www.independent.co.ug/east-african-community-to-add-kiswahili-french-as-official-languages/

Institute for Statistics, UNESCO. 2021. "Literacy Rate, Adult Female (% of Females Ages 15 and above)—Sub-Saharan Africa." https://data.worldbank.org/indicator/SE.ADT.LITR.FE.ZS?locations=ZG&most_recent_year_desc=true

Jaji, Tsitsi Ella. 2020. *Mother Tongues.* Evanston, IL: Northwestern University Press.

James, Adeola. 1990. "Introduction." In *In Their Own Voices: African Women Writers Talk*, edited by Adeola James, 1–6. London: James Currey.

James, Adeola, and Rebeka Njau. 1990. "Rebeka Njau." In *In Their Own Voices: African Women Writers Talk*, edited by Adeola James, 102–8. London: James Currey.

Kabira, Wanjiku, Alice Nderitu, and Nkatha Kabira. 2020. "African Feminist Mentorship Pedagogies and Praxis: Baseline and Scoping Study Leading to a Pan African Feminist Mentorship Toolkit." Nairobi: Akili Dada.

Kalu, Anthonia. 2020. "Women's Literature in African History." In *Oxford Research Encyclopedia of African History.* 29. Oxford: Oxford University Press. https://doi.org/10.1093/acrefore/9780190277734.013.346

Kameri-Mbote, Patricia. 2007. "Access, Control and Ownership: Women and Sustainable Environmental Management in Africa." *Agenda: Empowering Women for Gender Equity* 72: 36–46.

Kandel, Matt. 2017. "Land Conflict and Social Differentiation in Eastern Uganda." *Journal of Modern African Studies* 55 (3): 395–422. https://doi.org/10.1017/S0022278X1700026X

Kanengoni, Alex. 1997. *Echoing Silences.* Harare: Baobab Books.

Kanogo, Tabitha. 1987. *Squatters and the Roots of the Mau Mau 1906–63.* Nairobi: Heinemann.

Kelly, Jill E. 2018. *To Swim with Crocodiles: Land, Violence, and Belonging in South Africa, 1800–1996.* East Lansing: Michigan State University Press.

Kenny, Christina. 2016. "'She Is Made of and Coloured by the Earth Itself': Motherhood and Nation in Yvonne Adhiambo Owuor's *Dust.*" In *Researching Africa in Australasia–The Way Forward!*, proceedings of the 40th Annual Conference of the African Studies Association of Australasia and the Pacific, Adelaide, Australia.

Kenyatta, Jomo. 1962. *Facing Mt. Kenya.* New York: Vintage.

Kibera, Valerie, and Marjorie Oludhe Macgoye. 1987. "Afterword." In *The Present Moment*, 157–85. New York: Feminist Press.

Kiguli, Juliet, and Susan Kiguli. 2007. "2017: Empowering and Engendering the Future." In *Under the Tree of Talking: Leadership for Change in Africa*, edited by Onyekachi Wambu, 184–92. London: Counterpoint.

Kiguli, Susan. 2012. "Theorising Craft: Reading the Creative through the Critical in the Works of Okot p'Bitek and Ngũgĩ wa Thiong'o." In *Rethinking Eastern African Literary and Intellectual Landscapes*, edited by James Ogude, Grace A. Musila, and Dina Ligaga, 73–90. Asmara, Eritrea: Africa World Press.

Kilonzo, Susan Mbula. 2022. "Women, Indigenous Knowledge Systems, and Climate Change in Kenya." In *African Perspectives on Religion and Climate Change*, edited by Ezra Chitando, Ernst M. Conradie, and Susan Mbula Kilonzo. London: Routledge.

Knudsen, Eva, and Ulla Rahbek. 2017. "An Afropolitan Literary Aesthetics? Afropolitan Style and Tropes in Recent Diasporic African Fiction." *European Journal of English Studies* 21 (2): 115–28.

Kobusingye, Doreen Nancy, Mathijs van Leeuwen, and Han van Dijk. 2017. "The Multifaceted Relationship between Land and Violent Conflict: The Case of Apaa Evictions in Amuru District, Northern Uganda." *Journal of Modern African Studies* 55 (3): 455–77. https://doi.org/10.1017/S0022278X17000106

Koech, Martha. 2020. "An Examination of Gender Gaps in Systems of Land Ownership in Kenya." MA thesis, University of Nairobi. http://erepository.uonbi.ac.ke/bitstre am/handle/11295/153622/Koech_An%20Examination%20Of%20Gender%20Gaps %20In%20Systems%20Of%20Land%20Ownership%20In%20Relation%20To%20F ood%20Security%20In%20Kenya.pdf?sequence=1

Krings, Matthias. 2010. "A Prequel to Nollywood: South African Photo Novels and Their Pan-African Consumption in the Late 1960s." *Journal of African Cultural Studies* 22 (1): 75–89.

Kumalo, R. Simangaliso. 2020. "The Other Side of the Story: Attempts by Missionaries to Facilitate Landownership by Africans during the Colonial Era." *Studia Historiae Ecclesiasticae* 46 (2): 1–17.

Kurajian, Olivia. 2022. "The Serengeti-Mara Ecosytem: Interactions between Human and Non-Human Species." In *Posthumanist Nomadisms across Non-Oedipal Spatiality*, edited by Java Singh and Indrani Mukherjee. Wilmington, DE: Vernon Press.

Kurtz, John Roger. 1998. *Urban Obsessions, Urban Fears: The Postcolonial Kenyan Novel.* Trenton, NJ: Africa World Press.

Kurtz, John Roger. 2005. *Nyarloka's Gift: The Writing of Marjorie Oludhe Macgoye.* Nairobi: MvuleAfrica Publishers.

Kurtz, John Roger. 2007. "Debating the Language of African Literature: Ethiopian Contributions." *Journal of African Cultural Studies* 19 (2): 187–205.

Laloyo, Stell Apecu, and Mulyampiti Tabitha. 2021. "Women, Land Tenure Security and Livelihoods in Amuru District." *African Journal on Land Policy and Geospatial Sciences* 5 (1). https://doi.org/10.48346/IMIST.PRSM/ajlp-gs.v5i1.30519

"Land, n.1." 2021. In *OED Online.* Oxford University Press. www.oed.com/view/Entry /105432

"Landscape, n." 2021. In *OED Online.* Oxford University Press. www.oed.com/view/En try/105515

Lazarus, Neil. 2011. "What Postcolonial Theory Doesn't Say." *Race Class* 53 (3): 3–27.

Lazarus, Neil. 2004. *Cambridge Companion to Postcolonial Literary Studies.* Cambridge: Cambridge University Press.

Leduka, R. C., M. Ntaote, and S. N. Takalimane. 2018. "Land Governance in Lesotho." In *2019 Land Governance in Southern Africa Symposium*, 60. Windhoek, Namibia. https://nelga.org/wp-content/uploads/2020/09/Land-Governance-Lesotho.pdf

Lefebvre, Henri. 1991. *The Production of Space*. Translated by Donald Nicholson-Smith. Malden, MA: Blackwell.

Lentz, Carola. 2013. *Land, Mobility, and Belonging in West Africa*. Bloomington: Indiana University Press.

L'Éthiopie Rurale: Hier et Aujourd'hui. 1978. Addis Ababa: Comite d'Information et de Propaganda.

Liberti, Stefano. 2013. "Senegal's Shady Farmland Agreement." *AlJazeera*, December 23. https://www.aljazeera.com/features/2013/12/23/senegals-shady-farmland-agreem ent/

Likimani, Muthoni. 1985. *Passbook Number F.47927: Women and Mau Mau in Kenya*. Basingstoke: Macmillan.

Likke, Senay. 1977. *Tasks, Achievements, Problems, and Prospects of the Ethiopian Revolution*. Addis Ababa: Ethiopian Revolution Information Center.

Loomba, Ania. 2015. *Colonialism/Postcolonialism*. 3rd ed. New York: Routledge.

Løvschal, Mette, and Marie Ladekjaer Gravesen. 2021. "De-/Fencing Grasslands: Ongoing Boundary Making and Unmaking in Postcolonial Kenya." *Land* 10 (786). https://doi.org/10.3390/land10080786

Lugones, Maria. 2008. "The Coloniality of Gender." *Worlds and Knowledges Otherwise*, 1–17.

Lugones, Maria. 2010. "Toward a Decolonial Feminism." *Hypatia* 25 (4): 742–59.

Luig, Ute, and Achim von Oppen. 1997. "Landscape in Africa: Process and Vision. An Introductory Essay." *Paideuma*, no. 43: 7–45.

Maathai, Wangari. 2007. *Unbowed: A Memoir*. New York: Anchor.

Maathai, Wangari. 2010. *The World We Once Lived In*. New York: Penguin Random House.

Macgoye, Marjorie Oludhe. 1977. *Song of Nyarloka and Other Poems*. Nairobi: Oxford University Press.

Macgoye, Marjorie Oludhe. 1986. *Coming to Birth*. Nairobi: Heinemann Educational Books.

Macgoye, Marjorie Oludhe. 1995. "For Miriam." In *African Women's Poetry*, edited by Stella Chipasula and Frank Chipasula, 118. Portsmouth, NH: Heinemann.

Macgoye, Marjorie Oludhe. 1998. *Make It Sing and Other Poems*. Nairobi: East African Educational Publishers.

Madhavan, Anugraha, and Sharmila Narayana. 2020. "Violation of Land as Violation of Feminine Space: An Ecofeminist Reading of Mother Forest and Mayilamma." *Tattva–Journal of Philosophy* 12 (2): 13–32. https://doi.org/10.12726/tjp.24.2

Maina, Paul. 1977. *Six Mau Mau Generals*. Nairobi: Gazelle Books Company.

Majanga, Michael. 2017. "This Is the Canaan I Want for You–Raila 'Joshua' Odinga." *Citizen Digital*, May 28. https://citizentv.co.ke/news/this-is-the-canaan-i-want-for-you-raila-joshua-odinga-166939/

Makhulu, Anne-Maria. 2015. *Making Freedom: Apartheid, Squatter Politics, and the Struggle for Home*. Durham: Duke University Press.

Mama, Amina. 1995. *Beyond the Masks: Race, Gender, and Subjectivity*. New York: Routledge.

Mama, Amina. 2019. "African Feminist Thought." In *Oxford Research Encyclopedia of African History*. https://doi.org/10.1093/acrefore/9780190277734.013.504

Mamdani, Mamhood. 2020. *Neither Settler nor Native: The Making and Unmaking of Permanent Minorities*. Cambridge, MA: Harvard University Press.

Mangwanda, Khombe. 2002. "Re-Mapping the Colonial Space: Yvonne Vera's Nehanda." In *Sign and Taboo: Perspectives on the Poetic Fiction of Yvonne Vera*, edited by Robert Muponde and Mandi Taruvinga, 141–54. Harare: Weaver Press.

Manji, Ambreena. 2020. *The Struggle for Land and Justice in Kenya*. London: James Currey.

Mariam, Mengistu H. 1978. "Fourth Anniversary of the Ethiopian Revolution." Speech. Addis Ababa.

Mariam, Mengistu H. 1979. "Towards Economic and Cultural Development in Ethiopia." Speech. Addis Ababa.

Mariam, Mengistu H. 1980. "Report Delivered to the First Congress of COPWE." Speech. Addis Ababa.

Mariam, Mengistu H. 1986. "Towards Formation People's Democratic Republic." Speech. Addis Ababa.

Marwa, Nyankomo W. 2014. "Tanzania's Language of Instruction Policy Dilemma: Is There a Solution?" *Mediterranean Journal of Social Sciences* 5 (23): 1262–68. https://doi.org/10.5901/mjss.2014.v5n23p1262

Marzec, Robert. 2007. *An Ecologic and Postcolonial Study of Literature: From Daniel Defoe to Salman Rushdie*. New York: Palgrave Macmillan.

Massey, Doreen. 1994. *Space, Place, and Gender*. Minneapolis: University of Minnesota Press.

Massey, Doreen. 2005. *For Space*. New Delhi: Sage Publications.

Maughan-Brown, David. 1985. *Land, Freedom and Fiction: History and Ideology in Kenya*. London: Zed Books.

Mazrui, Alamin M. 2007. *Swahili beyond the Boundaries: Literature, Language, and Identity*. Athens: Ohio University Press.

Mazrui, Ali A., and Alamin M. Mazrui. 1998. *The Power of Babel: Language and Governance in the African Experience*. Nairobi: East African Educational Publishers.

Mbembe, Achille. 1992. "Provisional Notes on the Postcolony." *Africa: Journal of the International African Institute* 62 (1): 3–37.

McGiffin, Emily. 2019. *Of Land, Bones, and Money: Towards a South African Ecopoetics*. Charlottesville: University of Virginia Press.

Melesse, Tigist M., and Yesuf M. Awel. 2020. "Land Tenure, Gender, and Productivity in Ethiopia and Tanzania." In *Women and Sustainable Human Development: Empowering Women in Africa*, edited by Maty Konte and Nyasha Tirivayi, 89–108. Cham, Switzerland: Springer International Publishing. https://doi.org/10.1007/978-3-030-14935-2_6

Memmi, Albert. 1965. *The Colonizer and The Colonized*. New York: Orio Press.

Mengiste, Maaza. 2011. *Beneath the Lion's Gaze: A Novel*. New York: W. W. Norton.

Meroka-Mutua, A. 2022. "A History without Women: The Emergence and Development of Subaltern Ideology and the 'Land Question' in Kenya." *Feminist Legal Studies*. https://doi.org/10.1007/s10691-022-09488-4

Mesic, Selma. 2019. "The 'Green' Land Grabs—How the Rush for Biofuels Is Impacting Land Rights in Tanzania." MA thesis, Uppsala University. urn:nbn:se:uu:diva -384254.

Mies, Maria, and Vandana Shiva. 1993. *Ecofeminism*. London: Zed Books.

Mignolo, Walter. 2011. *The Darker Side of Western Modernity: Global Futures, Decolonial Options*. Durham: Duke University Press.

Mignolo, Walter, and Catherine Walsh. 2018. *On Decoloniality: Concepts, Analytics, Praxis*. Durham: Duke University Press.

Minh-ha, Trinh. 1989. *Woman, Native, Other: Writing Postcoloniality and Feminism*. Indianapolis: Indiana University Press.

Ministry of Information and National Guidance. *May Day*. 1977. Addis Ababa: Ministry of Information and National Guidance.

Mitchell, Peta, and Jane Stadler. 2011. "Redrawing the Map: An Interdisciplinary Geocritical Approach to Australian Cultural Narratives." In *Geocritical Explorations: Space, Place, and Mapping in Literary and Cultural Studies*, edited by Robert Tally Jr., 47–62. New York: Palgrave Macmillan.

Mitchell, W. J. T. 1994. *Landscape and Power*. Chicago: University of Chicago Press.

Mokgoatšana, Sekgothe, and Goodenough Mashego. 2020. "Why Our Ancestors Never Invented Telescopes." *HTS Teologiese Studies/Theological Studies* 76 (4). https://doi .org/10.4102/hts.v76i4.6116

Molvaer, Reidulf K. 1997. *Black Lions: The Creative Lives of Modern Ethiopia's Literary Giants and Pioneers*. Asmara, Eritrea: Red Sea Press.

Moolla, F. Fiona. 2016. "Introduction." In *Natures of Africa: Ecocriticism and Animal Studies in Contemporary Cultural Forms*, edited by F. Fiona Moolla, 1–26. Johannesburg: Witts University Press.

Moore, Donald. 1996. "Marxism, Culture, and Political Ecology: Environmental Struggles in Zimbabwe's Eastern Highlands." In *Liberation Ecologies: Environment, Development and Social Movements*, 1st ed., edited by Richard Peet and Michael Watts, 125–47. London: Routledge.

Mthatiwa, Syned. 2016. "Animals, Nostalgia and Zimbabwe's Rural Landscape in the Landscape in the Poetry of Chenjerai Hove and Musaemura Zimunya." In *Natures of Africa: Ecocriticism and Animal Studies in Contemporary Cultural Forms*, edited by F. Fiona Moolla, 276–303. Johannesburg: Witts University Press.

Mūchiri, Ng'ang'a. 2019. "Depictions of Kenyan Lands and Landscapes by 4 Women Writers." In *Routledge Handbook of African Literature*, 244–57. New York: Routledge.

Mūchiri, Ng'ang'a. 2020. "Interview with Kenyan Novelist Yvonne Owuor." *Africa Literature Today* 38: 134–40.

Mudimbe, Valentin. 1988. *The Invention of Africa: Gnosis, Philosophy, and the Order of Knowledge*. Bloomington: Indiana University Press.

Muganda, Clay. 2013. "Useless and Vile, Sheng Must Go." *Daily Nation*, February 19.

Mugo, Micere Githae. 1995. "I Want You to Know." In *African Women's Poetry*, edited by Stella Chipasula and Frank Chipasula, 128. Portsmouth, NH: Heinemann.

Muhonja, Besi Brillian. 2020. *Radical Utu: Critical Ideas and Ideals of Wangari Muta Maathai*. Athens: Ohio University Press.

Muigua, Kariuki. 2022. "Effective Application of Traditional Dispute Resolution Mechanisms in the Management of Land Conflicts in Kenya: Challenges and Prospects." *Alternative Dispute Resolution* 10 (1): 87–109.

Mukherjee, Upamanyu. 2010. *Postcolonial Environments: Nature, Culture, and the Contemporary Indian Novel in English*. New York: Palgrave Macmillan.

Müller, Melanie, and Laura Kotzur. 2019. "Sense of Frustration The Debate on Land Reform in South Africa." *SWP Comment* 22 (April). https://doi.org/10.18449/201 9C22v02

Mũngai, Mbũgua wa, Kimani Njogu, Johannes Hossfeld, and Tom Odhiambo. 2014. *Nairobi's Matatu Men: Portrait of a Subculture (Contact Zones Nairobi Book 7)*. Kindle. Nairobi: Goethe-Institut Kenya, Native Intelligence, Jomo Kenyatta Foundation.

Mungoshi, Charles. 1975. *Waiting for the Rain*. Harare: Zimbabwe Publishing House.

Musila, Grace A. 2012. "Farms in Africa: Wildlife Tourism, Conservation and Whiteness in Postcolonial Kenya." In *Rethinking Eastern African Literary and Intellectual Landscapes*, edited by James Ogude, Grace A. Musila, and Dina Ligaga, 223–43. Asmara, Eritrea: Africa World Press.

Musiyiwa, Mickias. 2016. "Shona as a Land-Based Nature-Culture: A Study of the (Re) Construction of Shona Land Mythology in Popular Songs." In *Natures of Africa: Ecocriticism and Animal Studies in Contemporary Cultural Forms*, edited by F. Fiona Moolla, 49–76. Johannesburg: Witts University Press.

Mutswairo, Solomon. 1983. *Mapondera: Soldier of Zimbabwe*. Harare: Longman Zimbabwe.

Mwaifuge, Eliah. 2001. "Beliefs and Human Behavior in the Theatre of Ebrahim Hussein." MA thesis, University of Dar es Salaam.

Mwangi, Evan. 2009. *Africa Writes Back to Self: Metafiction, Gender, Sexuality*. Albany: SUNY Press.

Mwangi, Evan. 2019. *The Postcolonial Animal: African Literature and Posthuman Ethics*. Ann Arbor: University of Michigan Press.

Mwangola, Mshai S. 2008. "Performing Our Stories, Performing Ourselves: In Search of Kenya's Uhuru Generation." *Africa Development/Afrique et Développement* 33 (3): 129–34.

Mwesigye, Francis, Madina Guloba, and Mildred Barungi. 2020. "Women's Land Rights and Agricultural Productivity in Uganda." In *Women and Sustainable Human Development: Empowering Women in Africa*, edited by Maty Konte and Nyasha Tirivayi, 71–88. Cham, Switzerland: Springer International. https://doi.org/10.1007/978 -3-030-14935-2_5

Nasta, Susheila. 2004. "Moyez Vassanji." In *Writing across Worlds: Contemporary Writers Talk*, edited by Susheila Nasta, 69–80. London: Routledge.

Nations, United. 2021. "The Sustainable Development Goals Report 2021." https://unsta ts.un.org/sdgs/report/2021/

Nderitu, Alexander. 2021. *The Talking of Trees*. Nairobi: Self-published.

Nfah-Abbenyi, Juliana Makuchi. 1998. "Ecological Postcolonialism in African Women's Literature." In *Literature of Nature: An Internatiopnal Sourcebook*, edited by Patrick D. Murphy, Terry Gifford, and Katsunori Yamazato, 344–49. Chicago: Fitzroy Dearborn Publishers.

Ngũgĩ, Mukoma wa. 2018. *The Rise of the African Novel: Politics of Language, Identity, and Ownership*. Ann Arbor: University of Michigan Press.

Nicholls, Brendon. 2010. *Ngũgĩ wa Thiong'o, Gender, and the Ethics of Postcolonial Reading*. Burlington, VT: Ashgate.

Nixon, Rob. 2011. *Slow Violence and the Environmentalism of the Poor*. Cambridge, MA: Harvard University Press.

Njau, Rebeka. 1995. "The Village." In *African Women's Poetry*, edited by Stella Chipasula and Frank Chipasula, 117. Portsmouth, NH: Heinemann.

Nyaga, Evanson Njiru, George Mose, Anthony Ichuloi, and Pia Okeche. 2020. "Challenges to Secure Land Ownership and Their Implications to Social Cohesion in Nakuru County, Kenya." *International Journal of Research and Scholarly Communication* 3 (4): 7–23.

Nyamfukudza, S. 1980. *The Non-Believer's Journey*. Nairobi: Heinemann Educational Books.

Nyamu-Musembi, Celestine. 2008. "Breathing Life into Dead Theories about Property Rights in Rural Africa: Lessons from Kenya." In *Women's Land Rights and Privatization in Eastern Africa*, edited by Birgit Englert and Elizabeth Daley, 18–39. Nairobi: East African Educational Publishers.

Nyeko, Monica Arac de. 2003. "In the Stars." *Nation*, August 28. www.thenation.com/ar ticle/archive/stars

Nyeko, Monica Arac de. 2004. "Strange Fruit." *Author-Me.Com*. http://www.author-me .com/fict04/strangefruit.htm

Nyeko, Monica Arac de. 2005. "Ugandan Monologues." *Agenda: Empowering Women for Gender Equity*, no. 63: 100–103.

Nyeko, Monica Arac de. 2008. "The Banana Eater." *AGNI Online*. www.bu.edu/agni/fict ion/africa/arac-de-nyeko.html

Obradovic, Nadezda. 1993. "Review of Uhuru Street by M. G. Vassanji." *Canadian Journal of African Studies* 27 (2): 327–28.

Odhiambo, E. S. A. 2003. "Matunda ya Uhuru, Fruits of Independence: Seven Theses on Nationalism in Kenya." In *Mau Mau and Nationhood: Arms, Authority, and Narration*, edited by E. S. A. Odhiambo and John Lonsdale, 37–45. Oxford: James Currey.

Odinga, Oginga. 1967. *Not Yet Uhuru: Au Autobiography*. Nairobi: Heinemann Educational Books.

Ogola, Margaret. 1994. *The River and the Source*. Nairobi: Focus Books.

Ogot, Grace. 1966. *The Promised Land*. Nairobi: East African Publishing House.

Ogot, Grace. 1968. *Land without Thunder and Other Stories*. Nairobi: East African Educational Publishers.

Ogude, James. 1999. *Ngugi's Novels and African History: Narrating the Nation*. London: Pluto Press.

Ojwang, Dan. 2000. "The Pleasures of Knowing: Images of 'Africans' in East African Asian Literature." *English Studies in Africa* 43 (1): 43–68.

Ojwang, Dan. 2012. "Exile and Estrangement in East African Indian Fiction." *Comparative Studies of South Asia and the Middle East* 32 (3): 523–42.

Orenstein, Ronald. 2013. *Ivory, Horn and Blood: Behind the Elephant and Rhinoceros Poaching Crisis*. Ontario: Firefly Books.

Oslund, Karen. 2011. "Introduction: Getting Our Hands Dirty." In *Cultivating the Colonies: Colonial States and Their Environmental Legacies*, edited by Christina Ax, Niels Brimnes, Niklas Jensen, and Karen Oslund, 1–16. Athens: Ohio University Press.

Otieno, Wambui W. 1998. *Mau Mau's Daughter: A Life History*. Edited by Cora A. Presley. Boulder: Lynne Rienner.

Owuor, Yvonne. 2014. *Dust*. New York: Vintage.

Oyěwùmí, Oyèrónkẹ́. 1997. *The Invention of Women: Making an African Sense of Western Gender Discourses*. Minneapolis: University of Minnesota Press.

Pankhurst, Richard. 1966. *State and Land in Ethiopian History*. Addis Ababa: Institute of Ethiopian Studies.

Patel, Shailja. 2009. "Interview with Monica Arac de Nyeko." *Pambazuka*, no. 421 (February). http://pambazuka.org/en/category/African_Writers/54418

Pepper, Rachel, and Harry Hobbs. 2020. "The Environment Is All Rights: Human Rights, Constitutional Rights and Environmental Rights." *Melbourne University Law Review* 44 (2).

Philipson, Robert. 1989. "Drama and National Culture: A Marxist Study of Ebrahim Hussein." PhD diss., University of Wisconsin.

Phillips, Layli. 2006. "Introduction. Womanism: On Its Own." In *The Womanist Reader*, edited by Layli Phillips, xix–lv. New York: Routledge.

Plastow, Jane. 1996. *African Theatre and Politics: The Evolution of Theatre in Ethiopia, Tanzania, and Zimbabwe—A Comparative Study*. Atlanta, GA: Rodopi.

"Prevalence Of Gender-Based Violence in Selected Public Universities In Kenya." 2020. Akili Dada.

"The Politics of African Freehold Land Ownership in Early Colonial Zimbabwe, 1890–1930." n.d. Accessed October 7, 2019. https://muse.jhu.edu/article/734359/summary

Quayson, Ato. 2000. *Postcolonialism: Theory, Practice or Process*. Malden, MA: Blackwell.

Rabaka, Reiland. 2020. "Introduction: On the Intellectual Elasticity and Political Plurality of Pan-Africanism." In *Routledge Handbook of Pan-Africanism*, 1–32. New York: Routledge.

Ramlagan, Michelle. 2011. "(Re)Placing Nation: Postcolonial Women's Contestations of Spatial Discourse." PhD diss., University of Miami.

Ranger, Terence. 1999. "The Fruits of the Baobab: Irene Staunton and the Zimbabwean Novel." *Journal of Southern African Studies* 25 (4): 695–701.

Ranger, Terence. 2010. *Bulawayo Burning: The Social History of a Southern African City 1893–1960*. Harare: Weaver Press.

Rastogi, Pallava. 2008. *Afrindian Fictions: Diaspora, Race, and National Desire in South Africa*. Columbus: Ohio University Press.

"Report on the Prospects of European Settlement in the East Africa Protectorate, Compiled and Submitted in Accordance with a Confidential Circular." 1908.

Ricard, Alain. 2000. *Ebrahim Hussein: Swahili Theatre and Individualism*. Dar Es Salaam: Mkuki na Nyota.

Rinkanya, Alina. 2014. "Woman for President? 'Alternative' Future in the Works of Kenyan Women Writers." *Tydskrif Vir Letterkunde* 51 (2): 144–55. http://dx.doi.org/10.43 14/tvl.v51i2.11

Roane, J. T., and Justin Hosbey. 2019. "Mapping Black Ecologies." *Current Research in Digital History* 2. https://doi.org/10.31835/crdh.2019.05

Rushton, Amy. 2017. "No Place Like Home: The Anxiety of Return in Taiye Selasi's *Ghana Must Go* and Yvonne Owuor's *Dust*." *Études Anglaises* 70 (1): 45–62.

Rwegasira, Abdon. 2012. *Land as a Human Right: A History of Land Law and Practice in Tanzania*. Dar Es Salaam: Mkuki Na Nyota.

Sahle Sellassie, Berhane M. 1968. *The Afersata*. Nairobi: Heinemann Educational Books.

Sahle Sellassie, Berhane M. 1974. *Warrior King*. Nairobi: Heinemann Educational Books.

Said, Edward. 1979. *Orientalism*. New York: Vintage.

Said, Edward. 1990. "Yeats and Decolonization." In *Nationalism, Colonialism, and Culture*, 69–94. Minneapolis: University of Minnesota Press.

Said, Edward. 1993. *Culture and Imperialism*. New York: Alfred A. Knopf.

Sandilands, Catriona. 1999. *The Good-Natured Feminist: Ecofeminism and the Quest for Democracy*. Minneapolis: University of Minnesota Press.

Schama, Simon. 1995. *Landscape and Memory*. New York: Vintage.

Scoones, Ian, Nelson Marongwe, Blasio Mavedzenge, Jacob Mahenehene, Felix Murimbarimba, and Chrispen Sukume. 2010. *Zimbabwe's Land Reform: Myths and Realities*. London: James Currey.

Simatei, Peter. 2000. "Voyaging on the Mists of Memory: M. G. Vassanji and the Asian Quest/Ion in East Africa." *English Studies in Africa* 43 (1): 29–42.

Simatei, Peter. 2011. "Diasporic Memories and National Histories in East African Asian Writing." *Research in African Literatures* 42 (3): 56–67.

Siwila, Lilian C. 2022. "An African Ecofeminist Appraisal of the Value of Indigenous Knowledge Systems in Responding to Environmental Degradation and Climate Change." In *African Perspectives on Religion and Climate Change*, edited by Ezra Chitando, Ernst M. Conradie, and Susan Mbula Kilonzo. London: Routledge.

Slaughter, Joseph. 2004. "Master Plans: Designing (National) Allegories of Urban Space and Metropolitan Subjects for Postcolonial Kenya." *Research in African Literatures* 35 (1): 30–51.

Slaughter, Joseph. 2005. "Becoming Plots: Human Rights, the Bildungsroman, and the Novelization of Citizenship." In *Postcolonialisms: An Anthology of Cultural Theory and Criticism*, edited by Gaurav Desai and Supriya Nair, 86–139. New Brunswick, NJ: Rutgers University Press.

Soja, Edward W. 2010. *Seeking Spatial Justice*. Minneapolis: University of Minnesota Press.

South Africa, Republic of. 1996. *Constitution of the Republic of South Africa, 1996—Chapter 1: Founding Provisions*. https://www.gov.za/documents/constitution/chapter-1-founding-provisions

Stahl, Michael. 1977. *New Seeds in Old Soil: A Study of the Land Reform Process in Western Wollega, Ethiopia 1975–76*. Research Report No. 40. Uppsala: Scandinavian Institute of African Studies.

Steinbach, Daniel. 2011. "Carved Out of Nature: Identity and Environment in German Colonial Africa." In *Cultivating the Colonies: Colonial States and Their Environmental Legacies*, edited by Christina Ax, Niels Brimnes, Niklas Jensen, and Karen Oslund, 47–77. Columbus: Ohio University Press.

Styles, Megan. 2019. *Roses from Kenya: Labor, Environment, and the Global Trade in Cut Flowers*. Seattle: University of Washington Press.

Sunday News. 2016. "Death of Jason Ziyapapa Moyo," January 10. https://www.sundaynews.co.zw/death-of-jason-ziyapapa-moyo/

Tally, Robert, Jr. 2011. "Introduction: On Geocriticism." In *Geocritical Explorations: Space, Place, and Mapping in Literary and Cultural Studies*, edited by Robert Tally Jr., 1–9. New York: Palgrave Macmillan.

Tamale, Sylvia. 2020. *Decolonization and Afro-Feminism*. Toronto: Daraja Press.

Tareke, Gebru. 1996. *Ethiopia: Power and Protest—Peasant Revolts in the Twentieth Century*. Asmara, Eritrea: Red Sea Press.

Tarisayi, Kudzayi Savious. 2019. "Divergent Perspectives on the Land Reform in Zimbabwe." *Journal for Contemporary History* 44 (1): 90–106. https://doi.org/10.18820/24150509/JCH44.v1.5

Thiong'o, Ngũgĩ wa. 1975. *Secret Lives and Other Stories*. New York: Lawrence Hill.

Thiong'o, Ngũgĩ wa. 1977. *Petals of Blood*. Nairobi: Heinemann.

Thiong'o, Ngũgĩ wa. 1986. *Decolonising the Mind: The Politics of Language in African Literature*. Nairobi: East African Educational Publishers.

Thiong'o, Ngũgĩ wa. 1993. *Moving the Centre: The Struggle for Cultural Freedoms*. Portsmouth, NH: James Currey.

Thiong'o, Ngũgĩ wa. 2004. *Mũrogi wa Kagogo*. Nairobi: East African Educational Publishers.

Thiong'o, Ngũgĩ wa. 2006. *Wizard of the Crow*. New York: Pantheon Books.

Thiong'o, Ngũgĩ wa. 2010. *Dreams in a Time of War: A Childhood Memoir*. New York: Pantheon Books.

Thiong'o, Ngũgĩ wa. 2013a. "Rũrĩmĩ Na Karamu: Ithoga Harĩ Athamaki a Abirika." *Journal of African Cultural Studies* 25 (2): 151–57.

Thiong'o, Ngũgĩ wa. 2013b. "Tongue and Pen: A Challenge to Philosophers from Africa—a Translation of 'Rũrĩmĩ Na Karamu: Ithoga Harĩ Athamaki a Abirika.'" *Journal of African Cultural Studies* 25 (2): 158–63.

Thompson, Leonard. 2000. *A History of South Africa.* 3rd ed. New Haven: Yale University Press.

Touval, Saadia. 1966. "'Treaties, Borders, and the Partition of Africa.'" *Journal of African History* 7 (2): 279–93. https://doi.org/10.1017/S0021853700006320

"Transgress, v." n.d. In *OED Online.* Oxford University Press. Accessed June 26, 2020. www.oed.com/view/Entry/204775

Tsikata, Dzodzi, and Dede-Esi Amanor-Wilks. 2009. "Editorial: Land and Labour in Gendered Livelihood Trajectories." *Feminist Africa* 12: 1–9.

Tuan, Yi-Fu. 1977. *Space and Place: The Perspective of Experience.* Minneapolis: University of Minnesota Press.

Tuck, Eve, and K. Wayne Yang. 2012. "Decolonization Is Not a Metaphor." *Decolonization: Indigeneity, Education and Society* 1 (1): 1–40.

United Nations. 2015. United Nations Framework Convention on Climate Change.

UN-Habitat. 2003. "The Challenge of Slums: Global Report on Human Settlements 2003."

Vambe, Maurice. 2002. "Spirit Possession and the Paradox of Post-Colonial Resistance in Yvonne Vera's *Nehanda.*" In *Sign and Taboo: Perspectives on the Poetic Fiction of Yvonne Vera,* edited by Robert Muponde and Mandi Taruvinga, 127–38. Harare: Weaver Press.

Varma, Rashmi. 2012. *The Postcolonial City and Its Subjects: London, Nairobi, Bombay.* London: Routledge.

Vassanji, Moyez. 1991. *Uhuru Street.* Nairobi: Heinemann Educational Books.

Vera, Yvonne. 1993. *Nehanda.* Harare: Baobab Books.

Vera, Yvonne. 1998. *Butterfly Burning.* New York: Farrar, Straus and Giroux.

Vera, Yvonne. 2002a. *The Stone Virgins.* New York: Farrar, Straus and Giroux.

Vera, Yvonne. 2002b. *Without a Name and under the Tongue.* New York: Farrar, Straus and Giroux.

Wabuke, Hope. 2016. *The Leaving.* New York: Akashic Books.

Wachira, James Maina. 2016. "Animal Oral Praise Poetry and the Samburu Desire to Survive." In *Natures of Africa: Ecocriticism and Animal Studies in Contemporary Cultural Forms,* edited by F. Fiona Moolla, 97–117. Johannesburg: Witts University Press.

Walker, Alice. 2011. *In Search of Our Mothers' Gardens: Prose.* New York: Open Road.

Walraven, Klaas van, and Jon Abbink. 2003. "Rethinking Resistance in African History: An Introduction." In *Rethinking Resistance: Revolt and Violence in African History,* edited by Jon Abbink, de Brujin, and Klaas van Walraven. Boston: Brill.

Watson, Elizabeth E. 2009. *Living Terraces in Ethiopia: Knoso Landscape, Culture and Development.* London: James Currey.

Wear, Andrew. 2011. "The Prospective Colonist and Strange Environments: Advice on Health and Prosperity." In *Cultivating the Colonies: Colonial States and Their Environmental Legacies*, edited by Christina Ax, Niels Brimnes, Niklas Jensen, and Karen Oslund, 19–46. Columbus: Ohio University Press.

Weaver-Hightower, Rebecca. 2011. "Geopolitics, Landscape, and Guilt in Nineteenth-Century Colonial Literature." In *Geocritical Explorations: Space, Place, and Mapping in Literary and Cultural Studies*, edited by Robert Tally Jr., 123–38. New York: Palgrave Macmillan.

Wegerif, Marc C. A., and Arantxa Guereña. 2020. "Land Inequality Trends and Drivers." *Land* 9 (101). https://doi.org/10.3390/land9040101

Weitzberg, Keren. 2017. *We Do Not Have Borders: Greater Somalia and the Predicaments of Belonging in Kenya*. Columbus: Ohio University Press.

Welch, Cameron. 2018. *"Land Is Life, Conservancy Is Life": The San and the N‡a Jaqna Conservancy, Tsumkwe District West, Namibia*. Basel: Basler Afrika Bibliographien. https://www.baslerafrika.ch/product/land-is-life/

Wenzel, Jennifer. 2020. *The Disposition of Nature: Environmental Crisis and World Literature*. New York: Fordham University Press.

Westling, Louise H. 1998. *The Green Breast of the New World: Landscape, Gender, and American Fiction*. Athens: University of Georgia Press.

West-Pavlov, Russell. 2017. "From the Spatial Turn to the Spacetime-Vitalist Turn: Mahjoub's *Navigation of a Rainmaker* and Owuor's *Dust*." In *The Routledge Handbook of Literature and Space*, edited by Robert Tally Jr., 291–302. New York: Routledge.

Westphal, Bertrand. 2011a. "Foreword." In *Geocritical Explorations: Space, Place, and Mapping in Literary and Cultural Studies*, edited by Robert Tally Jr., ix–xv. New York: Palgrave Macmillan.

Westphal, Bertrand. 2011b. *Geocriticism: Real and Fictional Spaces*. Translated by Robert Tally Jr. New York: Palgrave Macmillan.

Williams, Raymond. 1973. *The Country and the City*. London: Chatto and Windus.

Wood, Molara. 2007. "Caine Prize Interview: Monica Arac de Nyeko." *Africa Beyond: Celebrating African Arts in the UK* (blog).

Wu, Cheryl Coral. 2016. "Towards an Ecocriticism in Africa: Literary Aesthetics in African Environmental Literature." In *Natures of Africa: Ecocriticism and Animal Studies in Contemporary Cultural Forms*, edited by F. Fiona Moolla, 141–65. Johannesburg: Witts University Press.

Wubneh, Mulatu, and Yohannis Abate. 1988. *Ethiopia: Transition and Development in the Horn of Africa*. Boulder, CO: Westview Press.

Younger, Paul. 2009. *New Homelands: Hindu Communities in Mauritius, Guyana, Trinidad, South Africa, Fiji, and East Africa*. Oxford: Oxford University Press.

INDEX